"Frederick Buechner famously wro[...] the captain of a ship 'who is the only one aboard who . . . does not know that the waves are twenty feet high.' Preaching to pain clearly indicates that we understand that there are waves. Confessing our own pain as part of that process indicates that we have had to navigate the waves too. Matthew Kim addresses the waves and rides them with his readers to teach us all how to navigate life's storms by the light of our Savior's heart."

—**Bryan Chapell**, pastor emeritus, Grace Presbyterian Church; president emeritus, Covenant Seminary; author of *Christ-Centered Preaching*

"Our congregations need not only truthful exegesis and engaging preaching but also emotional discipleship. Each week, the people in our pews carry with them loss, grief, and suffering, and they long for a way to meet God in the midst of their struggles. When sermons focus only on the victory of the Christian life, this makes walking the way of Jesus more difficult for those who are in pain. Kim helps those of us who preach to address various types of suffering with wisdom, compassion, and the hope of Christ. He helps us take up the holy responsibility of proclaiming that every part of our lives—including our sorrow and pain—is something that we address as a church and is, more importantly, a place to encounter God."

—**Tish Harrison Warren**, Anglican priest; author of *Liturgy of the Ordinary* and *Prayer in the Night*

"Matthew Kim, an experienced pastor, preacher, and teacher of preaching, has written an insightful and beautifully instructive book on preaching to people who experience pain—on all sorts of levels. Kim deftly demonstrates the preacher's responsibility to understand his or her own personal pain and the pain of his or her listeners. As a result, the preacher is enabled to empathize with them and out of her own pain preach the hope of the Scriptures to them. *Preaching to People in Pain* is an important contribution to pastoral ministry, to preaching, and to the field of homiletics. Kim is to be commended for addressing this tender and fragile but often overlooked aspect of the preaching task."

—**Scott M. Gibson**, professor of preaching, David E. Garland Chair of Preaching, and director of the PhD program in preaching, Truett Seminary, Baylor University

"*Preaching to People in Pain* could also be called *Preaching to Humans*. In a culture which makes us believe something is wrong with us when we experience suffering, preachers have a choice: to provide shallow promises or to trust in the truth of our story—that resurrection only comes after death. With wisdom and courage Matthew Kim invites preachers to name their own pain for the sake of their own health and the health of their congregations. We're presented with the hopeful possibility that together we have the capacity for the challenges of life and that as we face them, we find the truth of our story in solidarity with our suffering (and resurrected) Lord."

—**Mandy Smith**, pastor and author of *The Vulnerable Pastor*
and *Unfettered: Imagining a Childlike Faith beyond
the Baggage of Western Culture*

Preaching
to
PEOPLE
IN PAIN

How Suffering Can Shape Your Sermons

and Connect with Your Congregation

Matthew D. Kim

Baker Academic

a division of Baker Publishing Group
Grand Rapids, Michigan

Published by Baker Academic
a division of Baker Publishing Group
PO Box 6287, Grand Rapids, MI 49516-6287
www.bakeracademic.com

Printed in the United States of America

Library of Congress Cataloging-in-Publication Data
Names: Kim, Matthew D., 1977– author.
Title: Preaching to people in pain : how suffering can shape your sermons and connect with your congregation / Matthew D. Kim.
Description: Grand Rapids, Michigan : Baker Academic, a division of Baker Publishing Group, [2021] | Includes bibliographical references and index.
Identifiers: LCCN 2020042372 | ISBN 9781540961297 (paperback) | ISBN 9781540964304 (casebound)
Subjects: LCSH: Preaching. | Pain—Religious aspects—Christianity. | Suffering—Religious aspects—Christianity.
Classification: LCC BV4211.3 .K55295 2021 | DDC 251/.56—dc23
LC record available at https://lccn.loc.gov/2020042372

21 22 23 24 25 26 27   7 6 5 4 3 2 1

To my wonderful parents-in-law,
Dr. Chung Hyun Oh and Mrs. Jung Sook Oh

Contents

Acknowledgments

This book arose out of witnessing the weekly pain and suffering of broken parishioners and making sense of my own pain as a disciple of Jesus, pastor, preacher, and teacher. In writing this book, I wish to mention several individuals who have helped me along the way.

First, I give thanks for the pastors who filled out a survey on preaching to people in pain. You know who you are, and I'm grateful for your continued friendship, partnership, and insights on this subject.

I'm grateful to Gordon-Conwell Theological Seminary for providing a generous sabbatical program and to my colleagues in the preaching department: Jeffrey Arthurs, Patricia Batten, and Pablo Jiménez, who served in various capacities in my stead. A word of thanks is also due to Larry Torres, my research assistant, who found articles and books to consider for use in this book.

Thanks to Baker Publishing Group, especially Robert Hosack, Eric Salo, Sarah Gombis, Paula Gibson, Kara Day, and Shelly MacNaughton. You saw the need for this book and helped it come to fruition. Thank you so much for the encouragement and expertise that I am blessed to enjoy as a member of the Baker author family.

My parents, Ki Wang Kim and Taek Hee Kim, are always in my corner rooting for me. Thank you for your ceaseless love, faithfulness, timely words, and prayers. I love you both so much. To my brother Dennis Daniel Kim, I'm so thankful for your love, encouragement, humor, and generosity. I love you very much, Dennis. Thanks also to my late brother, Timothy

David Kim—though he's no longer with us, he reminds me each day of Jesus's sacrificial love.

Sarah, my beautiful wife, and three delightful sons, Ryan, Evan, and Aidan, always sacrifice much time in allowing me to keep researching and writing for the sake of the academy and the church. I love you more than words can express. Thank you so much.

Finally, I give praise and thanks to God for my wonderful parents-in-law: Dr. Chung Hyun Oh and Mrs. Jung Sook Oh. You've loved me and lifted me up over two decades with prayer as well as financial and emotional support during my doctoral studies, my service as a pastor, and my work as a seminary professor. Words cannot express how much you've done for me that I can never repay. It's an honor for me to dedicate this book to you. Thank you for modeling what it means to love people in the midst of their pain: by healing physical pain as a surgeon and by caring for spiritual, relational, and emotional pains as elders of God's church. I love you and thank God for you!

Introduction

Imagine that you have the following choice to make for your listeners. This decision will have an impact on your congregants' church experience for the rest of their lives: (1) They can listen to sermons that only address the topic of success in the Christian life, or (2) they can listen to sermons that only discuss the issue of pain and suffering. Which type of sermon do you think *they* would prefer? Which message would *you* rather preach?

While this hypothetical situation is extreme, my guess is that most North American Christians would choose the former: sermons on success. Why? The overarching metanarrative in North America is one of triumphalism and victory.[1] We tend to celebrate individualism, success, and other virtues that support upward mobility, progress, and advancement. Many North American congregations champion these sanguine values as well—and I am not just talking about proponents of the prosperity gospel. Do we frequently raise the homiletical banner of success but seldom preach sermons about suffering? Why are we so allergic to suffering?

Another question: Might sermons about suffering and pain resonate with you and your listeners more deeply than the narrative of success and progress? In the Gospels, Jesus speaks more about suffering than about success. Perhaps he knew something about the human condition that we do not. This book provides an important corrective to the American Dream story line, which permeates many Christian churches today. In this book,

1. See Mark Charles and Soong-Chan Rah, *Unsettling Truths: The Ongoing, Dehumanizing Legacy of the Doctrine of Discovery* (Downers Grove, IL: InterVarsity, 2019), 8.

I encourage pastors to preach less pain-free sermons and to preach more pain-full sermons where preachers disclose their own suffering and pain, which allows space to encourage listeners to identify and share their suffering in Christian community for the ultimate purpose of healing and transformation.

Over the last several years, I have experienced various types of pain and suffering. Scattered throughout this book, I share those specific hardships in greater detail. You have your own stories to tell, and I hope that you'll find the freedom to write to me and share your pain with me.[2] In addition, I have preached about success and about suffering many times. Here is what I have learned about the differences between them: suffering is ubiquitous; success is not. Everyone experiences some form of suffering. Not everyone gets to experience accomplishment. Suffering brings people together. Success can separate the closest of friends.

I have divided this book into two parts. In part 1, I invite you into an open and honest conversation about the ways that pastors and parishioners suffer and experience pain, and I articulate a process for preaching on this pain.

In chapter 1, one of my goals is to persuade you that preaching on pain and suffering is vital for your personal well-being as well as for the congregation's potential for life transformation. While it seems counterintuitive to preach regularly on suffering, sharing our pain with the congregation from the pulpit may be the very vehicle that drives congregational change. The chapter addresses various types of pain for pastors/preachers and offers a road map for discovering and wisely disclosing pains in the pastor's life.

In chapter 2, we explore the numerous types of pains and suffering that listeners embody every single day and bring with them into the worship service. If we are honest, we preachers witness discouragement on the countenances of our listeners. As a pastor, I was often perplexed by my listeners' perceived apathy and despondency toward the Christian faith. "Why is their Christian life so depleted of spiritual vitality?" I would think to myself as I poured out sermonic energies each Sunday. However, when I understood my listeners' experiences and suffering, I began to have more grace for them. This second chapter names the sufferings and pains

---

2. I invite you to share your stories with me at matthewdkim@gmail.com.

of our listeners—and when appropriate, I include examples from other ethnicities and cultures.

Chapter 3 offers a plan for preaching on pain. I suggest nine foundational questions for exegeting pain in Scripture and in the congregation. These questions serve as prework before we preach on suffering and double as a working blueprint for the major chapters in the latter half of the book. I also suggest some general principles and reminders for preaching on the topic of pain.

In part 2, we will explore six different types of pain that listeners commonly harbor in their souls. First, chapter 4 identifies painful decisions. Every listener comes to church with a "past," which is occasionally checkered. Albert Camus, the French philosopher and author, once said, "Life is a sum of all your choices." Sometimes the decisions we made in the past are painful and linger on as the bane of our existence. We cannot seem to move past these backdated mistakes and sins. They resurface at the most inopportune moments—usually when we are on the brink of a spiritual breakthrough. This chapter identifies some of the painful decisions our listeners have made, considers how we can show them God's grace in spite of their poor choices, and provides suggestions for helping them in the sermon to move toward healing and transformation.

In chapter 5, we name some pains wrought by ill-advised and unintentional financial decisions. Money is one of the most difficult topics to preach on. Pastors know that tension all too well. The state of our listeners' finances often seems to be a taboo topic. Yet, what if we preach messages that encourage godly stewardship in light of unwise or unavoidable financial choices? That will be the subject of this chapter on painful finances.

Painful health issues are the subject of chapter 6, where we discuss matters related to our physical and mental health. We are living in an age of grave health concerns. Close to 40 percent of Americans will be diagnosed with cancer at some time in their life.[3] Millions of Americans live with chronic pain and medical conditions such as ALS, diabetes, osteoporosis, vertigo, nerve pain, fibromyalgia, arthritis, glaucoma, and much more. Mental health is also an explosive area that the church needs to be more intentional about addressing even from the pulpit. Suicide continues to curtail lives at every stage of life. Myriad health issues plague the members

3. "Cancer Stat Facts: Cancer of Any Site," National Cancer Institute, accessed June 25, 2020, https://seer.cancer.gov/statfacts/html/all.html.

of our churches. They are lamenting: "Why me, God?" How can we encourage Christians amid physical and mental hardships as well as care for others who experience such challenges?

In chapter 7, we recognize that listeners live with losses of all kinds: death of grandparents, parents, a spouse, children, siblings, relatives; loss of jobs; loss of promotions; loss of retirement savings; loss of homes; loss of respect and status; loss of marriage; loss of pregnancy; infertility; and much more. How can we bring the hope of the gospel into such experiences and feelings of loss? The chapter addresses various forms of loss and demonstrates how to preach with greater empathy and hope.

With regard to painful relationships, chapter 8 reminds us that God created us as social beings to be in relationship with one another. The trouble is that not all relationships flourish. We suffer because of fragile and fractured relationships with parents, a spouse, our children, friends, neighbors, bosses and coworkers, church members, and others. Our relationships with others are divided on a number of different levels, including race, gender, ethnicity, culture, politics, denominations, socioeconomics, beliefs, interests, hobbies, and more. The chapter names and articulates ways forward in addressing painful relationships.

Last, in chapter 9, we look at the power of the sin that holds us captive. Satan eagerly seeks opportunities to discourage Christians about past and current struggles with sin. Listeners vacillate between victories over and relapse into particular sinful behaviors. These sins are a confounding source of pain and shame. How can we address sin in sermons and even share some personal struggles with the congregation as well? The chapter helps pastors see the value in lovingly naming personal and corporate sins and recommends ways to overcome them by the power of the Holy Spirit.

Yet this book seeks not to dwell in the land of theory alone. I want to show us that preaching on pain and suffering is very much an expression and outworking of lived theology. In each chapter, I share stories, draw from the experiences of others, identify relevant Scripture texts that impart biblical wisdom, and offer best practices. At the conclusion of each chapter, I provide discussion questions and a sample sermon that integrates some of the practical suggestions in the main chapters. In the appendix, a worksheet is available for exploring personal pain as well as corporate suffering in our congregations.

We need not preach on only success or only suffering. Preaching on success, at times, is necessary. But so is preaching on suffering and pain. I hope that after reading this book you will agree with me that speaking on suffering regularly, and as your preaching pericope warrants, will contribute to increased vulnerability and congregational change. "Preaching on pain" sounds like an oxymoron, but it is not. It's actually the soothing balm that brings healing and life to weary souls who may identify more with suffering than with success. Let's begin the journey toward suffering successfully.

PART 1

Naming
THE PAIN

1

The Preacher's Pain

In nearly ten years of serving in pastoral ministry as a youth pastor, college pastor, and senior pastor, I can count on one hand the number of times that a church member asked me how I was doing and actually cared enough to listen to my pain and suffering. Why has this lack of care for pastors become so normative in our society? The minister, as perceived by the average churchgoer, is the person who does the work of ministry, but rarely does he or she need a form of "listening ministry"[1] from others. Yet pastors are human too. As Chuck DeGroat observes, "Lost pastors can make it a long way on the fuel of the false self. They may be successful, influential, endearing, charming, and smart. But beneath the veneer are people deeply afraid, lost and lonely, powder kegs of unmet and neglected needs. They have stories that have never been explored, pain never acknowledged, violations of others unconfessed."[2]

In the seminary context, I have seen similar one-directional exchanges occur between students and me, also leading me toward the conclusion that opportunities are few and far between for Christian leaders like pastors, professors, teachers, counselors, and others to disclose their spiritual,

---

1. See Susan K. Hedahl, *Listening Ministry: Rethinking Pastoral Leadership* (Nashville: Abingdon, 2002); and Lynne M. Baab, *The Power of Listening: Building Skills for Mission and Ministry* (Lanham, MD: Rowman & Littlefield, 2014).

2. Chuck DeGroat, "Pastor, Why Are You Hiding?," *Christianity Today*, January 15, 2019, https://www.christianitytoday.com/pastors/2019/january-web-exclusives/pastor-why-are-you-hiding.html.

physical, relational, emotional, economic, and other ontological selves. Perhaps you have encountered comparable indifference from your congregants or students. They assume that—while you are not always perched on a spiritual mountaintop—you are doing just fine in your soul. The truth is that perhaps the most sequestered person—struggling the most at any given time within a congregation—is the pastor himself or herself. Yet, is your prolonged silence eating at your very existence?

Isn't it refreshing to be able to admit aloud, "I am human too," or to be able to say freely, "My pastor is human too"? Depending on your church culture or ethnic culture, divulging one's pain and suffering as a minister of the gospel may be simply taboo. However, suffering and pain are no respecters of persons. Some of the most horrifically painful stories I have heard are from pastors who have undergone or are presently experiencing immense suffering.

In preparing to write this book, I surveyed several church pastors about preaching on pain and suffering. One pastor battled a brain tumor and experienced a form of chronic pain resembling "cluster" headaches for over a decade—one of the worst pains known to humanity other than childbirth. Yet a different pastor is haunted by the hollowing effect of his parents' divorcing and remarrying, each more than once. Another pastor struggles to make sense of the heinousness of systemic racism and how the gospel challenges our sinfulness. One pastor laments the daily grind of having a child who suffers from a genetic disorder that has required numerous surgeries. Another pastor tries to make sense of birthing a child with Down syndrome later in life. One pastor shares about his wife having numerous miscarriages. Another pastor expresses the agony of internalizing the collective suffering of his congregants. One pastor that I know of lost his wife and children in a horrific car accident. Stories of suffering endured by pastors are endless. Pastors are not immune from encountering unspeakable tragedy and hardship. If we believe in the power of the local church, why, then, are we so reluctant to share struggles with our beloved Christian communities?

Part of the pastor's dilemma is how our culture reacts to the suffering of others. People frankly don't want to hear about it. Consider how we, at least in North America, commonly greet others. We ask a person, "How are you?," but it's merely a courtesy acknowledgment of their existence, just in question form. We expect the other person to respond with some trite retort such as "Good" or "Can't complain." In other words, we don't *really* want to know how the other is *really* doing. Admit it. Suffering is often painful, raw, shocking, gut-wrenching, lonely, maddening, exposing, annoying, confusing, and even volatile. The pain of others exacerbates these and other feelings of being downtrodden.

At the same time, not all suffering is identical. The mystery of pain is that no two people experience pain identically even in the midst of very similar trials. Pain is also polarizing and perplexing. There are generally two converse attitudes toward suffering. Either people love to tell others of (i.e., vent and revel in) their misery and feel entitled to complain or grumble incessantly as if they are the only ones on the planet going through the hells of life, or people may try to conceal it from others because they feel ashamed or don't want to be judged. It's no wonder why pastors often err on the side of silence.

Moreover, Christians often minimize suffering by putting on a happy face upon entering the sanctuary and fellowship hall on Sunday morning. Such is the existence of the average pastor. We may feel like being transparent about our hardships, but then we wonder if such vulnerability may somehow undermine our leadership or pastoral authority. We might plow ahead by telling ourselves, "There is no time for wallowing in my agony when there is gospel work to be done." But as theologian Kelly Kapic points out in his book *Embodied Hope*, "We can acknowledge the struggle of being a follower of Yahweh, the creator of heaven and earth, and having to deal with suffering as it is: real, tragic, and heartbreaking."[3] In many ways, suffering is the great equalizer. At some point, every human being suffers and experiences pain—both Christians and non-Christians alike. Pastors and preachers are no exception. We cannot allow ourselves to stand "above the congregation" as if we are better than they. We can admit and share our pain and suffering with judiciousness.

Since pain is ubiquitous, the pulpit can be a place to address the topic strategically with biblical, theological sophistication as well as with cultural sympathy and empathy.[4] But merely mentioning the pain while offer-

3. Kelly M. Kapic, *Embodied Hope: A Theological Meditation on Pain and Suffering* (Downers Grove, IL: InterVarsity, 2017), 17.

4. The sheer volume of books on pain and suffering is quite astounding. It seems like every Christian writer wants to share their particular take on the topic. Over the last six decades, for example, the deluge of ink spilled on suffering has amassed inspiring works such as C. S. Lewis's *The Problem of Pain*, R. C. Sproul's *Surprised by Suffering*, Randy Alcorn's *If God Is*

ing a few flavorful biblical tonics is not the end or the catchall solution. We pastors and preachers must make ourselves available to our people postsermon. It's not prudent to preach on pain from Scripture, dumping our demons on our listeners, and then run off to the fellowship hall for refreshments. We must walk with our people in their pain, through their pain, and after their pain, and even in moments when hopelessness resurfaces and they relapse into their pain. More about that later in chapter 2.

This opening chapter addresses various pains in your life as a pastor and offers a road map for discovering and disclosing those pains from the pulpit and as a member of congregational life. Let's pause briefly to entertain insights that Scripture offers about pain and suffering.

Scriptural Snapshots on Pain and Suffering

Pain and suffering enter Scripture's purview immediately after the fall in Genesis 3. Postfall, there is no reentry into God's perfect Eden. Adam and Eve are banished forever, never to return to the garden. Strangely, as Christians, however, we can temporarily forget that we live in a fallen, sinful, and broken world. We live today as if we deserve readmittance into an amusement theme park called "Utopic Universe"—that is, the prefallen state of the garden of Eden (Gen. 1 and 2).

God has, no doubt, been extremely patient with humanity. He is not surprised by our suffering, nor does he tune us out when we sinfully murmur and grumble against him. God is here among us and present in our suffering and pain. He is not distant even though it can feel like it. The Bible includes more verses about suffering than about joy, which tells of the somber reality of the Christian life in a postfall world. Turning the pages of Scripture, we read sporadically about existential enjoyment and the pursuit of pleasure—yes, God created us to enjoy his creation—and yet, more verses speak directly to suffering and pain in the Old and New Testaments. The portrait of discipleship brushed on the canvas of life by

---

Good, John Piper's *Suffering and the Sovereignty of God*, Timothy Keller's *Walking with God through Pain and Suffering*, Philip Yancey's *Where Is God When It Hurts?*, Elisabeth Elliot's *A Path through Suffering*, J. Todd Billings's *Rejoicing in Lament*, Joni Eareckson Tada's *A Place of Healing*, Gerald Sittser's *A Grace Disguised*, J. I. Packer's *A Grief Sanctified*, Soong-Chan Rah's *Prophetic Lament*, Sheila Wise Rowe's *Healing Racial Trauma*, and many others.

the very words of our Savior (such as in John 16:33) only reinforces our sense of a Christian life brimming with sweat and struggle.

The passages of Scripture on pain and suffering are copious indeed. Job might be one of the most referenced books of the Bible associated with pain and suffering, but Scripture is replete with countless characters who suffered in both great and small ways. In the Old Testament, Sarah, Rebekah, Rachel, Samson's mother, Hannah, and Michal (King David's first wife), and Elizabeth (the cousin of Mary and eventual mother of John the Baptist) in the New Testament were tortured by their barrenness or infertility. Some scholars have suggested that over 40 percent of the Psalms are songs of lament.[5] For example, King David is baffled by God's tolerance of his enemies. His imprecatory psalms throw down visceral, violent words against his foes. The Old Testament prophesies concerning the Messiah's impending suffering. Later in the Gospels, Jesus shares regularly about his suffering and pain. Paul writes extensively in portions of his letters about his suffering—for example, in 2 Corinthians. Jesus also foretells that his disciples will not escape suffering. At times, he sounds as if suffering was a prerequisite or precondition for any bona fide disciple. Many characters in Scripture encounter various forms of pain and suffering in their lifetime. The narratives of broken, pain-filled personalities are littered throughout the Gospels. Why, then, are we so astounded by suffering?

A Prosperity Gospel or a Pain-Full Gospel?

Perhaps, if we can be transparent, the problem with Christianity is not suffering and pain in and of themselves. Yes, it is perfectly acceptable and normal to mourn and lament. God expects to hear the cries of his children. At the same time, the tension is that we are also invited to embrace Christ's call to discipleship—to pick up our cross daily (with every Christian receiving a different form of the cross)! The gospel is a gospel that is saturated, steeped, in pain. Jesus's sacrificial death, burial, and resurrection remind us that the Christian is called to a daily death. As Jesus says plainly, suffering is normative rather than the exception to the rule for those who dare call themselves Christians, or "little Christs." He says, "Whoever wants to be

5. See Glenn Pemberton, *Hurting with God: Learning to Lament with the Psalms* (Abilene, TX: Abilene Christian University Press, 2012), 37, cited by Soong-Chan Rah, *Prophetic Lament: A Call for Justice in Troubled Times* (Downers Grove, IL: InterVarsity, 2015), 22.

my disciple must deny themselves and take up their cross and follow me" (Matt. 16:24). Moreover, Paul declares, "I have been crucified with Christ and I no longer live" (Gal. 2:20). The command to die daily is not simply for Jesus and Paul. It's a call for modern Christians as well. What if we, as Christ followers, were able to view and experience suffering differently from those who live without hope?

We, in the twenty-first century, internalize a love/hate relationship with the prosperity gospel. We surreptitiously covet what it claims but hate what it stands for (i.e., what Dietrich Bonhoeffer called "cheap grace"[6]). Our sinful nature craves comfort and the finer things of life. Nobody wants to be introduced to "Lady Suffering" personified. To God's chagrin, his children look more comfortable at times than the people who have yet to call him "Lord, Lord." Paul Borthwick and Dave Ripper helpfully point out in *The Fellowship of the Suffering*, "Scripture is emphatic: suffering, in all its forms, is an unequivocal, inescapable part of not only the fallen human condition but the Christian life."[7]

Next time you are at a social gathering, try greeting someone with "How are you *suffering* today?" instead of the proverbial "How are you *doing* today?" The person, now in utter shock or sheer confusion, will probably not know how to respond. They'll think they misheard you. Our culture is so pain-averse and pain-sensitive that any modicum of pain and suffering can render Christians helpless and hopeless. Simply put, we have forgotten that there is a God who is sovereign and who knows what he is doing. He is a God who permits pain. We, human beings, have a tough time making sense of this mystery.

While there is no reason to actively run toward pain and suffering, the difference for the Christian is in how we respond to our plight. How are Christians any different from those without hope? What if Christians walked or limped in stride with suffering, albeit gingerly at times, rather than allowing it to deter us and even cause us to lose our faith? What would it look like for disciples—the New Testament's Greek word for "disciples" literally means "learners"—to learn what it means to imitate Christ and participate in Christ's suffering, in all its varied forms?

6. See, e.g., Dietrich Bonhoeffer, *The Cost of Discipleship* (New York: Touchstone, 1995), 44–46.

7. Paul Borthwick and Dave Ripper, *The Fellowship of the Suffering: How Hardship Shapes Us for Ministry and Mission* (Downers Grove, IL: InterVarsity, 2018), 14.

Why Share Our Suffering?

Scripture exposes suffering and pain because God provides solutions for us and *is* the solution for the Christian. Jesus and Paul regularly shared their suffering so that we could share ours as well. The verb *to share* has two meanings in this book. First, we are talking about sharing or communicating with others regarding our pain and suffering. Second, *sharing* means participating in, feeling, and experiencing the turmoil of others and encouraging them and empathizing with them in the midst of it. Paul says to the Philippian believers, "I want to know Christ—yes, to know the power of his resurrection and participation in his sufferings, becoming like him in his death, and so, somehow, attaining to the resurrection from the dead" (Phil. 3:10–11).

As fellow journeymen and journeywomen, preachers have freedom to participate in the sufferings of Christ and the sufferings that reflect our humanness in a sinful world. J. Howard Olds writes, "To live is to struggle, to endure suffering, to come to grips with pain. Pastors are not immune from the common sufferings of humanity. We get sick physically, struggle emotionally, feel the strains of relationships, and work like everyone else to make ends meet. What others don't have to deal with is preaching the good news in the midst of personal pain."[8] Should pastors, then, preach on pain and suffering regularly, or even ever?

Pitfalls of Preaching on Pain

Let's begin with some reasons why we avoid preaching on pain. If you have a market-driven philosophy of ministry, preaching on pain is an evangelistic turnoff. Nobody wants to be reminded of their present difficult circumstances on Sunday morning—especially on their Sabbath or day off. You can imagine your congregant inviting her coworker on Monday morning: "Hey Lisa, would you like to come to church with me for the next six weeks and hear this fantastic sermon series on suffering?"

Daniel T. Hans raises a number of valid questions regarding preachers sharing their pain from the pulpit. He asks, "Does a preacher have the right to carry his or her own confusion and pain into the pulpit? Doesn't such

---

8. J. Howard Olds, "Preaching out of Pain," Ministry Matters, August 1, 2008, https://www.ministrymatters.com/preach/entry/68/preaching-out-of-pain.

transparency focus more upon the preacher than the Lord? Does not personal exposure in preaching turn the pulpit into a soap opera and denigrate the ministry of proclamation into self-aggrandizement?"[9] He continues by asking, "Shouldn't a human preacher be human in preaching?"[10] Admittedly, inviting people into our pain and practicing self-disclosure may generate unintended consequences. Let's quickly name four arguments against preachers' self-disclosure.

Self-Disclosure Damages Listeners' Faith in God

Depending on what struggles we share, some listeners out there may falter in their faith in God as a result of hearing about our troubles. We don't want to be the "millstone" around other believers' necks, which Jesus so vividly describes in the Gospels. While we know that pastors are human, most Christians want to believe that their pastor is somehow closer to Christ—not falling into the same discipleship snares that they do. Whether we like it or not, pastors are Christlike figures in their parishioners' eyes. A pastor who shares freely about his or her struggles may elicit an unwanted response from listeners and diminish their faith in God. They may even feel manipulated by the preacher who shares emotional pain in transactional form to get something from the listener in response. The naysayers and ecclesiological pundits would argue that pastors should never encourage or promote doubt among their listeners. What benefit is there to causing gratuitous suspicion in one's congregation about who God is and how he responds to or permits human suffering?

Self-Disclosure Diminishes Pastoral Authority

Second, some listeners may doubt our pastoral authority as ministers of the gospel and taper the trust we have with them. Again, Olds continues, "Preaching should not be a therapy session for the preacher. Congregations want their pastors to be real, but they are not interested in being dragged through all the painful details of our personal struggles."[11] If we are living an immoral life or participating in sinful practices that jeopardize

---

9. Daniel T. Hans, "Preaching through Personal Pain: What Can You Say When the Tragedy Is Yours?," *Leadership Journal* 10, no. 1 (Winter 1989): 35–39.

10. Hans, "Preaching through Personal Pain."

11. Olds, "Preaching out of Pain."

our pastoral calling, then we need to confess this to our church board and perhaps even leave the ministry (at least for a season or maybe permanently). In addition, the pulpit is not the appropriate setting to share certain struggles. Rather, a more fitting venue may be at a pastor's small group or with trusted friends.

Self-Disclosure Focuses the Sermon Too Much on the Preacher

Third, Haddon Robinson warns about the dangers of self-therapy preaching: "First, we can end up using the pulpit for self-therapy. One's style of preaching can change during a crisis. Often, along the way, a suffering pastor preaches a sermon that is nine-tenths his painful story and one-tenth Bible. . . . Preaching becomes a catharsis for his pain. . . . [The congregation is] not unsympathetic, but after a while the weekly service becomes an emotional downer. People don't follow for long leaders who can't handle their emotions."[12] Here, a couple of unintended consequences may be that the congregants believe you are one-upping them in "suffering comparison" when you unintentionally communicate that your problems are worse than theirs or that you are so consumed by your personal concerns that you cannot handle the congregation's struggles.[13]

Self-Disclosure Makes for Repetitive Sermons

Everyone can tolerate a gut-wrenching story once or twice, but after a while the recounting of it will tire the listener. I know a pastor who lost his daughter to cancer thirty years ago. My heart, of course, cries out for him and his unspeakable loss. In every sermon I have heard him preach (several times), he weaves into the message this incredible gut punch in his life. The premature death of his daughter is a woeful tragedy that no one should have to endure, but the pulpit is not the place to tell her story over and over again. The story of loss, while prominent in one's consciousness, eventually begins to lose its impact because of the sheer repetition. The listener inevitably becomes numb to the preacher's pain. Self-disclosure,

---

12. Haddon Robinson, "When You're in Pain," *Christianity Today*, May 19, 2004, https://www.christianitytoday.com/pastors/leadership-books/voiceinwilderness/mmpp03-8.html.
13. From a survey respondent who pointed me to the work of Carol Kent, who argues this. See, e.g., Carol Kent, *When I Lay My Isaac Down: Unshakable Faith in Unthinkable Circumstances*, updated and expanded ed. (Colorado Springs: NavPress, 2013).

when done inappropriately or laboriously, can be detrimental to one's preaching ministry. However, what are some possible benefits of sharing about your life from the pulpit?

Benefits of Sharing Our Suffering

Self-Disclosure Humanizes Us

For better or worse, our vocation and title as pastor places us in an "other" category. We are different, or at least people perceive us as different from every other Christian. Self-disclosure, within boundaries, shows the congregation that we, too, encounter and struggle with the everyday matters of Christian discipleship. The proverbial pastor on a pedestal who stands "six feet above contradiction" comes down from the platform to stand and sit among "average" disciples. We become "real people" in the eyes of the listener. The once prominent pastor of Madison Avenue Presbyterian Church in New York City, David H. C. Read, shares, "When I was in my teens I listened regularly to a preacher who never made personal references or recounted incidents in his life as a pastor. . . . But there was something lacking in those sermons. They were somewhat remote from our daily life. One felt, This is a *good* man—but does he ever have the kind of experiences *we* have? If I went to him with some practical question would he understand?"[14] In some ways, our "human moments" free us from the façade of being inauthentic, robotic, or superhuman.

Self-Disclosure Connects Us with People and Their Pain

In the chapters that follow, I share several personal examples of pain and suffering. This is not an attempt to throw a pity party or become a metric of comparison for who has suffered most. Rather, by doing so, I hope to show you that I am not simply an "armchair sufferer"—one who thinks he knows what suffering is about but has never played in the game of hard knocks. Over the years, as I have shared my pain from the pulpit, listeners have come up to me after the service and thanked me for my vulnerability. They make comments such as these: "This was the first

14. David H. C. Read, *Preaching about the Needs of Real People* (Philadelphia: Westminster, 1988), 25.

time I've heard a pastor share so honestly about his life," or, "I'm so glad I'm not alone in this," or, "I also have that condition," or even, "I feel like you really understand me."

As stated in the introduction, pain is the common denominator in life, but success—not so much. People rarely connect with me by rehearsing their résumés, noting their educational credentials, or floating a list of publications. Rather, they connect with me in my weaknesses. As Olds explains, "People connect with your weakness. I can't tell you how many times a person may be in the midst of describing their trouble to me when they stop and suddenly say, 'But you know—don't you? You really know.'"[15]

Timothy Beavis provides additional benefits for preaching through pain, especially for the preacher. Beavis concludes:

1. The preacher in pain holds to his divine call to preach as a source of strength and encouragement.
2. The preacher in pain experiences a deep sense of dependence on God's Word and a growing sense of preciousness of His promises.
3. The preacher in pain recognizes a growth in compassion for others.
4. The preacher in pain feels a greater sense of urgency in his work and proclamation.
5. The preacher in pain must make adjustments to his routine, responsibilities and rhythm if he is to sustain ministry.
6. The preacher in pain needs to move from isolation to greater interaction with his friends, counselors and elders.
7. The preacher in pain finds his future hope becoming a bigger theme in his life and ministry.[16]

Self-Awareness Is Necessary for Good Leaders

In 1955, psychologists Joseph Luft and Harrington Ingham created the Johari window, a grid for measuring and developing self-awareness used during counseling and therapy sessions.[17] In this exercise, a person chooses adjectives from a list to describe themselves, and then their peers

15. Olds, "Preaching out of Pain."

16. Timothy Beavis, "Preaching in Pain: How Chronic Illness Impacts the Preacher's Ministry" (DMin thesis, Gordon-Conwell Theological Seminary, 2013), 92–93.

17. Joseph Luft and Harrington Ingham, "The Johari Window: A Graphic Model of Interpersonal Awareness," in *Proceedings of the Western Training Laboratory in Group Development* (Los Angeles: University of California, Los Angeles, 1955).

also choose adjectives from that same list to describe that person. The responses are charted on the grid, which moves from the unknown, to the hidden, to blind spots, and ultimately to openness about one's blind spots. This model is a conceptual pathway to consider one's level of self-awareness in moving toward greater self-awareness.

The Johari Window

	Known to Self	Not Known to Self
Known to Others	OPEN	BLIND SPOTS
Not Known to Others	HIDDEN	UNKNOWN

Many leaders lack self-awareness because they have unknown or hidden areas or small-to-considerable blind spots, or they completely overestimate their leadership abilities. This commonly happens to leaders in any workplace environment. They assume everyone is following them, that they have influence, when in fact their employees act as "independent contractors" with little accountability and do as they please.

A lack of self-awareness also occurs among leaders in the context of the local church. The pastoral leader who is unaware of his or her pain and suffering is quite dangerous. This person who has not acknowledged or dealt with emotional issues may one day erupt on the congregation like a dormant volcano. Wisely sharing about one's pain and suffering demonstrates a healthy sense of self-awareness, which is highly beneficial for the entire congregation to witness on occasion. Without proper boundaries, however, the pulpit can become an open window into a weekly therapy session where the preacher unknowingly spills his or her pain via stream-of-consciousness communication. Therefore, the preacher needs apt self-awareness as well as trusted others speaking into his or her life.

Self-Disclosure Helps Us Model How to Overcome Suffering and Pain

Finally, perhaps most importantly, self-disclosure (if we have effectively overcome or are in the process of positively working through our pain) can serve as a productive testimony for our listeners. Christians want to follow those who have struggled and can speak honestly from lessons learned. Of course, that does not mean that we must have experiential knowledge of every type of sin and spiritual malady. Bill Elliff observes, "Pain breaks and molds, educates and deepens. Pain authenticates and prepares. Pain, rightly responded to, gives us something to say."[18] On a much grander scale, this is why the author of Hebrews writes concerning Jesus, "For we do not have a high priest who is unable to empathize with our weaknesses, but we have one who has been tempted in every way, just as we are—yet he did not sin" (4:15). Wise and select doses of self-disclosure can be a worthwhile homiletical strategy.

Pastor, How Are *You* Suffering Today?

We must distinguish at the outset of this book the four major types of suffering: (1) suffering for the sake of Christ, (2) suffering from various illnesses that are out of our control, (3) suffering because of demands placed on us, and (4) suffering on account of our own sinfulness, sinful desires, and poor decisions. These four forms of suffering are not equal.

First, there is the unique challenge of suffering for the sake of Christ.[19] Pastoral weight is real. Souls are at stake. Eternity is in the balance. Rejection is common. Conflict is inevitable. Self-denial—perhaps one of the most difficult aspects of the pastoral calling—is expected. Martyrdom is not a distant reality, especially on the mission field. Sheep bite and then walk or even run away in search of a better shepherd. We may feel the pain of being disrespected or unappreciated, whether verbally or monetarily, overhearing gossip about our spouse or children (more on this later), and much more.

Jesus understood well the emotional pains of ministry, especially seeing his own father turn his face away. Kelly Kapic observes, "The Son fuses himself with our pain, our weakness, our fears, our struggles. . . . In and through the incarnate Christ, God experiences human suffering, undergoing everything from misunderstandings to outright betrayal. . . .

---

18. Bill Elliff, "Preaching from Pain," Strategic Renewal, accessed June 25, 2020, https://www.strategicrenewal.com/preaching-from-pain.
19. Philip Wagner notices six common areas of pain and suffering for pastors, including criticism, rejection, betrayal, loneliness, weariness, and frustration and disappointment. See Wagner, "The Secret Pain of Pastors," ChurchLeaders, September 5, 2018, https://churchleaders.com/pastors/pastor-articles/167379-philip-wagner-secret-pain-of-pastors.html.

Jesus constantly dealt with human agony, [others'] sin, and misery in his own life, and therefore with judgment and death for all the years leading to his own death."[20]

Second, there is suffering that is out of our control. For instance, we may suffer from physical maladies acute to ministers such as stress and anxiety, diabetes, hypertension, high blood pressure, high cholesterol, ocular challenges, and more. Furthermore, we cannot choose whether we become another victim of cancer or some other illness—terminal or otherwise.

Third, the relentless demands of ministry leave us beaten down and weary. Church leadership and congregants can present impossible demands and expectations. Nonpastors do not and cannot understand the emotional toil and spiritual warfare that come from serving God through full-time pastoral ministry. We are on call twenty-four hours a day and even during holidays and vacations. Even when we are technically off the clock, we lose sleep over Mrs. Johnson's recent cancer diagnosis. We incur financial deficits and duress such as college and seminary loans to be repaid and other economic burdens, so we become bivocational or slog through life living in the red rather than in the black. We seldom save money because our budgets are tightly constricted by hospital bills, medicines, car repairs, and water heaters that need replacement.

Fourth, as we will discuss in chapter 4, we may suffer from poor decision making. Wisdom is a perpetual need in the pastorate and for the Christian. We question God's character in allowing suffering in our lives when in fact we have created our own pain and demise with careless thinking, behaving, and living.

In addition, more specifically, there are at least six possible areas where a preacher could explore his or her pain and suffering in greater depth. In my book *Preaching with Cultural Intelligence*, I provide a short template for "exegeting the preacher" with respect to a pastor's own personal journey and how that affects one's life and preaching.[21] I encourage a two-step process to facilitate self-exegesis: (1) creating and reflecting upon one's personal time line of highs and lows and (2) writing journal reflections about one's sufferings, especially family dysfunctions, ethnic background, cultural attitudes, and pain.

20. Kapic, *Embodied Hope*, 90–91.
21. See Matthew D. Kim, *Preaching with Cultural Intelligence: Understanding the People Who Hear Our Sermons* (Grand Rapids: Baker Academic, 2017), 45–61.

Here the goal is to consider pain more intentionally for yourself. Your gut reaction is to probably avoid thinking about pain and painful moments. This is only natural because grief and pain are not linear, one-and-done ordeals. As a goal-oriented person, I do not appreciate setbacks. However, it's clear that pain has setbacks, even prolonged or interminable ones. Suffering comes and goes with the seasons, with every holiday, milestone, and celebration, with annual reminders, birthdays, and anniversaries. I wish that I could begin the journey of grief and healing and have it come to a definitive end—where I stop reliving that issue, moment, decision, trauma, episode, loss, or experience. However, as we know, grief, pain, and suffering don't operate that way. Grief, pain, loss, suffering, and trauma all come in waves and at both expected and unexpected times.

So, how can we take steps forward in this nebulous journey called pain? I would like for us to consider six areas of our lives that may need introspection and healing. Take some time to pray and ask the Holy Spirit to lead you in a process of acknowledging the pain in your life and begin the process toward healing. These areas are (1) physical, pertaining to bodily health, (2) psychological, regarding mental health and well-being, (3) emotional, dealing with heartache and trauma, (4) relational, pertaining to relationships with others, (5) economic, dealing with financial balance and boundaries, and (6) spiritual, having to do with the spiritual warfare and spiritual battles that come with serving God in full-time pastoral ministry.[22] In the appendix, you will find a concise worksheet to guide you in this process of self-exploration.

I invite you over the next several weeks to address one of these potential areas of pain and suffering in your life. It is safe to conjecture that you are suffering in at least one of these six areas. Preaching to people in pain includes preaching to ourselves. We are not immune or exempt from various trials. For instance, Rae Jean Proeschold-Bell and Jason Byassee interviewed a number of clergy in preparation of their book *Faithful and Fractured: Responding to the Clergy Health Crisis*. They found that pastors are some of the most physically unhealthy people, reporting that "there is a true crisis in clergy physical health. We believe it stems from the stressors pastors face today and the expectations other people have

22. Kim, *Preaching with Cultural Intelligence*, 58.

of pastors, paired with pastors' expectations of themselves."[23] Not to mention that pastors are often a direct target of spiritual warfare from the enemy. Satan wants every pastor to fall or give up. Start a journal and assess how you are doing in each of these painful pitfalls. If necessary, find a trusted friend or Christian counselor to dig deeper into the lingering trauma or troubles that would benefit from external expertise.

How Is Your Family Suffering?

For pastors who are married and have children, suffering can take on additional challenging forms. Our spouse and children may feel neglected by us because our first allegiance can easily appear to be a marriage to the church. We can act as a nurturing father or mother or caretaker for our parishioners more than for our own children. Rather than attending our kids' events and functions, we sit at church leading business meetings and prayer gatherings. Peter Cha shares the following story: "During my doctoral study years, I (Peter) was also a busy church-planting pastor, making it challenging for me to spend time with my family. One evening, during our dinner, my five-year-old son suddenly blurted out, 'Dad, I think you should get a new job.' Wrestling with feelings of guilt, I asked, 'What kind of job do you want me to get, Nathaniel?' 'Garbage man, Dad,' came the quick reply. Surprised and puzzled, I asked him why, and my young son explained cheerfully, 'Because the garbage man works only on Wednesdays!'"[24] It's easy for our spouse and children to feel neglected or abandoned by us. Ministry is relentless and sometimes all-consuming. There were times in pastoral ministry, and there are times now in my work as a seminary professor, when I was so drained by the day's preparations, activities, and events that I had little physical and relational energy left for my family. These are real concerns in vocational pastoral ministry.

Our spouse and children also suffer from our humble salaries. Most pastors live within financial restrictions such that additional income streams are few and far between. "Other kids get to go to fill-in-the-blank-vacation.

23. Rae Jean Proeschold-Bell and Jason Byassee, *Faithful and Fractured: Responding to the Clergy Health Crisis* (Grand Rapids: Baker Academic, 2018), xxi.
24. Peter T. Cha and Al Tizon, introduction to *Honoring the Generations: Learning with Asian North American Congregations*, ed. M. Sydney Park, Soong-Chan Rah, and Al Tizon (Valley Forge, PA: Judson, 2012), xiii.

Why can't we do those things?" they cry. Our spouse may hint at dissatisfaction with living modestly or meagerly. Due to our financial limitations, our families may not be able to enjoy some commonplace activities, recreation, or choice clothing, eat at restaurants, or purchase technology and gadgets like our parishioners, and this vacuum of pleasure can be devastating for those we love. Maybe we have transitioned to another pastorate but the timing could not have been worse for our children, ripping them away from their friends, social networks, school system, community, and home during the middle of a semester or during their middle school—or, worse, high school—years.

Family members may also encounter the pain of living up to parishioners' expectations, or what F. Belton Joyner Jr. calls "life in the fish bowl."[25] Church members expect not only the pastor but also the pastor's spouse and children to speak and behave in certain ways. Often these expectations are culturally perpetuated notions of an ideal pastor's spouse and kids. For example, an unhealthy sense of comparison can be made between the previous and current pastor's spouses. The spouse's and children's attire, accessories and adornments, hairstyles, and sense of fashion; the type of car they drive; their choice of college or lack of education; their occupation, their daily routines—all become gratuitous stumbling blocks for some congregants. And their disapproval makes itself known and felt.

Conclusion

In this first chapter, I have argued for the necessity of self-exploration and self-disclosure among preachers. As key members of the church body, we serve an integral function in helping our congregations deal with and heal from pain and suffering. Our honesty and vulnerability will show the church that it's permissible to be human and not "have it all together." The preacher's self-disclosure of which we are speaking is not a harping on the negative aspects of ministry that only leaves us venting to no avail or even embittered. The sermon isn't a weekly venting session to spew onto the pews one's repressed feelings of anger and resentment and pain.

---

25. See F. Belton Joyner Jr., *Life in the Fish Bowl: Everyday Challenges of Pastors and Their Families* (Nashville: Abingdon, 2006).

And yet there may be positive outcomes from sharing one's life with the church in a way that is communicated winsomely and in ways that don't sound like retaliation or wounding weaponry. Sharing our suffering from the pulpit—with wisdom and timeliness—may be the first step in helping to create a church culture of vulnerability, empathy, and healing. We will speak more of this in the next chapter.

Discussion Questions

1. What kinds of pain are you experiencing today or have you encountered in the past?
2. What areas of pain in your life still need healing from God? Are there any chronic pains that won't go away?
3. How is your family suffering today?
4. Do you feel comfortable sharing your pain from the pulpit? Why or why not?

2

The Listeners' Pain

"Do You Love People?"

Picture, in a seminary class or at an ordination council, a master of divinity student or a future ordained minister being asked, "Do you love people?" and responding to this straightforward question by mumbling something to the following effect: "Well, my goal in ministry is to be the preaching pastor of a large church so that I won't have to be bothered with people and their problems. I can just leave that mundane burden for my associate pastors." The audacity of this person is probably the thought that comes immediately to mind.

Perhaps in the inner recesses of our minds, however, we may not want to admit that we occasionally resonate with this comment. People are tough to deal with. They can often be quite challenging to love. Their problems almost inevitably become our problems. Their issues consume us to the point of sleeplessness. When we succumb to this flawed mindset that people are a nuisance, it gradually leads to pastoral and congregational despondency. We wonder, "Why bother with ministry?" This pejorative attitude toward people has contributed to the slow and steady suffering of souls in our congregations. Christians who lack genuine pastoral shepherds are hurting across the country and around the globe. As Paul tells the Philippians, there are very few pastors like his protégé, Timothy. In fact, Paul says, "I have no one else like him, who will show genuine concern for your welfare" (Phil. 2:20).

At times, pastors might like the stage on which to preach but no longer want to serve as a pastor to others and be involved in their painful, messy lives.[1] What we need more of today in our emotionally fragile and volatile churches is for the pastor to remember to act as a "soul watcher" (see Heb. 13:17).[2] We watch others' souls as we guard our own. As the Puritan pastor Richard Baxter once encouraged pastors, "See that the work of grace be thoroughly wrought in your own souls."[3]

Every Sunday, a mixed bag of congregants enters the sanctuary. This motley crew comes to church for any number of reasons: some come to see their friends, some to experience community, some out of religious obligation, some because they enjoy the worship music, and hopefully some because they also value biblical sermons. This eclectic group also needs a genuine pastoral shepherd just as much as it needs a genuine preacher of the Bible. These listeners walk gingerly into the worship service as they navigate their broken worlds—vacillating from moment to moment between being upbeat and being cynical, between feeling downtrodden and feeling optimistic, between realistic and pessimistic, sleepy and engaged, discouraged and hopeful, meandering and purposeful, splendid and suffering. As pastors and preachers, do we understand our listeners' pain? Do we hear their remote whimpers and their silent groans? Do we ask them questions about their lives? Do we really care? Do we really love people?

David H. C. Read became an early trailblazer for the necessity of "pastoral preaching"—preaching borne out of a life pastoring God's people. Read boldly contends, "If none of our sermons ever offers a hint that we are daily in contact with real people, daily sharing their experiences, and available for serious conversations that go beyond the chitchat of a coffee hour, *then the Word is not being truly preached*."[4] He later recounts a conversation with a parishioner who said, "Preachers seem always to be offering answers to questions I never ask."[5] How well do *we* know *our* congregants? To better understand our people and their pains, we want to remind ourselves of the original ecclesiology modeled for us in the early church.

---

1. See Harold L. Senkbeil, *The Care of Souls: Cultivating a Pastor's Heart* (Bellingham, WA: Lexham, 2019).

2. I'm grateful to my colleague Jeffrey D. Arthurs for this insight. Listen to Arthurs, "Pastors Are Soul-Watchers," *Preaching Points* (podcast), https://www.spreaker.com/user/9987846/57-mp3.

3. Richard Baxter, *The Reformed Pastor*, revised and abridged ed. (New York: American Tract Society, 1829), 89.

4. David H. C. Read, *Preaching about the Needs of Real People* (Philadelphia: Westminster, 1988), 26 (emphasis added).

5. Read, *Preaching about the Needs of Real People*, 71.

Re-creating an Acts 2 Church Culture

Today, pain and suffering can often be sources of great shame. Rather than exposing our challenges and struggles, we often keep them concealed—especially from those who may use our painful narratives as unwarranted gossip trails. Intellectually, we know that the Christian life necessitates living in community with fellow believers. Yet this same communal lifestyle invites everyone to be vulnerable and honest with themselves and with others. Christian community directly defies the notion of individualism and purports a sense of belonging to one another. Mandy Smith observes in *The Vulnerable Pastor*, "When one person is willing to step into vulnerability, it disrupts forever the cycle that traps us, giving us permission to share our fears, creating a space for others to be human and for God to be God."[6]

Teeming with vulnerability is the narrative of Acts 2:42–47, where Luke describes the inner workings of the post-Pentecost early church. This newly formed congregation—infused with the Holy Spirit—was a selfless, others-focused community. As Luke records, "They devoted themselves to the apostles' teaching and to fellowship, to the breaking of bread and to prayer" (2:42). This Spirit-led church loved each other deeply and even "sold property and possessions to give to anyone who had need. Every day they continued to meet together in the temple courts. They broke bread in their homes and ate together with glad and sincere hearts" (2:45–46). This Christlike community didn't have osmosis per se, but they were still able to see each other through the eyes of Jesus: being filled with empathy, generosity, hospitality, and joy. While it is up for debate whether this portrait of the early church is only descriptive of that time or whether, in addition, it is prescriptive for today, most professing Christians would agree that this is the type of church they long to be part of. Don't you? This early congregation was cared for not only by its leaders but also by its members, in body, mind, and soul.

Fast-forward two thousand years, and in his book *Discernment* Henri Nouwen reminds his readers, "Today, more than ever, I think of all of you as a community. I belong to you and you to me, and we to each other, whether we know each other or not, whether we have met or not, whether

---

6. Mandy Smith, *The Vulnerable Pastor: How Human Limitations Empower Our Ministry* (Downers Grove, IL: InterVarsity, 2015), 13.

we have embraced or not. We have been brought together by the goodness of God for reasons beyond our choosing and for the purposes of God."[7] Nouwen, a well-known scholar who taught at some of the leading universities in the world, continues: "My achievements did not impress [others]. What they cared deeply about was how consistently I showed up for them and showed them how much I loved them."[8]

Even in the twenty-first century, we can replicate this spirit of selflessness and other-centeredness in our local churches with the help of the Holy Spirit. Part of our pastoral responsibility as preachers is to know our people and to identify, sympathize with, and even empathize with their pain. We can create a congregational culture of compassion and love. Our people are in pain. What is the pastor and preacher to do?

Create an Inventory of Listeners' Pains

In part 2 of this book, we will explore in greater detail six universal types of pain and suffering among God's people and those outside the fold of God. These six types are (1) painful decisions, (2) painful finances, (3) painful health issues, (4) painful losses, (5) painful relationships, and (6) painful sins. It would be foolish to promise you that we could address in this book every single type of pain and suffering. Nor would it be prudent to preach on pain and suffering every Sunday. One of the ways that we can exegete our congregations is to create and develop a church inventory of pain and suffering. Perhaps quarterly or twice per year, sit down with a church membership roster and take stock of how your people are suffering. You could create an Excel spreadsheet that looks something like this:

Individual Inventory of Pain and Suffering

Member	Type of Pain	Length of Pain
Johnny Gomez	Finances: Lost job	6 months
Stacy Ward	Losses: Abortion	2 years

7. Henri Nouwen with Michael J. Christensen and Rebecca J. Laird, *Discernment: Reading the Signs of Daily Life* (New York: HarperOne, 2013), xxv.

8. Nouwen, Christensen, and Laird, *Discernment*, 65.

Conrad Jacobs	Health issues: ALS	3 months
Melissa and Tom Leong	Relationships: Divorce	18 months
Nancy Capistrano	Decisions: Gambling addiction	16 years
Amanda Rogers	Sins: Same-sex behavior	1.5 years

This individualized inventory assumes that we know most or many, if not all, of our congregation members and their struggles. I understand that this would be more challenging in more sizable churches. But we can start with the people we know the best. If there are blank spaces, we will eventually figure out which members we will want to spend more time with. A number of individuals may have more than one type of pain. We will want to take note of those persons and document their varied concerns.

Another beneficial inventory may be to record and pray for the collective pains of our congregation as a community in a corporate setting. For instance, how is our church feeling after the abrupt removal of the previous senior pastor due to moral failure? What lingering emotions have been unresolved with the recent church decision to lay off members of the church staff? How are we doing emotionally and spiritually after witnessing the tragic loss of a high school congregant to suicide? The corporate pain that an entire congregation feels is just as important to explore as individual forms of suffering.

Church Inventory of Pain and Suffering

Type of pain	Length of pain
Pastor's moral failure	4 Months
Staff layoffs	1 Year
Suicide of youth group member	7 Months
Church split	3 Years
Others	

Our congregants and congregations experience myriad challenges in their lives. These pains are certainly palpable and even discouraging. Left unattended, however, pain and suffering lead many to doubt their faith, leave the faith, and even lose the desire to live. Sometimes we suffer more acutely because we allow our perspective on suffering to obscure our thinking and our attitudes.

Why Do We Suffer?

There's the old adage that "lightning never strikes the same place twice." However, this statement is scientifically unsupported. Lightning can strike and has struck the same location more than once during a single storm or even years apart.[9] This saying is often used to assure people that bad things, or even good things, don't happen twice. Yet we've witnessed the same person get struck by the figurative lightning bolts of suffering more than twice, and frequently his or her suffering never quits. When considering the topics of pain and suffering, we are often plagued and pestered by questions about the goodness of God. Theologians call the challenge of responding to these questions *theodicy*, or sometimes *God and the problem of evil*.[10] Every person on the planet wrestles with common universal questions, whereas more specific questions depend on the individual. Here I do not intend to minimize the pain of suffering, for indeed human suffering can be discouraging and even devastating.

Timothy Beavis observes four primary reasons why people experience pain:

1. We experience pain as a result of divine discipline and our own sinful actions.
2. We experience pain as a proving of our faith.
3. We experience pain as a result of the sinful actions of others.
4. We experience pain because we live in a broken and fallen world where even the fabric of the created universe has been marred and distorted.[11]

Kate Bowler, a professor at Duke Divinity School, was diagnosed with stage 4 colon cancer at the age of thirty-five. She chronicles her experi-

9. Nora Gonzalez, "Can Lightning Strike the Same Place Twice?," Britannica, accessed June 25, 2020, https://www.britannica.com/story/can-lightning-strike-the-same-place-twice.

10. For a helpful resource, see Chad Meister and James K. Dew Jr., eds., *God and the Problem of Evil: Five Views* (Downers Grove, IL: IVP Academic, 2017).

11. Timothy Beavis, "Preaching in Pain: How Chronic Illness Impacts the Preacher's Ministry" (DMin thesis, Gordon-Conwell Theological Seminary, 2013), 103.

ences in the bestselling book *Everything Happens for a Reason: And Other Lies I've Loved* and asks some of the questions we ask ourselves: "Why do some people get healed and some people don't? Why do some people leap and land on their feet while others tumble all the way down? Why do some babies die in their cribs and some bitter souls live to see their great-grandchildren?"[12] In spite of her incurable illness, she embraces life to the best of her ability: cherishing each day with her husband and son, pursuing excellence in teaching and scholarship. In many ways, we all live in this creative tension. We enjoy certain blessings and yet experience tremendous hardships. Questions abound. Questions confound. Questions remain. To our chagrin, many questions have no earthly answers.

In the rest of this chapter, I would like to name some tacit reasons why our listeners might be encountering high intensities of pain, often due to incorrect attitudes toward suffering. One strategy to improve our listeners' spiritual and emotional conditions is to preach on pain and suffering regularly and to help reorder their biblical and theological thinking regarding their challenges.

Preach to Expect Suffering

Why are Christians so surprised by suffering when they know cognitively that suffering is a by-product of living in a sinful, fallen world? Post-Eden, there is no going back to the way things were prior to Genesis 3. The denial of existential suffering or the desire for exemption from it only leads to negative responses to suffering. As Paul Borthwick and Dave Ripper relate in their book, *Fellowship of the Suffering*, "I think that too often suffering or things not being perfect or not as we think they should be can lead us to bitterness."[13] Suffering comes as a surprise to the novice and seasoned Christian alike. The foul and acerbic taste of suffering renders the Christian resentful and embittered toward God. Often we live as if we don't expect suffering to strike us down or even that we should be exempt from it. Suffering isn't a problem unless it comes to disrupt *our* lives.

12. Kate Bowler, *Everything Happens for a Reason: And Other Lies I've Loved* (New York: Random House, 2018), xiii.
13. Paul Borthwick and Dave Ripper, *Fellowship of the Suffering: How Hardship Shapes Us for Ministry and Mission* (Downers Grove, IL: InterVarsity, 2018), 46.

Instead, Jesus made it plain to his followers that suffering should be expected by all believers who choose the way of Christ. "Suffering," "persecution," "self-denial," and "pain" are some of the descriptors used by Jesus to explain what the kingdom of God would include. As Nicholas Perrin observes, "Suffering would not only mark the entrance to the kingdom but would be *the* defining feature of the kingdom itself."[14] Perrin continues: "In the first-century world, a suffering Messiah would have been countercultural for all kinds of reasons, but for that very reason Mark had no choice but to hammer the point home." Similarly, today's listeners want to view "a suffering Christian" as equally oxymoronic.[15]

But our model for discipleship is Jesus, who regularly preached about the kingdom of God, likening it to a kingdom of suffering. Jesus didn't entertain the riches of material comforts. In fact, he said surprisingly in Matthew 8:20, "Foxes have dens and birds have nests, but the Son of Man has no place to lay his head." Most of us have living spaces with more than one possible place to lay our heads. He didn't promise a pain-free, trouble-free, or suffering-free existence. Rather, Jesus says in John 16:33, "I have told you these things, so that in me you may have peace. In this world you will have trouble. But take heart! I have overcome the world." The trouble in the world is counteracted by Jesus himself, who alone is the administrator of peace. We suffer not alone but with Christ, who grants peace to his believers. This emboldens the believer to take courage, or to "take heart."

In addition, Jesus never promised a self-indulgent, libertarian existence. Instead, Jesus says in Luke 9:23, "Whoever wants to be my disciple must deny themselves and take up their cross daily and follow me." The remedy for the prosperity gospel or "prosperity-mindedness," which permeates many pulpits today—and not just among "prosperity" preachers—is preaching a commitment to sacrificial living. This involves daily cross-bearing. The preacher who preaches to pain reminds listeners to expect suffering of myriad shapes and forms. We may need to normalize pain and suffering in our preaching to help listeners see them as normal and not an aberration. A Christian's experience of suffering doesn't mean there's something wrong with them. This is true of every living person. Each person suffers but suffers differently.

14. Nicholas Perrin, *The Kingdom of God: A Biblical Theology* (Grand Rapids: Zondervan, 2019), 88.
15. Perrin, *Kingdom of God*, 108.

Preach to Lower One's Expectations

We also exacerbate our feelings of suffering when we expect too much from ourselves and from others. My wife likes to say it this way: "No expectation, no disappointment." We must expect that people will disappoint us. We must expect to feel disappointed by God as well. For example, over the years in my position as a seminary professor in the area of preaching, I have met a number of well-known pastors and preachers. No need to mention names. Early on in my teaching ministry, I would become quite nervous prior to meeting these larger-than-life ministers. To be blunt, after meeting certain individuals I would feel disappointed with the person because of our less-than-ideal social interaction. Before our actual conversation, I would have an imaginary conversation with the person. When they didn't meet my preconceived expectations, I was disappointed. Sometimes they only talked about themselves and never asked me about my life. All people are human, including well-known preachers. Curtly stated, people are people, and people are sinful. Scott M. Gibson reminds us, "As pastors and preachers, when we recognize that people are people we aren't surprised by disappointments or failures because we are people, too."[16] People—pastors and parishioners alike—will disappoint us.

We also suffer sometimes because we disappoint ourselves. We assume pressures to live up to our own self-induced and self-serving expectations. We want everything and want to do everything. In short, when we are being idealistic, "we've set ourselves up for a devastating fall. I'll pray more. I'll share my faith at work. I'll read my Bible from Genesis to the maps in the back of the book. I'll trust God without questioning."[17] Maybe we experience pain because we couldn't save our marriage, we got laid off, we didn't go to college or finish our degree, we gave up on a fractured friendship, and much more. Failures in life can lead to various gradations of suffering and pain.

Preach against Entitlement and Ingratitude

Entitlement in today's culture creates another source of pain. Audrey Borschel shares a past encounter with a parishioner. When she was called

16. Scott M. Gibson, "A Preacher Looks Back after 30 Years," *Preaching* 34, no. 1 (Fall 2018): 33.
17. Sheila Walsh, *It's Okay Not to Be Okay: Moving Forward One Day at a Time* (Grand Rapids: Baker Books, 2018), 15.

to become the senior minister of a church, a congregant asked her, "Are you going to preach what we want to hear or what we need to hear?"[18] The same question might be useful for our consideration. Are we preaching sermons that people want to hear or sermons that they need to hear? Over the last half century, in particular, we have witnessed an uptick in what we might call a culture of entitlement. Paul calls this the culture of "itching ears" (2 Tim. 4:3). We see this regularly in the seminary context when students are unwilling or unable to put forth the effort and yet still feel entitled to receive good grades for their submitted work and exams. We see this in churches where congregants only want to hear sermons about love and grace and not holiness and judgment.

Sociologist Brené Brown notices a significant source of pain in what she describes as "the scarcity principle," a feeling that we never have enough. For instance, she says people have internal struggles with feeling like they are never good enough, never perfect enough, never thin enough, never powerful enough, never successful enough, never smart enough, never certain enough, never safe enough, never extraordinary enough.[19] Similarly, this scarcity principle is reflected well in the biblical narrative of Exodus 16. Those who complain the most are not those who have nothing but rather those for whom God has provided something. That something becomes what we scorn. We want something different. Remember God's provision of sweet water and manna from heaven to the Israelites? Instead of being grateful for their miraculous sustenance, the Israelites moaned about having to eat the same meal again. They later disobeyed God by pocketing too much manna and quail for themselves and not trusting in his daily provision. Many of our congregants, including ourselves, lack gratitude. This attitude of ingratitude exacerbates our sense of pain and suffering.

The other side of the same coin of ungratefulness is comparison. Comparison asks the question, What has God done for me versus what has God done for him or her? Once we bring others into the conversation, we have compared ourselves with them. We have told God that our suffering

---

18. Audrey Borschel, "Preaching in Times of Conflict," *New Theological Review* 19, no. 1 (2006): 78.

19. Brené Brown, *Daring Greatly: How the Courage to Be Vulnerable Transforms the Way We Live, Love, Parent, and Lead* (New York: Avery, 2012), 25. Brown is a secular scholar at Houston Baptist University whose research is often employed by Christian scholars sometimes without much discernment. While insightful and quite popular, Brown's work must not be appropriated without a critical lens.

is too much to handle because that person over there has suffered less than we have.

Preach to Educate and Reconcile the Church

A silent pain for many of our listeners is overt and subtle forms of prejudice: it could be based on our ethnicity, culture, race, gender, class, disability, education, political views, or something else. Bryan Loritts's book *Insider Outsider: My Journey as a Stranger in White Evangelicalism and My Hope for Us All* is a clarion call to all churches that struggle to navigate difference and to deal with our common sin of bigotry. No church culture would admit to having such superiority and judgment toward others who are different. However, Loritts identifies one of the church's defining conundrums: "The problem with [a majority theological group] is not that it has an accent, but that it fails to see the ethnic theological accent it possesses. This glaucoma of sorts leads [them] . . . to normalize their hermeneutical biases while wielding them as a tool of oppression where anyone who doesn't see it the way they do tends to be castigated, ostracized, blogged about, or ignored."[20]

Similarly, speaking to any dominant culture for a moment, a person doesn't know they're different unless they have experienced sticking out from the majority. Those in any minority group will suffer silently in your church. In many cases, they are ignored, overlooked, marginalized, despised, unappreciated, invalidated, discouraged, and more, even though they may attend regularly. To preach to pain in the twenty-first century involves a pastor figuring out who is marginalized and ignored in the congregation. The minority and majority need reconciliation. This ongoing source of pain in the church will be discussed further in chapters 8 and 9, on painful relationships and painful sins, respectively.

Preach a Big God and Small Problems

When tragedy strikes and pain emerges seemingly out of the blue, the magnitude of the problem engulfs our vision, and simultaneously we see

20. Bryan Loritts, *Insider Outsider: My Journey as a Stranger in White Evangelicalism and My Hope for Us All* (Grand Rapids: Zondervan, 2018), 23–24.

a diminutive God. The pain, struggle, and concern overwhelms us to the point that that is all we can see. Try an experiment with me: Put your hand in front of your face. The hand represents the problem or pain in your life. Can you see much of anything else? Not much. The problem dominates your vision. In some cases, our suffering begins to define us and we assume a new identity. We become captives to our hardships. As something difficult happens to people, God becomes smaller and smaller in their eyes. Suffering incites the doubting of God. Chad Meister and James K. Dew Jr. explain: "This poses a tenacious problem for those who believe in a God who is perfectly good and loving, all-powerful, and infinitely smart. For surely a God who is good and loving would not want there to be widespread pain and suffering in the world. And surely a God who is omniscient and omnipotent could ensure that no such world would exist. But such a world does exist. Our world."[21]

In the book of Job, as the narrative unfolds, our hearts go out to Job. How could one (righteous) person endure so much heartache? Although Job is valid in his lament toward God from a human perspective, the literature on the book of Job seems to suggest that God is rather cold and heartless in his response toward Job's suffering. In fact, God shows up and speaks with almost a sarcastic tone beginning in Job 38. After hearing out Job's complaints in the previous chapters, God demands a rhetorical answer starting in 38:3: "Brace yourself like a man; I will question you, and you shall answer me. Where were you when I laid the earth's foundation? Tell me, if you understand. Who marked off its dimensions? Surely you know! Who stretched a measuring line across it? On what were its footings set, or who laid its cornerstone—while the morning stars sang together and all the angels shouted for joy?" And the Lord carries on for several chapters in this candid fashion. In God's defense, he is not insensitive to Job's cries and duress, but rather he is simply straightforward in reminding Job of his—God's— incalculable nature. When we see the greatness of God, our problems and pains become a little smaller in our eyes. Indeed, our focus is still myopic and life remains challenging. But preaching big problems and a small God is the antithesis of what a preacher ought to be doing on Sunday mornings.

21. Meister and Dew, *God and the Problem of Evil*, 1.

Preach Lament without an Immediately Happy Ending

While holding on to the previous preaching principle, we must give our listeners the time they need to vent and wallow in their lament. The tendency of the positively minded, solution-oriented preacher is to leap toward the resolution for every human need and problem in the sermon: Jesus! While Jesus is the philosophically and theoretically correct answer to all positive and negative existential realities, we still have to grind through our myriad pains day by day, week after week, month by month, and year after year.

Growing up in the church, we would often sing at Vacation Bible School the song associated with 1 Peter 5:7, which says: "Cast all your anxiety on him [Jesus] because he cares for you." Peter does not say, "Cast all your anxiety on him because he dissects that part of your brain's recall." Jesus doesn't magically dilute the pain or expunge our painful memories. Rather, we hand our worries to him because he walks alongside us as a source of encouragement and comfort to help us get through yet another day.

What is the worst possible form of pain imaginable for you? Would it help you as a listener if someone immediately offered you Jesus as the silver lining? Probably not! In the same way, we want to exhibit pastoral empathy, at times, to let people in pain lament without being told that there is an immediate happy ending—when we cast our burdens on Jesus or, with regard to delayed gratification, when we get to our heavenly home.

Preach for Spiritual Maturity

Trying to wrap our minds around why we suffer is as hopeless as looking for a golf ball in four feet of prairie grass at night. Yet somehow through suffering, God produces spiritual maturity in us.[22] Mark DeVries, in *Family-Based Youth Ministry*, compares what an immature Christian looks like with what a mature one looks like. For example, he presents childhood faith as believing that "good Christians don't have pain or disappointment" and presents mature adult faith as recognizing that "God uses our pain and disappointment to make us better Christians"; alternatively, childhood faith believes that "faith will help us always explain what God is doing (things always work out)," whereas mature faith understands that

22. A helpful resource on preaching and spiritual maturity is Scott M. Gibson, *Preaching with a Plan: Sermon Strategies for Growing Mature Believers* (Grand Rapids: Baker Books, 2012).

"faith helps us stand under God's sovereignty even when we have no idea what God is doing."[23] How are we doing, and in what areas do our listeners need to mature as they encounter and experience pain and suffering?

Conclusion

Suffering is ubiquitous whenever people are involved. The pains of our listeners are too numerous to count and more than we can bear as pastors and preachers. In fact, we were never meant to bear the weight of the world on our shoulders. Only Jesus is able to do that. Yet taking requisite time to familiarize ourselves with our listeners' and congregation's pains is a worthwhile pastoral endeavor. Each congregation faces individual pains—some are kept silent and some readily recognized. Simultaneously, the challenges permeating the collective consciousness at one congregation are distinctive and will not be on the radar for the church down the street. Once we know the struggles of our people, how do we plan on preaching to their pain? That will be the focus of our next chapter.

Discussion Questions

1. Do you love people? How do you demonstrate love for God's people?
2. What are some of the urgent and long-term challenges/pains of your church members?
3. How often do you preach on the topic of pain and suffering? Might it be possible to preach on pain more regularly?
4. Beyond the pulpit, in what ways could pain and suffering be addressed in congregational life: in the context of worship, fellowship, and discipleship?

23. Mark DeVries, *Family-Based Youth Ministry*, revised and expanded ed. (Downers Grove, IL: InterVarsity, 2004), 27.

3

A Plan for Preaching on Pain

Ad hoc sermon planning seldom works effectively. Wise preaching pastors create a preaching calendar for the year's sermons and develop sermon series.[1] Depending on your church or denomination's traditions, prayerful guidance from the Holy Spirit, and input from your pastoral staff or leadership, you probably have a system already in place for determining the content of your messages for a given year. Some will preach only through entire Bible books, others lean toward topical or thematic series only, and some prefer to go back and forth between Bible books and topical series. In certain traditions, the lectionary serves as one's guide for selecting preaching texts.

Regardless of our particular approach, we will want to construct and implement some type of plan for preaching on the topic of pain. This chapter invites us to consider some of the key elements for preaching on pain and an initial pathway for how we can preach on pain intentionally and effectively. This pathway will become the preaching template for chapters 4 through 9, which deal with specific topics related to pain and suffering in our congregants' lives.

In this book, I am not arguing that every single sermon must address pain and suffering. This would be unfair, unwise, and unfaithful to

---

1. For assistance on sermon planning, see Scott M. Gibson, *Preaching with a Plan: Sermon Strategies for Growing Mature Believers* (Grand Rapids: Baker Books, 2012); and Stephen Nelson Rummage, *Planning Your Preaching: A Step-by-Step Guide for Developing a One-Year Preaching Calendar* (Grand Rapids: Kregel, 2002).

Scripture and its assortment of genres and passages. Not every single text in Scripture speaks about pain and suffering. At the same time, however, our preaching can be so focused on celebration and positivity that we fail to address or we avoid the pain and suffering evident in particular Bible passages. As a general rule of thumb, we can preach on pain and suffering when the sermon text addresses it.

Preparatory Questions to Preach on Pain

The following nine questions serve as a guide or template to preach more intentionally on pain and suffering that we will later employ in chapters 4 through 9.

1. Which Passage Will I Preach On?

As expositors, we must first select a passage for our sermon. As mentioned above, we select texts using a variety of methods depending on whether we are preparing an exposition of a book, a topical sermon, a sermon on a lectionary passage, or another context. Sometimes the topic of pain and suffering explicitly emerges from the text. At other times, the topic of pain and suffering is implied but not expressed outright. Either way, we begin the sermon process by choosing a text.

2. What Type of Pain/Suffering Is Revealed in the Text?

In his widely used textbook for homiletics, *Christ-Centered Preaching*, Bryan Chapell encourages preachers to consider what he calls the Fallen Condition Focus in every sermon and preaching text. Chapell argues that Scripture passages often name or describe our sinfulness and depravity or fallen condition, which needs redemption and grace through the person and work of Jesus Christ. We might view pain and suffering in a similar light by asking, What type of pain or suffering is revealed in this text? To provide a concrete biblical example, let's consider the painful exchange between Hagar and Sarai in Genesis 16.

One of the first things we want to do when preaching on pain is to explore whether our Scripture text addresses the issue either intentionally or unintentionally. The biblical accounts of Hagar and her son Ishmael might appear to be sideshows or strange tangents to the real crux of the narratives of God's promise to Sarai and Abram. Yet God is working even in the lives of secondary characters such as Hagar and Ishmael. For Hagar, the Egyptian maid of Sarai, pain is real. Sarai gives Hagar to her husband Abram because Sarai is unable to conceive a child of her own. Hagar has no choice in the matter. Seen as property, she isn't consulted as to whether she wants to have this child with Abram. On top of this, Sarai resents her for having sexual relations with her husband and ultimately for being able to have his child—something infertility prevented her from doing herself. Moses records in Genesis 16:6, "Then Sarai mistreated Hagar; so she fled from her." The specific forms of abuse are not recorded, but we can imagine that Sarai—at the least—verbally accosted her.

It would strengthen the sermon to also consider Sarai's pain and suffering as she witnesses Abram, the man that she loves, share sexual intimacy with her servant. Sarai feels betrayed by Abram even though it was her idea for them to consummate. She probably feels abandoned and rejected by God, as he has not opened her womb. Since having offspring was so important in this culture, Sarai might escape some cultural shame by Abram having an heir even if the heir doesn't come from her own body.

3. How Does the Bible Character or Biblical Author Deal with the Pain?

Clearly, this situation speaks into the pain that arises from human conflict. Psychologists tell us that when there is tension, we typically respond by fighting or fleeing. Hagar, abused by Sarai, flees from Abram and Sarai's home. An angel of the Lord later finds her in the wilderness near a spring of water (Gen. 16:7).

Sarai responds to her dilemma with fight as she holds her ground and lashes out at Hagar. Sarai demonstrates outwardly the pain that she feels inwardly. When people feel pain, they may vent or even hurt others with their words and actions. We might say that Hagar is the scapegoat for Sarai's internal frustrations and perhaps anger toward God and Abram.

4. How Does This Pain in the Text Relate to Our Listeners' Pain?

The pain or suffering in any given Scripture passage may relate to one of these common human struggles: the sin-related, the economic, the physical, the emotional, the psychological, the relational, and the spiritual.

The pain in this narrative might hit home to our listeners on different levels. First, it addresses the pain of infertility. We will address the topic of infertility in greater detail in chapter 6. Second, the passage speaks into betrayal and rejection by those we love. Sarai experiences rejection by Abram and even Hagar, her maid. This story, in modern terms, explores the realm of marital unfaithfulness and adultery. Third, related to the previous two, this narrative delves into the pain of shame—in this case the cultural shames of infertility and betrayal.

5. What Does This Pain Say about God and His Allowance of Pain?

Preaching to people in pain requires a theological grounding in who God is in his character. One of the most beautiful elements in this Genesis 16 story is how it reveals God's individual attention and care for all people—including those whom society deems "invisible." He hears the cries not only of Sarai, the main protagonist, but also of Hagar, who is essentially a dispensable Egyptian slave woman. Richard E. Averbeck explains: "Slave women sometimes were used as surrogates to bear children for men whose wives (apparently) were infertile or whose status did not allow it. . . . In the Bible, Hagar is an example of a chattel slave woman whom Sarai gave to Abram for this purpose."[2] We sense and experience as the story unfolds that God's love for Hagar is no less than his love for Sarai. God sees Hagar and comprehends her pain. Later Hagar offers her perspective on who God is to her: "You are the God who sees me" (16:13). God sees and hears the pain of all his creation—in particular, people who go unnoticed and are seemingly invisible to others.

6. How Does God / Jesus / the Holy Spirit Help Us in Our Suffering?

God understands exactly what Hagar is feeling at this moment, and the narrative reminds us that he has not abandoned Hagar in her time of need. Knowing Hagar's emotional and relational turmoil and abuse incurred at the hands of Sarai, God sends an angel to stop her from fleeing and to reassure her that this child in her womb also will receive God's blessing. God acknowledges her pain through this angel. God sends the

---

2. Richard E. Averbeck, "Slavery in the World of the Bible," in *Behind the Scenes of the Old Testament: Cultural, Social, and Historical Contexts*, ed. Jonathan S. Greer, John W. Hilber, and John H. Walton (Grand Rapids: Baker Academic, 2018), 428.

angel to lead her back to his plan and will. God wanted Abram to have a son in spite of his own sin of impatience and lack of trust by entering his slave woman Hagar. The angel of the Lord says to Hagar, "Go back to your mistress and submit to her." But God does not merely send her back to the source of her pain, Sarai; rather, he couples this instruction with a promise of blessing in verse 10, "I will increase your descendants so much that they will be too numerous to count." Our suffering is not in vain. Sometimes our suffering keeps us in the will of God. We are also reminded of and strengthened by God's promises.

7. How Can Our Preaching Show Care and Empathy?

Lenny Luchetti writes in *Preaching with Empathy*, "Homiletic empathy is the grace that enables preachers to imagine their way into the situational shoes of others, to understand the thoughts and feel the emotions of listeners. Only then can they preach in a manner most responsive to their listeners' deepest needs."[3] In this Genesis text, it is easy to minimize or omit emotional material regarding the feelings of Hagar because she is "less important" than Sarai. However, the text shouts of God's empathy toward the least of these. Pain is evident clearly in Sarai. Her own infertility and witnessing Hagar's ability to bear a child for Abram are too heartbreaking for her. In this sermon, we can take some time to acknowledge the grieving women and men in our congregations who battle daily the pain of infertility and miscarriage. Hagar's experiences also invite opportunities to demonstrate pastoral care and empathy to victims of various forms of abuse.

Ask probing questions to various listeners in the room. For instance, we might ask of "Sarais" in the sanctuary: "Are you currently experiencing, or in the past have you experienced, the pain of infertility and miscarriage?" "Do you feel like God has abandoned you?" For "Hagars" in the room: "Have you ever been abused, whether verbally, physically, emotionally, or sexually?" "Do you ever feel like Hagar, someone unnoticed or unimportant?" Allow those questions to sit in silence in the minds of your listeners. Permit them to acknowledge and deal with the suffering and pain. Later on in the sermon, we can offer up words of biblical encouragement

3. Lenny Luchetti, *Preaching with Empathy: Crafting Sermons in a Callous Culture* (Nashville: Abingdon, 2018), 11.

and hope to such couples and individuals who feel abandoned and neglected by God and society.

8. How Can We Share This Pain in Christian Community?

In our individualistic culture, we often consider suffering and pain as existential properties in isolation from others. As we address pain and suffering in this book, we want to be able to use the pulpit in such a way that we create an ecclesial culture in which pain and suffering are addressed, where appropriate, communally rather than merely individually. Infertility and abuse are highly internalized pains that people tend to suffer on their own rather than exposing them to the wider community. One of the ways that preachers can assist others in their pain is to foster a trusted, shame-free environment where over time parishioners and listeners can acknowledge their suffering and pray for each other even during the worship service and beyond. We can make the most of our pain as we find intentional ways to help others through their suffering. A modern-day paralytic, Mark R. Talbot encourages, "Stop asking, 'Why has God allowed this to happen to me?' Instead, be alert to those you can encourage because of how you are suffering, remembering that it is often only as we focus on relieving others' suffering that we ourselves find significant relief."[4]

9. How Will God Use Our Suffering to Transform Us and Bring Himself Glory?

This final question is probably not at the forefront of sufferers' inquiring minds, at least not immediately. Yet one of the aims of our pulpit ministry is to consider alongside our hearers how God will transform their lives and use their pain and suffering ultimately to bring glory to God. Some or many listeners might wonder, "How cruel and selfish of God to permit or ordain suffering in my life just so that I can return glory to him." John Piper explains the consuming or preoccupying nature of God for his own glory: "Probably no text in the Bible reveals the passion of God for his own glory more clearly and bluntly as Isaiah 48:9–11 where God says, 'For my name's sake I *defer my anger*, for the sake of my praise I *restrain*

---

4. Mark R. Talbot, "Redeeming a Life of Paralysis," in *When Suffering Is Redemptive: Stories of How Anguish and Pain Accomplish God's Mission*, ed. Larry J. Waters (Bellingham, WA: Lexham, 2016), 37.

it for you, that I may not cut you off. Behold, I have refined you, but not as silver; I have tried you in the furnace of affliction. For my own sake, for my own sake, *I do it, for* how should my name be profaned? My glory I will not give to another.'"[5]

God wants to transform us, and sometimes the best way to accomplish this is to permit pain and suffering in our lives. How will God transform us through this current and long-term circumstance or hardship? When we contemplate the fact that God created the entire universe—including humankind—for his glory, the natural by-product of pain and suffering is that our attitude and response to tribulations ought to bring him glory as well. The preacher to people in pain will spend prayerful time thinking through the appropriate application from the text that introduces the listener to life transformation and helps them see how their afflictions can bring glory to God.

General Principles for Preaching on Pain

In the second part of this chapter, I will offer seven general principles for preaching on pain and suffering and two reminders to be stated after we have preached the sermon. First, the principles.

1. Diagnose the Source of the Pain

One of the first questions a physician will ask upon our arrival at the office is, "What brings you in today?" He or she assumes there is a medical concern and wants to hear what's going on with us physically or sometimes mentally. By inquiring about our symptoms, the doctor can deduce conclusions about what the concern may be. Similarly, one of the first things we want to do as preachers is to diagnose the source of our listeners' pain and suffering. Carol M. Norén observes, "Unlike an *individual* seeking medical attention, the diagnostic questions we ask and the sermons we preach pertain to a congregation—*many* people. They won't all experience or describe their symptoms the same way. Some will want to put a brave face on it and pretend they feel fine. Others may be

---

5. John Piper, "Biblical Texts to Show God's Zeal for His Own Glory," Desiring God, November 24, 2007, https://www.desiringgod.org/articles/biblical-texts-to-show-gods-zeal-for-his-own-glory (emphasis original).

hypochondriacs, certain they are suffering more than anyone else. Still others may try to use the malaise or crisis as an opportunity to promote their own agenda."[6]

As mentioned in chapter 2, a host of diagnoses are possible among our varied parishioners. Depending on the movement of the Holy Spirit through prayer, the spiritual climate of the congregation, and sometimes the urgency of the life situation, event, or tragedy, the preacher can discern the type of pain or suffering that needs to be addressed in a particular sermon. Diagnose the source of the pain. Are there people in pain and suffering in the congregation who would benefit from such a sermon?

2. Preach on Pain When the Text Addresses It

Second, does this text that I'm preaching on address the topic of pain and suffering explicitly or implicitly? Preach on pain whenever the Scripture text mentions or refers to afflictions. In every genre of biblical literature, we find subtle and overt references to pain and suffering. Think out loud with me for a moment regarding the Bible's assorted genres: historical narratives, the law, wisdom literature, psalms, prophetic books, the four Gospels, the epistles, and apocalyptic literature. Allusions to and concrete examples of pain and suffering, whether human or divine, permeate Scripture. When studying a given pericope for preaching purposes, jot down any aspects of pain and suffering conveyed in the text. Prayerfully submit to God the most effective way to communicate what he has said to those living in biblical times and how this biblical truth relates to our listeners' world in the twenty-first century.

3. Preach on Pain When the Occasion Calls for It[7]

When tragedy and pain strike a congregation, writes Sondra Wheeler in *The Minister as Moral Theologian*, "to say nothing at such times is to do more than miss an opportunity; it is to leave parishioners with no help at all in bringing the world of the text and the world they must inhabit together. Your silence could even suggest that the faith you proclaim has

---

6. Carol M. Norén, "Preaching Hope to People in Pain," *Preaching* 33, no. 3 (Spring 2018): 28.

7. Some doctrinal topics with regard to pain and suffering that we might preach on include self-denial and crucicentrism, heaven and hell, the kingdom of God, God's holistic nature (justice and mercy, holiness and wrath), the importance of Christian community, and more.

nothing to say to frustration and grief, outrage and perplexity."[8] What does the Bible have to say about natural disasters like hurricanes, tsunamis, tornadoes, earthquakes, shootings, murders, unexpected deaths, diseases, hate crimes against humanity, and a plethora of other hardships?

A couple of caveats are in order here. First, not every personal event or life situation needs to be addressed from the pulpit. The preacher might engage in some "group processing" with the church's leadership as to whether they believe a sermon is warranted on a particular issue. Second, loving the people affected by a tragedy or painful crisis is also a chief consideration vis-à-vis whether or not I preach on pain. Perhaps it is best that I wait to preach on this topic or, in certain cases, that I not preach on it at all.

4. Help Listeners Receive Comfort from God (Triune God: Father, Son, and Spirit)

One of the most helpful passages in Scripture on how Christians can approach pain and suffering comes from 2 Corinthians 1:3–11, where the apostle Paul opens his second letter to the church at Corinth. This letter exposes the vulnerability of one of the greatest preachers in history, documenting his own sufferings for Christ in Asia (v. 8), which he describes in greater detail in 6:3–13 and 11:16–33.

Paul reminds the Corinthians in this text of the true source of comfort: God. He writes in verses 3–4 that God is "the Father of compassion and the God of all comfort, who comforts us in all our troubles." Sometimes, when we are suffering, we believe the lie that God is not actually the source of comfort but really the source of our pain. We immediately question and doubt God's omnipotence and sovereignty over all of creation. Our human tendency is to run away from God rather than run toward God when we are hurting. God seems far, far away during seasons of trial. Lewis Allen writes in *The Preacher's Catechism*, "Suffering is often a powerful test of who we really are. Suffering exposes our values, our faith, and our hearts."[9] We might say that how we handle suffering reveals whether we really believe in God or not.

---

8. Sondra Wheeler, *The Minister as Moral Theologian: Ethical Dimensions of Pastoral Leadership* (Grand Rapids: Baker Academic, 2017), 32.

9. Lewis Allen, *The Preacher's Catechism* (Wheaton: Crossway, 2018), 87.

How does God comfort us in our pain in this passage? In every sermon on pain, provide tangible expressions of how God comforts us in all of our troubles. Sometimes the comfort of God is divinely supernatural. Yet, most of the time, being comforted by God is not a one-and-done experience of healing. Although God can supernaturally heal emotional wounds, in the most mysterious and miraculous of ways, Paul uses the imagery of a loving, steady father who is always there for us to be a figurative shoulder to cry on. Only God is capacious enough to absorb the volume and duration of our questions, frustrations, anger, lament, nagging, vitriol, and cantankerousness. God's hands of peace and comfort wipe away our stream of tears. Yet sometimes God chooses to bring us comfort through other people.

5. Encourage Listeners to Comfort Others in Their Pain

Paul continues his spiritual prescription for coping with pain by telling the Corinthians that once they receive God's comfort, they can help comfort others in their pain as well. He tells the believers in verse 4 that God comforts us "so that we can comfort those in any trouble with the comfort we ourselves receive from God." The NIV's rendering of "so that we can" for the Greek word *dynasthai* (a present infinitive middle/passive verb) diminishes the emphasis of the root *dynamai*, which refers to the *power* to do something that we cannot conjure up by our own strength.

It is a gift of God to have the power to comfort others in their tribulations. God does not comfort us individually or in isolation. Rather, his gaze is upon all of his children, making the by-product of our reception of God's comfort the ability to assist others in their pain. As a form of sermonic application, envision with your listeners the ways in which they can come alongside others to comfort them in their pain. This is a corporeal way of serving the body of Christ that is a privilege and a gift from God to his beloved community.

6. Give Thanks to God in the Midst of Pain

Paul challenges the Corinthians at the beginning of the letter, in verse 3, to praise God and thank him for his compassion and comfort. This Pauline admonition to praise and thank God is almost unfathomable. How can Paul possibly thank God for anything related to pain and suffering?

Somewhere in the sermon the preacher can gently encourage listeners to give thanks to God in spite of their difficulties. We might say it this way: "Where would I be now if I didn't have God in my life?" or "How bad would my suffering be if God wasn't in the picture?" Like Paul, we hope that our listeners can respond in time: "Praise be to the God and Father of our Lord Jesus Christ, the Father of compassion and the God of all comfort!" Be patient with your listeners. Give them time to heal and continue to heal when setbacks and reminders come.

7. Urge Listeners to Glorify God through Their Pain

How might our listeners glorify God in the throes of their suffering? Paul's section on imitating Christ in Philippians 2:5–11, the Christ hymn, is a helpful reminder of Christlike attitude and humility. Even in Jesus's suffering, his greatest aim was to be obedient and to glorify the Father. "Therefore," Paul writes in verses 9–11, "God exalted him to the highest place and gave him the name that is above every name, that at the name of Jesus every knee should bow, in heaven and on earth and under the earth, and every tongue acknowledge that Jesus Christ is Lord, *to the glory of God the Father*." In all things, even in the midst of pain and suffering, our discipleship leads us to bring God glory. We can highlight in the sermon concrete ways that long-term optimistic attitudes and testimonies during even insufferable miseries can please and glorify God and enable others to witness his glory more fully.

Two Reminders

Pain Comes in Waves

As I have shared in a previous book, *Preaching with Cultural Intelligence*, my younger brother Timothy D. Kim was brutally murdered in the Philippines on November 7, 2015, on the night he was celebrating his thirty-sixth birthday.[10] Not a day goes by that I don't think about Tim. In fact, I don't ever want to stop thinking of him, so I keep a picture of his beautiful, smiling face in my pocket. Yet the reality about suffering and pain is that it comes in waves. The heartache erupts like a dormant

---

10. Matthew D. Kim, *Preaching with Cultural Intelligence: Understanding the People Who Hear Our Sermons* (Grand Rapids: Baker Academic, 2017), 216.

volcano every birthday, his birthday and mine, when he used to call to wish me a happy birthday from wherever he was in the world. The harrowing aide-mémoire reintroduces itself every Christmas and New Year's. It comes around when something reminds me of him: his intelligence, his creativity, his boldness, his selflessness, his warmth, his humor, his smile, his myriad talents. The pain of losing him resurfaces and triggers even at random moments. The trauma is still painfully fresh and raw even years later. The bite of suffering is infinitely more excruciating for our parents—in particular, for our mother.

I will continue to reexperience the pain of Tim's death in this life. It would be hard enough if he had died from natural causes. Nobody deserves to be murdered and have his or her life cut short prematurely. We don't have all of the information and answers surrounding his death, as earthly justice came to a crashing halt after a few mere weeks due to local and governmental corruption there. And yet, like Paul tells believers in 1 Thessalonians 4:13, "Brothers and sisters, we do not want you to be uninformed about those who sleep in death, so that you do not grieve like the rest of mankind, who have no hope." There is also this supernatural peace from God above, who whispers how he understands the pain of losing someone he loved—his one and only Son, who lived a perfect life and yet died a wrongful death, only on an infinitely greater scale. Pain comes in waves. For this reason, we preach to comfort those in pain, but we also remain close to them in their suffering.

Preach with Your Presence

The second reminder is to preach to them with your presence before and after the sermon. The well-known adage attributed to Saint Francis of Assisi is helpful here: "Preach the gospel at all times, and if necessary use words." The point is that our behavior and actions speak loudly and concretize and validate the gospel message. Similarly, congregants hear our sermons on Sundays, but our presence speaks louder in their lives, especially during times of trial and tribulation. We can preach with our presence when they need us most.

Preaching with our presence often entails sitting beside them in a hospital room, palliative care center, waiting room, home visitation, police station, courtroom, prison, and other physical locations where they are.

At the same time, perhaps preaching with our presence means a phone call because we cannot be physically present with them for various reasons. It's not enough to just preach a good sermon on suffering. In addition, our listeners need a listening ear, someone to pray with, and someone to sit with them in their grief—sometimes over and over again.

Conclusion

Preaching on pain is never easy. Being present with our listeners in their pain can be additionally taxing on the pastor's spirit. Yet, these are the "burdensome joys" of pastoral ministry and preaching.[11] Now that we have a basic plan for preaching on pain, we will move forward to part 2 where we will consider six universal painful hot spots for God's people: painful decisions, painful finances, painful health issues, painful losses, painful relationships, and painful sins.

Discussion Questions

1. What is your plan for preaching on pain?
2. How can you actively choose to praise God in the midst of your pain?
3. How will you help your congregants to embrace and even praise God in the midst of suffering?
4. In what ways can you provide opportunities for the entire church to hear testimonies of pain and suffering and stories of healing and restoration?

---

11. See James Earl Massey, *The Burdensome Joy of Preaching* (Nashville: Abingdon, 1998).

PART 2

Preaching ON PAIN

4

Painful Decisions

A church member who is a professing Christian visits you regularly in the church office to confess his stream of unhealthy relationships. Every time he describes his latest girlfriend, your pastoral intuition screams that she is less than God's best for him. From verbal abuse to sexual impropriety to wasted time and resources, the unequally yoked relationship teeters and totters and eventually comes to a crashing halt. He asks you with great puzzlement, "Why would God continue to put me in such bad relationships?" Mystified by this comment—which lacks self-awareness and perpetuates poor theology—you wonder about the sheer number of Christians who fall into the trap of making habitually unwise choices and later blame God for the ensuing chaos.

Life is ultimately about decisions, decisions, and more decisions. According to an article in *Psychology Today*, the average adult makes thirty-five thousand decisions every single day.[1] That equates to over two thousand decisions every waking hour (assuming eight hours of sleep per night). Some choices that we make are inconsequential during a single twenty-four-hour period. For instance, I may choose to splurge on a late afternoon bowl of my favorite Taro-flavored frozen yogurt. Satisfying my sugar craving is rather inconsequential for one day. However, if I choose to indulge in frozen treats for several days or even weeks in a row, my body will revolt somehow and tell me to stop.

1. Eva M. Krockow, "How Many Decisions Do We Make Each Day?," *Psychology Today*, September 27, 2018, https://www.psychologytoday.com/us/blog/stretching-theory/201809/how-many-decisions-do-we-make-each-day.

Some choices are no-brainers, whereas others are excruciatingly difficult to discern. The gray areas, however, engender additional layers of complexity. Emily P. Freeman observes in her book *The Next Right Thing*, "It's the *mights* and *maybes* of our lives that keep us awake at night. *Maybe I should accept the new position. Which schooling choice is best for my kids? How can I support my aging parents? What might happen if I choose wrong?*"[2] To extend her line of questioning, What if my choice today ruins my future? Every person on the planet has made some very poor choices in life. We all have and will continue to do so. Hollywood films involving a time machine or a mulligan capitalize on our proclivity to wallow in our misery, because these painful decisions haunt us potentially every day. For Christians, they inhibit our ability to move toward discipleship and to look more like Christ.

In this chapter, we explore some possible ways that Albert Camus's statement "Life is a sum of all your choices" rings true only to a certain extent for our listeners—who live with resurrection hope in the person of Jesus Christ. The brilliant cinema philosopher Forrest Gump articulates the mystery of life nicely when he says, "Life is like a box of chocolates. You never know what you're gonna get." Our listeners, similarly, don't know what life will bring, but what can they do with the life they've been granted by God? How do we assist our listeners in overcoming their poor decisions? How can we help them in our preaching ministry to make godly decisions going forward in a culture of hedonism, self-pity, and blame-shifting?

The possible topics related to decision making are essentially infinite. So let's put some boundaries around this discussion by focusing on four major life decisions that may produce pain for our church members. They are challenging to speak about from the pulpit but are spiritual areas, nonetheless, that test our allegiance to God and his Word. Second, we will briefly study a possible Scripture text for preaching on decision making. Third, we will consider how best to preach on the topic of painful decisions.

Sexual Sins, Abortion, and Adoption

Having served as a youth, college, and senior pastor, I've found that one of the most painful decisions in life regards engaging in sex and sexuality

2. Emily P. Freeman, *The Next Right Thing: A Simple, Soulful Practice for Making Life Decisions* (Grand Rapids: Revell, 2019), 12 (emphasis original).

outside of biblical boundaries set forth by God in Scripture. We are clearly living in a post-sexual-revolution era. In many areas of life, including sexuality, Christians behave no differently from nonbelievers.[3] Paul M. Gould observes correctly, "Even though Christians no longer stand under the penalty of sin, the desires of the flesh still have power."[4] The apostle Paul rightly names in Romans 7:15 the human predilection toward gratifying the flesh, a tendency that we cannot even understand ourselves: "I do not understand what I do. For what I want to do I do not do, but what I hate I do." What intensifies the human predicament is that in the case of sexual sin, people actually "love to do" the sin that they receive pleasure from. Frankly speaking, we as clergy would prefer not to be in the know. For this reason, it's easier to omit from our sermon calendars preaching on the topic of sex.

The vast brokenness of church members in the area of sexuality may be more surprising than we imagine. It's a taboo topic at church. It's almost verboten to ask, "Are you being sexually pure in both thought and deed?" Many professing Christians choose to engage in sex outside the covenant of a heterosexual marriage via premarital sex, adultery, homosexual relationships, and gratifying oneself through sex trafficking, to name just a few. The consequences of one's actions may not be losing one's virginity alone. The one who sins in such a way may now live the rest of life with a sexually transmitted disease or face the reality of an unplanned child. Other listeners, continuing in a sexually immoral lifestyle, long for you, the pastor, to turn your eye from their sexual indulgences. They don't want to hear a sermon from the pulpit about how they are "living in sin" and being disobedient to God. Perhaps some of our congregants have engaged in or are currently struggling with some type of LGBTQ behavior and feel shame and remorse over their thoughts and actions. Cohabitation is an ongoing struggle for Christians and non-Christians alike. Over the years, I have done premarital counseling with a number of soon-to-be-married couples. Many Christians today hold a strangely laissez-faire, normative perspective on cohabitation, while others regularly engage in premarital

3. See Paul M. Gould, *Cultural Apologetics: Renewing the Christian Voice, Conscience, and Imagination in a Disenchanted World* (Grand Rapids: Zondervan, 2019), 147; David Kinnaman and Gabe Lyons, *UnChristian: What a New Generation Really Thinks about Christianity . . . and Why It Matters* (Grand Rapids: Baker Books, 2007), 46–48.

4. Gould, *Cultural Apologetics*, 147.

sex without thinking twice about it. They combat biblical truth with, "So what? Everybody is sleeping together and living together." Adultery, fornication, sex addiction, stalking, sexual assault, homosexuality, pornography, prostitution, bestiality, virtual reality sex, and numerous other sexual sins are continually spiritual land mines among Christian men and women alike. Whether or not our listeners are conscious that these practices are sinful, these decisions have significant consequences.

Another important related topic concerns the decision of abortion. About one-third of all women in the church have had an abortion at some point in their lives. In her article "Preaching on Abortion," Nancy Kreuzer explains, "We know that one out of three women have had an abortion, and this means that they sit in the pews of our churches. The first baby step in healing from abortion is to know the truth about it so it can be confessed and healing can begin." Choosing to remain silent about abortion so as to not upset anyone may also prove to be an unhealthy pastoral action. Kreuzer continues: "Silence is a powerful weapon of the enemy. It is in silence that the enemy invades the territory of the post-abortive woman's heart. The enemy says, 'See what you have done. It is so horrible that no one can even mention it. You are alone. Completely alone. Even your pastor will not speak of it. . . . And if abortion is that terrible, you must be too.'"[5] On the opposite spectrum, others in your congregation might struggle with the fact that they gave up their "unwanted" child for adoption. The unsettling feeling of "I wonder what happened to him or her" never goes away. The various difficult decisions regarding sex, sexuality, abortion, and adoption abound in the congregation.

How do we minister and preach to those who feel lingering regret in these areas of decision making? In the case of abortion, postabortive syndrome is quite common among many women. In her study of postabortive women, Debra Susan Dacone found that they commonly used "words such as *grave sin, evil, shame, unwelcome, guilty, judgment, condemnation* and *church teaching* to describe current preaching. The words *hope, healing, forgiveness, pardon for those who are injured, freedom*, and *preached in love*, consistently appeared to describe what women wanted to hear."[6]

---

5. Nancy Kreuzer, "Preaching on Abortion," *Preaching Today*, January 2015, https://www.preachingtoday.com/skills/2015/january/preaching-on-abortion.html.

6. Debra Susan Dacone, "Healing Words: What the Post-Abortive Woman Can Teach the Preacher" (DMin thesis, Aquinas Institute of Theology, 2014), 52 (emphasis added).

When was the last time you preached on sex, sexual sins, abortion, and adoption, if ever? What did you say? How did you say it? How did the people respond to the sermon? How did you encourage those who are misbehaving sexually and postabortive women in your congregation? We will later discuss in this chapter how to preach the truth in love and with grace.

Adult Milestone Commitments (Education/College, Vocation, and Marriage)

A second major life category regards the "adult milestone commitments" we make as we enter adulthood, such as determining whether to go to college, selecting a college/university, deciding on a major, choosing a vocation and career path, and discerning whether to marry (and whom) or remain single. Our listeners most likely live with some form of regret in one or more areas of major milestone commitments. Have we ever asked ourselves this question: "What would my life have been like if I had just . . . ?" The Bible never prods us toward a particular college, major, occupation, or marriage partner. Brett McCracken writes, "Contrary to what some Christians maintain, the Bible neither endorses nor forbids all sorts of things it could have been clearer about."[7] In considering milestone commitments, we are not necessarily dealing with black-and-white decisions in all cases. Rather, a congregant might toss between two different gray areas, choose rightly or wrongly, and either delight in or bemoan his or her past decisions.

Sometimes milestone commitments are made for us. For instance, we don't receive the university scholarship we planned on, or a parent loses his or her job so the dream of a college education slips away. Perhaps our parents threaten not to pay for our education unless we pursue a particular occupational path. We may be forced into managing the family business when that's not the occupational choice we had in mind. Our parents may expect us to marry the child of a family friend who checks all of the boxes for an ideal son-in-law or daughter-in-law, or may push us into marrying someone of the same ethnic group even though that person is not

7. Brett McCracken, *Gray Matters: Navigating the Space between Legalism and Liberty* (Grand Rapids: Baker Books, 2013), 8.

a Christian. In most cases, when we give in to the person's or situation's control, we feel remorse and regret the decision that we must live with.

Milestone commitments are usually self-made and self-fulfilled—so we think. We made what we thought would be the best decision at the time, but we chose either correctly or erroneously. One of the ways that we can assist our listeners with milestone commitments is to help them make the most of their current situation or circumstance. Kyle Rohane observes, "A change in our exterior won't necessarily transform our interior. I'm prone to grass-is-always-greener-itis, an affliction that entices me to imagine how much better things would be if only *this* or *that* were different."[8] "If only I had chosen this college, career, or spouse, my life would be so much more fulfilling" is the lie that we often tell ourselves, and we become despondent and thus blind to the blessings we could enjoy. We can preach with a glass-half-full philosophy of life as a possible antidote to discontentment.

Priorities, Values, and Overcommitments

Painful decisions surface, thirdly, when there are misplaced priorities and values and the tendency to overcommit ourselves on things tangential to the Christian life. The North American culture is one of utter fatigue and exhaustion. We have depleted our energy resources to the point that we have no giddyup left to live the Christian life as God intended it. As a result of our depleted energy and mental fatigue, we tend to regularly make poor decisions and choices.

A clear struggle in North American Christianity is that we are following the wrong shepherd. The shepherd we often follow is the vexing voice of a Christless culture. Jesus plainly says in John 10:3–5, "The gatekeeper opens the gate for him, and the sheep listen to his voice. He calls his own sheep by name and leads them out. When he has brought out all his own, he goes on ahead of them, and his sheep follow him because they know his voice. But they will never follow a stranger; in fact, they will run away from him because they do not recognize a stranger's voice." Part of our fundamental struggle to make good decisions (based on false priorities, values, and commitments) lies in the fact that we cannot distinguish the voice of Jesus from the culture's voice. We don't spend enough time

8. Kyle Rohane, "In Search of Greener Grass," *CT Pastors*, March 19, 2019.

hearing from Jesus, and so our priorities and values are governed by the culture and strangers rather than by Christ, who is the Shepherd. We choose the culture over Christ.

As a pastor, I saw the overextended self in all sorts of ways. The formula for life burnout is quite simple: working fifty-five to seventy-five or more hours per week, saying yes to overtime hours to save for that tropical vacation or kitchen remodel, drinking with coworkers after work, getting less than six hours of sleep regularly, selecting unhealthy food options, living vicariously through their kids and putting them in every after-school activity imaginable, including more than one sport per season, instrument lessons, art lessons, community service, participating in sports games and practices on Sunday mornings, and other recreational activities, personal interests, and more. No wonder we have no time for Jesus and for the church.

In *No Is a Beautiful Word*, Kevin G. Harney explains that many people have difficulty saying no:

Maybe you have some of the same reasons for avoiding the word no.

- "I don't want to disappoint people. I like to make them happy."
- "I feel bad when others see me as being unable to help."
- "I care about people, and I don't want others to see me as lacking compassion."
- "I don't want to be seen as limited or weak."
- "I don't want to be left out."[9]

Harney goes on to say: "By saying no, you are creating margin for an essential and life-changing yes. . . . When you embrace this truth, you can say no because you are committed to saying yes to what matters most."[10]

When we can't say no, we feel trapped and don't know how to get out of the mess we're in. The consequence of our misplaced priorities and values is that we have no other recourse but to make continuously bad decisions. It's the ceaseless treadmill that won't stop even when we yank on the emergency cord. Congregants need a preacher who can help them

9. Kevin G. Harney, *No Is a Beautiful Word: Hope and Help for the Overcommitted and (Occasionally) Exhausted* (Grand Rapids: Zondervan, 2019), 22.
10. Harney, *No Is a Beautiful Word*, 25.

see their decision-making blind spots and move forward toward saying yes to things that mature them in the Christian life.

Breaking the Law

A fourth and final painful decision concerns breaking or keeping the law. *Regret* is the word that comes up most frequently whenever a person breaks the law. Church members will eventually get over a small traffic violation. However, misdemeanors like DUIs and felonies are impossible to live down. While God the heavenly judge will forgive us our trespasses, the earthly judge is not quick to pardon us.

On March 12, 2019, a news story broke about a college admissions scandal among fifty people who were charged by the US Department of Justice with "buying" their children's admissions to our nation's top colleges and universities.[11] Emily P. Freeman writes:

> I don't think parents wake up out of the blue one morning and say, "You know I think I'm going to cheat the system and bribe some people so my kid can get into a good college." Doing the next right thing happens one step at a time. So does doing the next wrong thing. It starts small. It grows slow. It may begin with a general belief that we deserve something we aren't getting or we're owed something that isn't coming easy. We make a compromise here, a self-deception there, and eventually, the rationalizations start to feel justified.[12]

In similar ways, equally egregious or small, our congregants face moral dilemmas every day in deciding between dealing honestly and getting ahead dishonestly—dilemmas such as whether to tell a "white lie" to make a profit or advance in their career. Every aspect of our lives is affected somehow by the ethical or unethical decisions we make.

The following disturbing reality must be acknowledged today as well: Sometimes our congregants or their loved ones, particularly African

11. Devlin Barrett and Matt Zapotosky, "FBI Accuses Wealthy Parents, Including Celebrities, in College-Entrance Bribery Scheme," *Washington Post*, March 12, 2019, https://www.washingtonpost.com/world/national-security/fbi-accuses-wealthy-parents-including-celebrities-in-college-entrance-bribery-scheme/2019/03/12/d91c9942-44d1-11e9-8aab-95b8d80a1e4f_story.html.

12. Emily P. Freeman, "Why I Can't Get That College Admissions Scandal off My Mind," *Emily P. Freeman* (blog), accessed June 25, 2020, https://emilypfreeman.com/college-admissions-scandal.

Americans, experience the pain of injustices administered by a broken legal system, even though they've done nothing to deserve the rendered punishment. Racial profiling and mass incarceration are systemic problems in the United States. Dominique DuBois Gilliard explains in his challenging book, *Rethinking Incarceration*, "Our nation's overcrowded jails, prisons, and detention centers are an indictment of our criminal justice system. It is impossible to visit these institutions and not be struck by the inhumane treatment of the people serving time and the disproportionate number of black and brown bodies confined in cages like animals. These men and women are America's latest crop of strange fruit."[13] Have we ever considered the pain of listeners who experience such injustice for crimes they or their loved ones did not even commit?[14]

I recognize that most of your congregants will not be in dire legal straits such as in the examples above. Nevertheless, we will find that some of our members are carrying the noose of a criminal record around their neck. Their impropriety and indiscretion will stay on their records for a long time or even permanently. Law breaking often cannot be expunged from our life histories, and we must live with the consequences of our actions. Some of your parishioners might be currently struggling emotionally with their past records. For example, every time they fill out a job application, they need to reluctantly check that box that says in no uncertain terms, "I'm a law breaker." Neil Anderson and Charles Mylander note that "painful memories nudge us toward regret and resentment—unless we forgive [ourselves and others] and find freedom in Christ."[15] When facing painful decisions, we wish that forgiving ourselves and receiving freedom through Christ's forgiveness were as easy as having him use heavenly Wite-Out to clean our earthly memory's curriculum vitae. How might your sermons assist your congregants in spite of their painful past decisions? How do we preach morality and making moral decisions in a corrupt, self-serving world?

13. Dominique DuBois Gilliard, *Rethinking Incarceration: Advocating for Justice That Restores* (Downers Grove, IL: InterVarsity, 2018), 3.

14. Due to limitations of space, I am unable to engage thoroughly with this discussion on racial profiling, mass incarceration, and related issues. However, Gilliard is right that as pastors and Christian leaders, we should not turn a blind eye to the problem and should seek to rectify it whenever we can. Perhaps in your congregation and community these are critical issues of pain that require pulpit engagement and collective activism.

15. Neil T. Anderson and Charles Mylander, *Setting Your Church Free: A Biblical Plan for Corporate Conflict Resolution* (Minneapolis: Bethany House, 2005), 149.

Preaching on Painful Decisions

Let's now consider preaching a sermon on painful decisions. Using the questions laid out in chapter 3, walk with me through the process of preaching on this type of pain.

1. Which Passage Will I Preach On?

A number of Bible verses address the topic of decision making. A well-quoted life passage for many Christians regarding decision making, for instance, is Proverbs 3:5–6. Many can recite it from memory. Although we could easily select a proverb like this as our sermon text, let's envision that we are preaching a short sermon series, "Life Lessons from Biblical Characters," on the topic of decision making. We're recounting the narratives of Bible characters who made right and wrong choices and asking what we can learn from them. The character for this week's sermon is King Saul, part of whose story appears in 1 Samuel 15.

In this genre of historical narrative, we find ourselves reading about a military battle between Israel and the Amalekites. God commanded Saul through the prophet Samuel in 1 Samuel 15:3, "Now go, attack the Amalekites and totally destroy all that belongs to them. Do not spare them; put to death men and women, children and infants, cattle and sheep, camels and donkeys." Rather than fully trusting God and obeying him completely, Saul exhibited partial obedience: he destroyed the Amalekite people with the sword (v. 8), but "Saul and the army spared Agag [the Amalekite king] and the best of the sheep and cattle, the fat calves and lambs—everything that was good. These they were unwilling to destroy completely, but everything that was despised and weak they totally destroyed" (v. 9).

2. What Type of Pain/Suffering Is Revealed in the Text?

The painful decision made by Saul was to obey God only halfway. God tests whether Saul's allegiance is to him or to material possessions. It's clear that initially the pain evoked in this text concerns God's response to Saul's disobedience. God says to Samuel, "I regret that I have made Saul king, because he has turned away from me and has not carried out my instructions" (1 Sam. 15:11). Samuel, the prophet, in turn feels pain: "Samuel was angry, and he cried out to the Lord all that night" (v. 11b).

Interestingly, Saul does not show any remorse until he hears that God has rejected him as king for his disobedience (v. 30). In fact, Saul insists that he has obeyed God and blames his army for not completing the mission of God. He even sets up a monument for himself to celebrate his accomplishments (v. 12). We're later reminded of the severity of Saul's indiscretion: "Samuel mourned for him. And the Lord regretted that he had made Saul king over Israel" (v. 35).

3. How Does the Bible Character or Biblical Author Deal with the Pain?

First, Saul denies any wrongdoing in the story, at least initially. When confronted by Samuel's question, "Why did you not obey the Lord? Why did you pounce on the plunder and do evil in the eyes of the Lord?" (1 Sam. 15:19), Saul responds, "But I did obey the Lord. . . . I went on the mission the Lord assigned me. I completely destroyed the Amalekites and brought back Agag their king" (v. 20). Notice how Saul spins the blame onto others for his iniquities: "*The soldiers* took sheep and cattle from the plunder, the best of what was devoted to God, in order to sacrifice them to the Lord your God at Gilgal" (v. 21). When called to account for a decision, humans naturally tend to blame others first and not take ownership. Remember Adam and Eve in the garden of Eden?

Second, as our narrative continues, Saul only admits wrongdoing after Samuel tells him of the consequences of his actions and that God had revoked the kingdom from him on account of his sin of disobedience. Saul then replies, "I have sinned" (v. 30). Yet his following statement demonstrates again his self-serving nature. "But please honor me before the elders of my people and before Israel." As readers, we only hope his desire to go back with Samuel and "worship the Lord" is authentic. Preservation of one's reputation is another way that individuals deal with painful choices. What, we ask, can I do to maintain some level of repute and dignity?

4. How Does This Pain in the Text Relate to Our Listeners' Pain?

Partial obedience or partial disobedience, however we communicate it, is something that all of our listeners can identify with. Specifically, the point of the story is that Saul chose not to completely follow God's instructions to destroy everything. This leads to Samuel's well-known observation, "To obey is better than sacrifice, and to heed is better than the fat of rams" (v. 22).

Many of our listeners have experiential knowledge and pain that comes from partial obedience and disobedience. How many have given a partial tithe rather than the entire amount? Ananias and Sapphira are an extreme example of lying to the Holy Spirit. How many have exaggerated or manipulated their accomplishments on a résumé, only to be found out later on, even after receiving the job or admittance into the university? How many have run away from God's call to ministry in some capacity—telling God they are willing to obey only in these areas or if these specific conditions are met? Jonah's partial obedience and disobedient spirit led to his own misery and suffering. Our listeners will have personal testimonies on how their decisions to only partially trust God led to pain and suffering.

5. What Does This Pain Say about God and His Allowance of Pain?

Saul, in many ways, is the Old Testament example of what Jesus describes in the New Testament as a person who received five bags of gold based on his ability.[16] Incredibly gifted, tall, and the prototypical leader, Saul became his own worst enemy. His self-reliance, self-glorification, self-affirmation, and other sins produced in the end a self-serving king who trusted in himself more than in God. God's patience with Saul wore thin, to the point that he grieved and mourned that he had crowned Saul king, because Saul had "turned away" and had "not carried out [God's] instructions" (1 Sam. 15:11).

God is not shy about allowing us to suffer for our misconduct. God's removal of Saul from his kingship is justified by his various actions. Although some may view God's permission of pain as punishment for sin or even vindictive, Saul apparently brought destruction upon his own leadership through his personal character struggles. These character issues linger on in the rest of 1 Samuel, ultimately leading to his decision to end his own life. I wonder what would have happened if Saul had repented and changed from his sinful patterns. Would God have called David to reign as king as early as he did? Might Saul have enjoyed a blessed and prosperous reign? It appears that God cares more about Saul's character

16. See Matt. 25:14–30, commonly called the parable of the talents.

in life than about his position and station in life. While difficult to accept, the same message holds true for us in our day.

6. How Does God / Jesus / the Holy Spirit Help Us in Our Suffering?

When we are living in disobedience or decide to disobey, God often sends a messenger to help us see and repent from our errant ways. God loves Saul dearly. God's sovereignty means that he was aware of Saul's deficiencies, and yet he permitted Saul to serve as the principal governing leader over Israel. Although the text says that God grieved that he appointed Saul king, we find little evidence of God's softer, empathetic side. Saul's example is a harsh one indeed. Later the biblical writer informs us that "the Spirit of the LORD had departed from Saul, and an evil spirit from the LORD tormented him" (1 Sam. 16:14).

How, then, does God help Saul in spite of Saul's misjudgment as narrated in this text and beyond? Here, Saul's example is one of God's demonstrations of harsh discipline. Sometimes the only way we learn to mature in our suffering is through our removal from leadership or positions of influence. In God's view, the best thing for Saul was to dethrone him. Though we may not fully understand, God knew the best course of action for Saul, and at times he affords us the same type of discipline.

7. How Can Our Preaching Show Care and Empathy?

When people make poor decisions that lead to significant adverse consequences, the manner and tone in which we preach will influence the listener positively or negatively. Our hearers make poor choices every single day. The consequences of our unwise actions may be small, significant, or delayed. Indirection might be the best course of action for preaching on difficult decisions. Instead of naming their specific situation and experience, we may address the same point by mentioning a related but different outcome. If the Spirit so leads, we can directly speak to the concern, especially in cases where we want to avoid poor decisions in the future.

Behind the scenes throughout the week, pray that God will use this sermon to convict the person and prick their conscience. This is particularly true in cases like Saul's, where the individual believes he or she is in the right and has done nothing wrong. Preach with a tone of gentle firmness. We can name the sin and disobedience while also embodying a message of grace with our words and tone of speech. In addition, we couple our words with our actions. Don't just preach, live out the message. Pray for the person privately and publicly. Invite them after the service for prayer and encouragement. Be present with them by listening to their pain. Coach them with reminders that there is always hope for them in Christ, even in their ominous circumstances.

8. How Can We Share This Pain in Christian Community?

Encourage your listeners to share their pain with trusted members in the congregation or others who are spiritually mature in whom they confide. The losses that come from significant decisions will cause ongoing frustrations and worries in their future, as in the four common examples mentioned earlier: sex, milestones, priorities, and the law, and others. Provide a bridge to your listeners by letting them know that they are not alone in their suffering. If they are presently not serving in a ministry or are not experiencing Christian community, it will be even more crucial to facilitate opportunities to cultivate strong connections and friendships to rely on going forward. Moreover, develop a church culture where decisions are made in community. Perhaps small groups are the perfect setting in which to bounce ideas off each other prior to making an important decision. The voices of others might be just what we need in order to make wise choices. My wife, prior to making the life-altering decision of whether to marry me, asked ten influential people in her life what they thought about this choice (I was a seminary student at the time). To her surprise and my delight, all ten people said yes. Over the years, we have known many people who have made major decisions in isolation and chose wrongly. How can we share in each other's decision-making processes more regularly as the body of Christ?

9. How Will God Use Our Suffering to Transform Us and Bring Himself Glory?

Platitudes abound concerning how God uses pain and suffering even for our good. Tod Bolsinger writes in *Canoeing the Mountains*, "Leadership is *a way of being* in an organization, family, team, company, church, business, nation (or any other system) that, in the words of Ronald Heifetz, '[mobilizes] people to tackle tough challenges and thrive.' Therefore, *leadership is always about personal and corporate transformation.*"[17] Leaders lead others. We, as pastoral leaders, are called to lead our people in such a way that they can and will overcome even the most trying of situations—sometimes over a long time. God will transform leaders, taking them from rock bottom to a higher ground, spiritually speaking. Saul chose to remain in the depths of despair. He didn't and couldn't traverse beyond his removal from leadership. Ultimately, Saul's life tragically failed to be restored and to bring glory to God. In the sermon, we want to prayerfully note constructive ways that our listeners can mourn over their pain, but also, secondly, to encourage them to channel their energy in order to ascertain how their struggles might glorify God in the end.

Principles for Preaching on Painful Decisions

Here are two guiding principles for preaching on painful decisions.

Preaching to People from Honor-Shame Cultures

Know whom you're preaching to. Often our decisions reflect who we are and are shaped by our cultural identities. Preaching on decisions and decision making can be taboo because at their core decisions deal with the dynamic of honor and shame. Jayson Georges and Mark Baker explain, "Honor-shame is the predominant culture type for most people in the world. . . . This data suggests that approximately 80 percent of the global population (i.e., Asians, Arabs, Africans and even Latin Americans) runs on the honor-shame operating system. Westerners (i.e., North Americans and Western Europeans) not familiar with honor and shame, globally speaking, are the odd ones out."[18] Furthermore, Curt Thompson, in *The Soul of Shame*, expresses his belief that to varying degrees everyone experiences shame.[19]

Being mindful of who is present on Sunday morning may to some degree alter how we preach to parishioners who come from honor-shame

17. Tod Bolsinger, *Canoeing the Mountains: Christian Leadership in Uncharted Territory*, expanded ed. (Downers Grove, IL: InterVarsity, 2015), 21 (emphasis original).

18. Jayson Georges and Mark D. Baker, *Ministering in Honor-Shame Cultures: Biblical Foundations and Practical Essentials* (Downers Grove, IL: IVP Academic, 2016), 18–19.

19. Curt Thompson, *The Soul of Shame: Retelling the Stories We Believe about Ourselves* (Downers Grove, IL: InterVarsity, 2015), 10–11.

cultures. In many cases, you will not have heard firsthand about the errant decisions or their outcomes. People from honor-shame cultures will do everything within their power to keep their shame to themselves and not let it be publicized. Does this mean that we shouldn't preach about painful decisions? Not necessarily.

It may, however, involve communicating against some of the shame-filled lies we believe about ourselves after shame-causing decisions. Thompson names two particularly destructive results of shame for the Christian: "It is the emotional weapon that evil uses to (1) corrupt our relationships with God and each other, and (2) disintegrate any and all gifts of vocational vision and creativity. . . . Shame is a primary means to prevent us from using the gifts we have been given."[20] Preach in such an encouraging way that your listeners will not close themselves off from serving God. The listeners' inner monologue will repeat the refrain: "You're worthless. God can't use someone like you." Our mantra for the message on painful decisions will require myriad forms of empathy, encouragement, and emboldening for our listeners. "God loves you. God wants to use you. God never fails you. God encourages you. God is able." Everyone falls. Not everyone gets up, as reflected in Saul's account.

Preaching on Postdecision Consequences and Predecision Deliberations

As a spiritual shepherd, the pastor is to help listeners make wise decisions. Peter Scazzero shares, "The early church fathers considered the most precious gift, or *charism*, in the church to be *discretion* (i.e. discernment). They understood that without *discretion*, we are dangerous—speaking too freely, giving people burdens they cannot bear, and offering superficial spiritual counsel."[21] The astute preacher considers preaching on decision making in two fundamental ways: (1) preach preventive messages to guide listeners toward making wise, biblical decisions; (2) preach on how to respond to the consequences of an unwise decision by someone else or one's own unwise decisions. Any type of decision requires biblical wisdom. Some sermons will invite dialogue with listeners either before or after a decision, and sometimes both.

20. Thompson, *Soul of Shame*, 13.
21. Peter Scazzero, "My Biggest Regrets: Part 2," *Emotionally Healthy Leader Podcast*, May 14, 2019, Emotionally Healthy Discipleship, https://www.emotionallyhealthy.org/my-biggest-regrets-part-2.

When preaching on the process of making decisions, serve as a sage to help them see what might have happened in the biblical narrative or passage if the character or author had done something differently. As when analyzing a movie screenplay, consider with them the turning points or pivots where godly decisions can be made biblically and with theological acumen. Point out choices by biblical characters that resemble modern-day choices and that offer an alternative to choosing evil.

When preaching on how to respond to the consequences of a poor decision, refrain from lingering too long on the source of one's shame. In most cases, listeners already know better than we do what they did wrong. They have felt the shocks and aftereffects of the poor-choice earthquakes. Help them see the light at the end of the Christian tunnel. Show them how to accept the consequences but also how to make the most of their lives in spite of them. If appropriate, have them internally say to themselves, "There is life after fill-in-the-blank." Spend a few more minutes on life application, "making the most of every opportunity" (Eph. 5:16; cf. Col. 4:5).

Conclusion

Every painful topic in this book will be challenging to preach on. Painful decisions are no exception. By sprinkling their message with wisdom, grace, and much patience, pastors can play an instrumental role in shaping the sanctification of their listeners in the realm of decision making. Don't miss out on this significant shepherding function because the culture seeks to silence us. Wisdom and godly decision making are much-needed biblical topics for today's Christians, whose sense of morality has been swayed by cultural norms and values. In winsome ways, we can encourage and even persuade our hearers to make decisions biblically and theologically. With the words of God, we can comfort those who have made poor decisions. We can guide them in such a way that our preaching enables them to avoid making harmful or unwise choices rather than live under the umbrella of a bad decision.

Discussion Questions

1. What decisions linger long in your consciousness, whether positive or destructive?

2. In what ways do painful decisions in your life hamper you from freely living the Christian life?

3. Which specific decisions do our listeners need help with in order to experience forgiveness and freedom in Christ?

4. How will you help others as they wrestle with painful decisions they have made in the past?

"The Anatomy of a Bad Decision"[1]

Sermon on 1 Samuel 15

> **HOMILETICAL IDEA:** Obey God completely and not your human wisdom, and offer him no half-hearted sacrifice.

Have you ever made a bad decision? Seems like a silly question. Of course, we all have at some point. Maybe it was last week when you took that risk in running the light only to get caught by that dreaded red-light camera. Perhaps it was the time that you bought that stylish winter jacket even though in hindsight you should've said no when the zipper didn't work the first or second time. Another decision might have been devastating, like saying "I do" to the wrong person against your better judgment. Decisions are a part of life. Some are small and some are big. An article in *Psychology Today* suggests that the average adult makes thirty-five thousand decisions every day. That doesn't seem possible! Sometimes we get those decisions right and sometimes we're wrong. We all make bad decisions from time to time.

When we make poor decisions, the consequences can be minimal, such as having to pay the dollar late fee for an overdue movie at the public library or getting the punishment of an extra chore for not listening to your parents. Other times they can be quite severe: divorce, time in prison, getting fired from a job, or becoming an addict. The Bible speaks quite frequently about the issue of decision making. One of those moments is found in 1 Samuel 15, where King Saul faces an important decision. Turn with me there as we read about the anatomy of Saul's decision and his choice either to obey God completely or not.

---

1. The title of this sermon borrows conceptually from Dave Carder's book *Anatomy of an Affair* (Chicago: Moody, 2017).

I. Remember, God hates sin and punishes sins.

It's quite a jarring scene. God sends word to Samuel to give King Saul an odd and violent command: Destroy all of the Amalekites for their sins, including women and children and everything they own.

Read with me 1 Samuel 15:1–3. Samuel said to Saul, "I am the one the LORD sent to anoint you king over his people Israel; so listen now to the message from the LORD. This is what the LORD Almighty says: 'I will punish the Amalekites for what they did to Israel when they way-laid them as they came up from Egypt. Now go, attack the Amalekites and totally destroy all that belongs to them. Do not spare them; put to death men and women, children and infants, cattle and sheep, camels and donkeys.'"

Really, God? You're asking Saul to do *what*? One of the reasons why Christians and non-Christians struggle sometimes with the character of God is the presence of passages like this in the Bible. We ask legitimate questions like, Why is the God of the Old Testament so harsh, violent, wrathful, and merciless? How can God command the wiping out of an entire people group? How can a loving God act so unlovingly? Aren't those women and children innocent?

The simple truth is that God hates sin and punishes sins. What did the Amalekites do to deserve such severe punishment? As you may know, there are many *-ites* in the Bible. You may recall some of them, such as the Canaanites, Hittites, or Jebusites. Here, by way of background, the Amalekites were the descendants of Esau. We're told in Exodus 17 and other passages that "the Amalekites came and attacked the Israelites at Rephidim" (v. 8). Because of the Amalekites' ambush on the Israelites, in Exodus 17:14 God foretells the elimination of the Amalekites when he says to Moses, "Write this on a scroll as something to be remembered and make sure that Joshua hears it, because I will completely blot out the name of Amalek from under heaven." As an omniscient God, he already knew the events of 1 Samuel 15 would happen.

As our story continues, Saul receives God's commands, and it seems that he wants to follow them. Eventually, in verse 6, Saul forces the Kenites to leave the area because they "showed kindness to all the Israelites when they came up out of Egypt." So that they did not get mistakenly killed among the Amalekites, Saul sent them away.

The first thing that our passage teaches us is that God hates sin and punishes sins. No one can understand the mind of God. Was this sin of attacking the Israelites worthy of mass execution? According to human wisdom, the answer is no. But what this story reminds us of is the hatred God has for sin and that sin is punishable even by death. While this sounds like a cop-out, what we do know is that throughout the Old Testament, certain sins were punishable by death, including breaking the Sabbath. For God, the Amalekites' attack on the unassuming Israelites was worthy of death. The short answer is that God's holiness cannot stand to see sin and wickedness.

What does that mean for us? We need to take sin seriously. This is not a message of behavior modification. The point of the sermon is not "Stop sinning." That's not possible. We will continue to sin on this earth. And yet God's command to obey him completely cannot be ignored or explained away. We want to obey God fully because we love him even when his commands make no human sense. And this is where Saul's decision making begins to falter in verse 8.

II. Remember, God demands complete obedience and not human wisdom and half-hearted sacrifice.

According to verses 8–9, Saul "took Agag king of the Amalekites alive, and all his people he totally destroyed with the sword. But Saul and the army spared Agag and the best of the sheep and cattle, the fat calves and lambs—everything that was good. These they were unwilling to destroy completely, but everything that was despised and weak they totally destroyed."

Let me quickly remind us of the historical situation. Saul became king in 1 Samuel 10 after the people of God cried out for an earthly ruler. God eventually gave them what they asked for. It wasn't God's initial desire to give the people an earthly king. He alone wanted to be king over the Israelites.

Eventually the earthly king he provides is Saul, a man of great promise. "There is no one like him among all the people," Samuel says to the people in 1 Samuel 10:24. But Saul was also a man prone to error, and he lacked wisdom. Some time before the attack on the Amalekites in chapter 15, a similar event occurs in chapter 13, when Samuel asks Saul to wait for him. Instead of waiting, Saul, because of Samuel's tardiness, acts according to his own will and gives a burnt offering against the wishes of Samuel—but, more importantly, against the will of God.

In 1 Samuel 15, we see a similar anatomy or pathway toward disobedience. Two causes led to Saul's failure to obey God completely. The first is relying on human wisdom rather than on God's. The second is thinking that God desires to receive our half-hearted sacrifice.

First, instead of fully obeying God's commands to destroy everything including the king, Saul relied on his own logic and wisdom. What he did makes a lot of common sense! Verse 9 says, "But Saul and the army spared Agag and the best of the sheep and cattle, the fat calves and lambs—everything that was good. These they were unwilling to destroy completely, but everything that was despised and weak they totally destroyed." Bible scholars explain that in ancient times, the army would pillage and loot whatever they could take with them after winning the battle. It was their so-called reward.

The heart can be deceptive. Morals can be compromised. Character can be threatened. My kids and I watched many of the episodes in a National Geographic TV series called *Brain Games*. One of the episodes showed what happened when a wallet was left on the ground in a busy courtyard-type area in a major city. Many picked up the wallet, some even looked around briefly to see if anyone had dropped it, but they eventually took off with the wallet. Have you ever found something and kept it for yourself? What does your heart tell you to do? We can rationalize pretty much any decision we make. We may even tell ourselves, "Finders keepers, losers weepers."

Perhaps Saul had a similar take on morality. I'm going to do what's seemingly right and sensible. Saul's error was to rely on his own human wisdom. First, he and the army spared King Agag. Second, he and the army spared all of the good, healthy animals. In terms of human wisdom, Saul is spot on. Maybe he wanted to ask Agag some questions. Why would you waste perfectly good animals? Humanly speaking, we would probably say that King Saul is in the right. But here's the problem: partial obedience is disobedience. We cannot engage in partial sin and think that it's complete obedience. God commanded Saul and the army to destroy the king of Amalek and every person and possession.

Have we ever done something similar? Have we ever obeyed the Lord with human wisdom rather than complete surrender? I empathize with Saul here. I could've made this error in judgment. For example, I hate wasting food—especially choice meat. What if God asked me to throw out perfectly good prime rib already sitting on my dinner plate? Would I eat it anyway because there are starving people all over this country and world? We can fall into sin when we rely on human wisdom rather than godly, complete obedience to his commands.

Going further, Saul's human wisdom caused him to celebrate his partial obedience to the Lord. It's clear that Saul is not remorseful over his disobedience. In fact, verse 12 says Samuel was told, "Saul has gone to Carmel. There he has set up a monument in his own honor and has turned and gone on down to Gilgal." When Samuel confronts Saul in verse 14 with his famous line, "What then is this bleating of sheep in my ears? What is this lowing of cattle that I hear?," Saul quickly comes to his own defense and shifts the blame in verse 15, "The soldiers [not I] brought them from the Amalekites; they spared the best of the sheep and cattle to sacrifice to the LORD your God, but we totally destroyed the rest." Samuel corrects Saul in verses 17–19 because Saul did not fully obey God in wiping out the Amalekites and all their possessions: "The LORD anointed you king over Israel. . . . And he sent you on a mission. . . . Why did you not obey the LORD?" Saul defends himself again, "But I did obey the LORD."

Dear church, are there areas of our lives that we think are surrendered fully to God but are not? Are we holding on to our sin while saying to ourselves, "But I did obey the Lord"? Maybe we have surrendered our finances to God only incompletely. Maybe we're holding on to certain sins such as greed, lust, pride, gossip, or self-reliance. What is it that God wants you to hand over to him today completely and with full honesty?

Second, instead of complete obedience, which means destroying everyone and everything, Saul gives God the sacrifice of a half-hearted obedience, as we learn in verses 22–23:

> But Samuel replied:
> "Does the LORD delight in burnt offerings and sacrifices
>   as much as in obeying the LORD?
> To obey is better than sacrifice,
>   and to heed is better than the fat of rams.
> For rebellion is like the sin of divination,
>   and arrogance like the evil of idolatry.
> Because you have rejected the word of the LORD,
>   he has rejected you as king."

God wants our full obedience. I hear the melody of the late Keith Green's song "To Obey Is Better Than Sacrifice." It's clear that God doesn't want our offering or sacrifice if we're unwilling to obey him completely, even if it's a good offering. Where are we relying on human wisdom, and where are we giving God sacrifices apart from full obedience? Remember, God demands full obedience and not human wisdom and half-hearted sacrifice.

And finally . . .

III. Remember, God can regret giving us his blessings and even take them away.

God regrets making Saul king of Israel. He says in verse 11, "I regret that I have made Saul king, because he has turned away from me and has not carried out my instructions." And verse 35, similarly: "And the LORD regretted that he had made Saul king over Israel." To be king of Israel was a tremendous blessing for Saul. And yet we must remember that God can regret giving us his blessings and even take them away when we fail to obey him.

Similarly, as the Lord's prophet, Samuel grieves over Saul's sin of disobedience. Verse 11 tells us, "Samuel was angry, and he cried out to the Lord all that night." Samuel's sorrow over Saul does not end here. In verse 35 we learn, "Until the day Samuel died, he did not go to see Saul again, though Samuel mourned for him." The word translated "mourned" here, *hitabbel*, used only once in the Hebrew Bible, meant "regarded Saul as if dead."[2] In Samuel's mind, hereafter, God had completely rejected Saul.

In moments of desperation, we may try to confess our sin, but what matters more is that we obey God in the first place. Saul admits in verses 24 and 30 that he has sinned. In verse 24, he confesses that he feared men over God. He cared more about what his men thought of destroying perfectly good animals than about the necessity of surrendering to God's command. Then in verse 30 Saul confesses his sin again, but then he still wants to be honored by his people. God's punishment is pending and certain. Saul will soon be removed from his throne. Saul's focus has become one of self-reliance, self-preservation, and eventually self-glorification. In short, Saul has forgotten the Lord. This doesn't mean that we should not confess our sins. We should confess our sins daily and seek repentance.

2. See note at 15:35 in *The NIV Study Bible* (Grand Rapids: Zondervan, 1995), 394.

But the biblical principle here is that we ought to first seek to please and obey the Lord rather than commit a sin and confess it later.

Indeed, Samuel in verse 33 is the one to fully obey the Lord when he puts King Agag to death before the Lord at Gilgal. When we are blinded to our own sin, sometimes God sends us a messenger, just like Samuel was sent to Saul. This was not the only time Saul disobeyed the Lord. On several occasions, Saul failed to keep God's commands completely. The harshest punishment of all comes later in 1 Samuel 16:14, which says that "the Spirit of the LORD had departed from Saul, and an evil spirit from the LORD tormented him."

Conclusion

The anatomy of a bad decision or even sinful disobedience can often begin with human wisdom and half-hearted obedience and sacrifice. If we are not careful, God may, as with Saul, regret giving us certain blessings and may even take them away. We all make mistakes. We all make bad decisions. We all commit sins. But what this passage wants to teach us going forward is this: Obey God completely and not your human wisdom, and offer him no half-hearted sacrifice. If we love God completely, we will desire to obey him and please him completely. Everyone makes bad decisions. It's impossible not to do so. And yet God loves us so much that he wants us to listen to him and obey what he says fully, completely, wholeheartedly. What are the areas of our lives where we are prone to rely on human wisdom and where are we giving him half-hearted obedience and sacrifice? May we ask the triune God—Father, Son, and Holy Spirit—for his help to live a life of complete obedience to him! Obey God completely and not your human wisdom, and offer him no half-hearted sacrifice.

5

Painful Finances

Winston Churchill receives credit for saying, "We make a living by what we get, but we make a life by what we give."[1] Sermons on the subject of money typically champion investing in heavenly treasures by using one's economic resources for the church and for overseas missions and missionaries. This approach is to be expected since churches are not self-funding and need congregants' money for daily operations: salaries, benefits, utilities, and general maintenance are part and parcel of the church's budgetary needs. Moreover, pastors occasionally seek additional funding for renovations, building additions, the purchasing of land and other properties, and more, which require princely sums, more often than not from paupers. Missionaries, too, need consistent financial support. Therefore, the only time preachers talk about money is when they are addressing congregational needs in the form of tithes, offerings, missionary giving, balancing a church budget in the red, and building projects.

When it comes to personal finances, many skeletons remain as fixed accessories hanging in our economic closets. How many Christians would have the humility and candor to admit financial failures to anyone at church other than a spouse—and perhaps not even our spouse? We feel

1. Churchill did not likely say this, but he nonetheless widely receives credit for it. "Quotes Falsely Attributed to Winston Churchill," International Churchill Society, accessed October 16, 2020, https://winstonchurchill.org/resources/quotes/quotes-falsely-attributed.

extraordinary remorse and shame or beat ourselves up as we ponder questions like the following:

"If I give God this offering, how will I have enough to put food on the table?"

"How am I going to give to the church when I'm in so much debt that I don't know what to do?"

"Why did I buy the more expensive home?"

"The seven-year financing on that living room furniture set put me in a deep hole. The monthly payment sounded so affordable. Why did I do it?"

"Why did I cosign on my cousin's business? Now I'm going to have to file for bankruptcy."

"Why was I so stupid as to get trapped into that Ponzi get-rich-quick scheme?"

"Now that I'm actually calculating my monthly budget, do I really spend that much on my pets?"

"What if people knew how many credit cards I've maxed out?"

"Why do I keep buying lottery tickets even though I know gambling is a sin?"

"How did I lose my job, and why can't I get gainfully employed?"

Who hasn't bought something that they later regretted? Who hasn't made a financially irresponsible decision? Who hasn't succumbed to the temptation to make a rash, spontaneous purchase? Who is ever satisfied with their income?

Not only does money cause suffering due to our mental lapses in decision making; sometimes monetary challenges strike us in unforeseen, out-of-our-control ways: a corporate restructuring involves demotions or layoffs, which lead to foreclosing on our home; the landlord increases rent out of the blue; illness or accidents suddenly lead to astronomical hospital bills; a recession hits the planet such as in 2008 or in 2020 with COVID-19; we need to replace the roof or HVAC system; an aging parent requires assisted living; and so on. Money is often a source of immense pain and suffering whether one is a Christian or not. Whether rich or poor, white collar or blue collar, generous or miserly, money causes pain for everyone. Most people are living paycheck to paycheck, and something's got to give—as the saying goes.

In this chapter, the goal is not to encourage shaming or to scold our listeners for splurging on their recent purchase. Shaming from the pulpit is easy to do unintentionally and hard to avoid, especially regarding money. Nor is our intention to pour salt on emotional wounds from job layoffs and other financial crises or to guilt parishioners into giving more in order to satisfy various line items in the church's budget.

Rather, the objective here is to guide us in thinking about how we preach on finances and whether we are helping or hurting our listeners by what we say, how we say it, and what we choose not to say. Staying true to the meaning and intention of Scripture, we want to preach messages that convict rather than condemn and that edify rather than exasperate. We want to be pastoral in our approach to sermons concerning finances and offer a clear vision for how Christians might view money going forward as an integral part of discipleship. Let's start by naming five common practices of preaching on finances and consider how we can be more effective in our sermonic craft and reach.

Preach a Theology of Money, and Not Just Giving

The phrase *theology of money* is often perceived as an oxymoron. Money is profane and dirty, whereas theology (relating directly with God and his nature) is holy and spotless. How can the two be associated with each other? Craig Satterlee observes, "Stewardship preaching is *practical theology* in the truest sense of the term. Its spiritual aim is to help people deepen their faith and grow in grace by giving in response to the gospel. . . . The *practical* and *theological* aims of stewardship preaching are regularly at odds with each other."[2] Our listeners, then, will probably compartmentalize how they feel about God and money. For instance, some might hotly contend, "God didn't go to work this week. I did. I earned this income, which means I can do as I please with it."

Money is essentially a symbol that represents something different to each person. When our bank accounts are full, it can mean power,

---

2. Craig A. Satterlee, *Preaching and Stewardship: Proclaiming God's Invitation to Grow* (Herndon, VA: Alban Institute, 2011), 12–13.

prestige, privilege, access, authority, admiration, and much more. When our account balance is depleted, we can assume just the opposite. In its basic form, money is an idol for many. As Timothy Keller says, "Money is one of the most common counterfeit gods there is. When it takes hold of your heart it blinds you to what is happening, it controls you through your anxieties and lusts, and it brings you to put it ahead of all other things."[3] The challenge is that money is not always objective: it can be quite subjective. Janet Jamieson and Philip Jamieson explain: "The problem [of money] cannot be merely objectified and thus solved by a system or in some pain-free way by asking others to sacrifice. The subjective dimension of money is extremely powerful. All individuals participate in the worldly power of money, and thus all are corrupted by it by default. Thus, the problem is not an external one but is located in the heart of each person."[4] Any time an object like money becomes objectified, the devastation of not having it or losing it spawns greater attachments of loss and pain. When a bandage is left on the skin too long, it sticks and becomes extraordinarily difficult to peel off, even tearing the skin. In the same way, if money is not a treasured commodity in one's heart, one can peel away from it with less pain. The problem is that it is a treasured commodity for nearly every person on the planet—including pastors. If we could take down our masks for a moment, we would admit that we wish we had more money.

In order to ameliorate current attitudes among Christians toward finances, it would be beneficial to concretize and preach a theology of money or Christian stewardship[5] rather than only talking about money when asking for financial gifts (tithes, offerings, special gifts, missionary pledges, building funds, etc.). For example, twentieth-century philosopher Jacques Ellul argued that Protestant Christians have developed two primary theologies of money, which can be somewhat problematic.[6] One is that "money is a blessing" provided by the hand of God. If we take this view literally, we naturally assume that if we don't have much money, we

---

3. Timothy Keller, *Counterfeit Gods* (New York: Dutton, 2009), 58.

4. Janet T. Jamieson and Philip D. Jamieson, *Ministry and Money: A Practical Guide for Pastors* (Louisville: Westminster John Knox, 2009), 39.

5. Aubrey Malphurs and Steve Stroope suggest the same in *Money Matters in Church: A Practical Guide for Leaders* (Grand Rapids: Baker Books, 2007), 21.

6. Jacques Ellul, *Money and Power*, trans. LaVonne Neff (Downers Grove, IL: InterVarsity Press, 1984), 15, cited by Jamieson and Jamieson, *Ministry and Money*, 39–41.

are not blessed by God. If we are materially wealthy, we are blessed. The prosperity gospel has perpetuated this theology of money.

Second, money is often associated with a theology of stewardship. Specifically, we must be clear about how we define stewardship. Satterlee observes, "My first point about preaching stewardship is that preachers and congregational leaders need to define stewardship for themselves and for their hearers. . . . 'If you mean money, say money.'"[7] A common disconnect can occur if listeners don't include money under the purview of stewardship, because they have been trained to think of stewardship as only creation care or other important categories unrelated to money. Also, with regard to economic stewardship, Christians often believe they are stewards of—that is, responsible for—only their tithe, or 10 percent, which means the remaining 90 percent is theirs to do with as they please.[8] Beyond notions of blessing and stewardship, what other principles of a theology of money are crucial to teach and preach about?[9] To provide a corrective, it would be helpful to preach on a kingdom vision.

Preach on a Kingdom Vision

There are particular moments in a church's life cycle when a pastor must search his or her motivations for asking congregants to give and give more. A sensitive area is the amount of congregational funds employed for building projects in North America and augmenting and expanding facilities.[10] What is the return on investment for adding a balcony or a parking garage or purchasing properties or constructing a gymnasium or another wing? Does our congregation really need the additional space or fancier amenities? Could we spend less on the accoutrements or perhaps be more frugal? Is our congregation already stretched beyond its financial limits? Could we

7. Satterlee, *Preaching and Stewardship*, 7.
8. Satterlee, *Preaching and Stewardship*, 41.
9. Several topics come to mind with regard to a theology of money: biblical stewardship, tithes and offerings, the uses of money for good and evil, power and authority, various destructive sins caused by greed and money, giving to the poor as lending to the Lord, idolatry, values, priorities, poverty and riches, cheerful giving, capitalism and socialism, Christian views on economics and finances, incurring debt, identity, treatment of others, God's faithfulness and provision, and others.
10. John Starke, "Should Churches Spend Money on Nice Buildings?," Gospel Coalition, July 6, 2011, https://www.thegospelcoalition.org/article/should-churches-spend-money-on-nice-buildings.

be contributing unintentionally to listeners' financial woes? Are we preaching by using the "give till it hurts" philosophy? Is now really the best time?[11]

When we employ the 80/20 rule, also known as the Pareto principle, we can make the generalization that 80 percent of the church's budget is provided by 20 percent of its most charitable members.[12] This doesn't mean, though, that we let the remaining 80 percent off the hook. David King notes, "Stewardship is not simply paying our dues; rather it is tending our souls so that we can see our wealth properly as an instrument to invest in God's kingdom. It is also working diligently to combat the subversive power money can often play in our lives, which causes us to believe that our net worth can be equated to our self-worth."[13] Most Christians can't imagine giving away their wealth because having less diminishes their earthly sense of identity and worth. Money is a safety net that replaces ultimate trust in God's sovereignty and provision.

Therefore, preach and educate the entire congregation on God's heart for maximizing kingdom resources for evangelism, discipleship, and reaching the nations with the gospel message. Wisdom in spending is a central biblical matter. Many Christians in North America have been blessed to receive not just daily bread but a premium selection of daily sustenance. We can teach our listeners how to live modestly, frugally, and generously with what they already have in their possession—rather than follow the proverbial "I'll give when I have just a bit more margin."

Preach by Example

A few well-known pastors took preaching by example to the next level by giving away 90 percent of their income or selling their home and possessions in order to provide a live demonstration of generous or radical kingdom living.[14] These models of sacrificial giving are commendable; however,

11. I recognize that pastors can make the argument go the other way in that it's never a "good time" to give.

12. David Murray, "The Pareto Principle for Churches," *HeadHeartHand* (blog), March 13, 2017, http://headhearthand.org/blog/2017/03/13/the-pareto-principle-for-churches.

13. David P. King, "Stewardship of Money and Finances: Practicing Generosity as a Way of Life," in *Beyond the Offering Plate: A Holistic Approach to Stewardship*, ed. Adam J. Copeland (Louisville: Westminster John Knox, 2017), 39.

14. Rick Warren, David Platt, and Francis Chan are some recent examples of pastors who have modeled sacrificial giving for one's congregation. I applaud them for heeding God's desire for them to give in such ways. However, the same expectations cannot be placed on every believer.

pastors and preachers can also share with the congregation smaller, less extravagant measures of living with kingdom values.

Perhaps we can use as a sermon illustration an example of how we came to decide which of two big-ticket items to purchase, such as which home, car, or computer, or how we chose between less significant purchases like a phone, a pair of shoes, or even groceries. In many years of listening to sermons, I don't think I have ever witnessed a preacher lead by example in such concrete, tangible, and practical ways. While arguments can be made to support either product or either name brand, what matters is the kingdom value with which one makes economic decisions. We can also lead by sharing what not to do and disclosing one or two poor choices we've made over the years financially (with prayer, wisdom, and discernment). Third, be vulnerable about your own struggles and temptations with the love of money. Pastors are not so pious as to be immune to such fiscal cravings. Be genuine with your parishioners.

Preach on Contentment to the Haves, Have-Nots, and Have-Somes

Economic disparities exist within any local church context. Depending on your church's location (urban, suburban, or rural), some of your congregants will have seven-figure incomes, some four figures.[15] The natural human tendency is to compare ourselves with others. We compare ourselves with pretty much everything. But as Theodore Roosevelt once rightly quipped, "Comparison is the thief of joy." Allow me to provide a somewhat tangential and lighthearted example. The other day I was walking downhill at the seminary campus. When walking alone down a hill, you often feel tall. Standing in at a whopping 5'10", I felt larger than life as I walked in isolation from others. Later, when I entered the mail room, however, the very first person I saw was the tallest student on campus, who is about 6'9". The brief satisfaction of believing I was tall vanished as I compared myself to him and was reminded of the normalcy and averageness of my height.

We humans usually compare ourselves with other people by comparing our external, quantifiable, objective things with theirs: homes, cars,

---

15. For additional discussions on preaching and location, see Matthew D. Kim, *Preaching with Cultural Intelligence: Understanding the People Who Hear Our Sermons* (Grand Rapids: Baker Academic, 2017), 157–83.

educational and professional pedigrees, salaries, the size of their television, vacation destinations, memberships at clubs, the restaurants they frequent, maybe even the physical attractiveness of one's spouse, and so on. How can we preach on contentment to the various levels of finances represented in the congregation? How do we preach to those who seemingly have it all, to the helpless and hopeless, to the other "blessed-nots," and to those nestled in the middle class?

The apostle Paul suggests to the Philippian Christians one of the primary, lasting ways to be content: "I am not saying this because I am in need, for I have learned to be content whatever the circumstances. I know what it is to be in need, and I know what it is to have plenty. I have learned the secret of being content in any and every situation, whether well fed or hungry, whether living in plenty or in want" (Phil. 4:11–12). Paul is able to be content because focusing on Jesus gives him the strength to carry on (v. 13). Our listeners come from various financial levels. Although it seems cliché to say this, we must help our listeners be content by focusing on Christ, who gives them the strength no matter how little or how much they have. If Paul can write this from a dismal and dreary first-century prison cell, we can aspire to be content as well. This is easier said than done, for certain. However, the key is to train ourselves to stop comparing ourselves with others and to be thankful for our blessings.

Preach the Truth about Money with Empathy and Love

Preachers are tasked to preach the truth of God's Word accurately. This is what we have been trained to do in Bible college and seminary. At the same time, we can preach accurate biblical sermons that remain impractical and heady. Timothy Keller acknowledges this tension in *Preaching: Communicating Faith in an Age of Skepticism*: "Unless the truth is not only clear but also real to listeners, then people will still fail to obey it. Preaching cannot simply be accurate and sound. It must capture the listeners' interest and imaginations; it must be compelling and penetrate to their hearts."[16]

How can we preach practical, real sermons on the significance of finances? Most Christians have heard their share of sermons on the dangers

---

16. Timothy Keller, *Preaching: Communicating Faith in an Age of Skepticism* (New York: Viking, 2015), 157.

of money and riches. Jesus identified these dangers quite plainly when he said, "It is easier for a camel to go through the eye of a needle than for someone who is rich to enter the kingdom of God" (Matt. 19:24 // Mark 10:25 // Luke 18:25). The analogy seems exaggerated. We all know plenty of rich people, and they will enter heaven's gates because of their faith in Christ alone. Lenny Luchetti explains: "From a distance, empathy is hard to muster. Empathy is best cultivated in us through engagement that is up close and personal, face-to-face, and life-to-life."[17] One of the most effective ways to show listeners empathy is through verbalizing disappointment in life. Cliché phrases like "This too shall pass," "It was just meant to be," "You'll grow from this," "You'll come out stronger," "God is just refining you," "Isn't Jesus enough?" and others can be crushing to the spirit, especially when listeners are going through serious financial hardships. Instead, we want to acknowledge the pain and suffering of their current circumstances. Gift them the freedom to lament and vent to God their frustrations, angers, and heartaches. Sometimes a good cry is the best medicine. Provide the biblical response later, after they have had moments to express their emotions and pain.

Preaching on Painful Finances

Let's now consider preaching a sermon on painful finances. Using the questions laid out in chapter 3, walk with me through the process of preaching on this type of pain.

1. Which Passage Will I Preach On?

As we are aware, the Bible has more to say about money and finances than perhaps any other major subject in life. The Old Testament is littered with examples, and so is the New Testament. One author asserts that over twenty-three hundred Scripture verses regard the subject of money.[18] Take, for example, the parables of Jesus. Many of them relate to the issue of

---

17. Lenny Luchetti, *Preaching with Empathy: Crafting Sermons in a Callous Culture* (Nashville: Abingdon, 2018), 61.

18. See Dick Towner, "Money Management That Makes Sense," *Church Executive*, July 2005, http://www.churchexecutive.com, cited in Malphurs and Stroope, *Money Matters in Church*, 14.

money and stewarding our resources.[19] While you have plenty of Scripture passages to choose from, the passage you select on finances will depend on the original author's meaning and purpose.

As preachers, we can preach directly on financial principles from a parable per se, or we can take an indirect approach and encourage the congregation in the midst of painful financial situations through a topical sermon, such as one on contentment. Depending on the circumstances, both strategies are effective and worthwhile. As referenced above, Philippians 4:10–20 may be a relevant, indirect pericope to accomplish this sermonic goal. Imagine with me that your sermon this Sunday will be based on this text on painful finances.

2. What Type of Pain/Suffering Is Revealed in the Text?

The apostle Paul wrote this letter to the Philippians from the harsh confines of a tiny prison cell. He was incarcerated for causing a public disturbance for the sake of Christ. At the time of his writing, Paul was awaiting his sentence and possible execution. What kinds of pain might Paul have been feeling as he wrote this portion of the letter? A number of immediate concerns are plausible: loneliness and isolation, hunger pangs, cuts and bruises from the chains of bondage, physical discomfort from being in a first-century prison, emotional pain of missing his ministry colleagues, the suffering that comes from being misunderstood—death, and more, is clearly on his mind as he awaits pending execution.

3. How Does the Bible Character or Biblical Author Deal with the Pain?

In this text, Paul models two primary ways in which Christians can handle situations of pain and suffering. First, we notice that he surprisingly focuses much of his extant energy on others. He begins this section by praising the Philippians and rejoicing in God for their renewed interest in him and concern for his ministry (Phil. 4:10). Later, rather than embodying and communicating a woe-is-me perspective, Paul is again other-centered in his outlook. He commends their faith and thanks them for their generosity expressed through financial support in Macedonia and Thessalonica (vv. 15–16). He encourages them through verbal commendation when

---

19. Clay Stauffer, *Preaching Politics: Proclaiming Jesus in an Age of Money, Power, and Partisanship* (St. Louis: Chalice, 2016), chap. 2.

he says, "They [the gifts] are a fragrant offering, an acceptable sacrifice, pleasing to God" (v. 18). He reminds them also that God will take care of them as they have cared for him: "And my God will meet all your needs according to the riches of his glory in Christ Jesus" (v. 19).

Second, Paul looks to Christ, not to things and circumstances, as the source of his contentment. The pivotal verse in this passage is the oft-quoted and oft-misapplied Philippians 4:13, where Paul asserts boldly, "I can do all this through him who gives me strength." It's not that Jesus provides him with supernatural strength that enables him to conquer the world. Instead, Paul replaces worry and anxiety and suffering in this prison cell with the cloak of Christ, who covers him in the darkest recesses of life. When our gaze is centered on Jesus, we can be content no matter what we have or don't have. As Chuck Swindoll explains, "His letter to the Philippians showed them that by centering their lives on Christ, they, too, might live in true joy."[20] This spirit of rejoicing permeates the passage and the entire letter as Paul reminds the believers that—even while he is in prison and stripped of every material comfort—Christ is his ultimate sufficiency and reward. Now that will preach!

4. How Does This Pain in the Text Relate to Our Listeners' Pain?

While our listeners are not in physical bondage and captivity, many, if not all of them, are held captive to material possessions and seeking comfort of various kinds. Perhaps some of our listeners have lost the ability to rejoice in God due to repeated financial trials. They can't seem to catch an economical break in life. They lose their job. Their mortgage is foreclosed. They can't pay their monthly car payment. Their exorbitant student loan repayments persist for what seems like an eternity. They have a child unexpectedly. Medical bills are insurmountable. For those who are in such dire financial straits, giving seems utterly impossible, and when they do give, they do so uncheerfully. They may even encounter pain because they want to give to the Lord but don't know how it will be possible without incurring added monetary strains to an airtight budget.

---

20. Chuck Swindoll, "Philippians," Insight for Living Ministries, accessed June 25, 2020, https://www.insight.org/resources/bible/the-pauline-epistles/philippians.

5. What Does This Pain Say about God and His Allowance of Pain?

The hard reality is that sometimes God permits his children to remain in prison, whether literally or figuratively. Notice he doesn't deliver Paul from his prison cell. In fact, Paul was imprisoned several times, and for long stretches of time, for the sake of Christ. Philippians is one of four epistles he wrote in captivity (i.e., Ephesians, Philippians, Colossians, and Philemon). God allows Paul to experience suffering in this way for precise reasons only known to him. However, we can surmise that God was using these trials of imprisonment to refine Paul's character and to present Paul as a model of discipleship for the Christians he loved in those church plants. Perhaps God was even testing Paul to see what attitude emerged out of his situational darkness and to see in whom he would trust during prospective moments of hopelessness.

6. How Does God / Jesus / the Holy Spirit Help Us in Our Suffering?

This passage marks a couple of different ways that God aids and comforts us in our time of suffering. First, he brings to remembrance the people we care about who have been there for us in the past. Even though Paul spent only a few months, give or take, in Philippi, bonds of Christian friendship formed quickly between him and the Philippians—notably Lydia and others (see Acts 16:11–15). When we remember other people, we remember that we are not alone. There are people out there who care for me and love me. Sometimes God even physically sends colaborers to visit us in troubled times: Epaphroditus visited Paul (Phil. 4:18). Are there any friends God can send our way in times of trouble?

7. How Can Our Preaching Show Care and Empathy?

When Christians are going through financial difficulties or are gripped by the idol of comfort and materialism, pastors can refrain from offering economic solutions and preaching about a "light at the end of the tunnel"—at least not at the beginning of the sermon. The listener may be doing mental gymnastics thinking about all of the ways their finances have gotten out of control and about how they feel engulfed with guilt, shame, remorse, and even anger. The last thing they want to hear from the pulpit is the promise of a quick fix or an admonition that their priorities are in the wrong place.

Allow them the opportunity to be still with God and do two things: first, give them time during the sermon to lament about their current situation. Do they feel that somehow God is responsible for their fiscal plight? What could they have done differently to avoid this situation, if anything? Apart from winning the lottery, what realistic approaches could be taken to reverse or correct their circumstances over time? Second, help them bring their pain to the Lord. Help them surrender their finances completely to God. Encourage them to seek first God's kingdom so that everything else will be put into balance when they rely on Paul's promise in Philippians 4:19 as well as on what Jesus promised in Matthew 6:33: "Seek first [God's] kingdom and his righteousness, and all these things will be given to you as well."

Perhaps a final way to encourage our listeners is to guide them to discuss their personal finances not with the pastor but rather with Christian organizations that advise and coach believers on financial health, such as Crown Financial Ministries, whose vision is "to see believers all over the world committed to managing all that we are, have, and influence for His glory so that lives are transformed, economies flourish, and the Gospel is spread to all nations."[21] The Oikonomia Network is another valuable Christian organization for pastoral support. They state that they are "dedicated to raising up church leaders who help people develop whole-life discipleship, fruitful work and economic wisdom for God's people and God's world."[22]

8. How Can We Share This Pain in Christian Community?

Evidence of the importance of Christian community is widespread throughout this portion of Philippians. We cannot help our brothers and sisters in Christ if we are unaware of their financial hardships. The body of Christ exists to assist others—and, yes, even in financial terms, where applicable. Adam Copeland writes: "With how many people have you discussed your annual salary? How many friends know how much you gave to charity last year? What members of your family know about your true financial condition? Since we so rarely address money in public settings, it makes sense that money talk in church makes many of us a bit

---

21. See Crown Financial Ministries, accessed August 2, 2020, https://www.crown.org/about.
22. See "Who We Are," Oikonomia Network, accessed August 2, 2020, https://oikonomia network.org/about/who-we-are.

uncomfortable. And so church leaders, out of their desire not to ruffle too many feathers, approach stewardship apologetically."[23]

Let's say a couple at your church encounters a variety of financial pressures. They didn't know whom to turn to for assistance. Cognizant of the state of affairs, the leaders pray and decide to take up a "love offering" to address two or three of their immediate concerns. Members of the congregation enthusiastically chip in to lighten the financial burden of this couple. Understandably, the church cannot "bail out" every person who exposes an empty purse or wallet, but we can embolden our listeners to share with discretion what they are going through. This might not be publicized openly in a worship service, but perhaps we can create a culture where vulnerability occurs in a small group or through sharing freely with a trusted church leader.

9. How Will God Use Our Suffering to Transform Us and Bring Himself Glory?

I personally have not spent any time in a literal prison cell, but I know a few people who have. More commonly, many Christians can relate to being in a figurative prison, in the sense that they are shackled by money. Ultimately, as our final verse (v. 20) makes clear, Paul understood that everything, including suffering, can be used to give God glory. What can financial hardships teach us about dependence on God? How might he be able to use our fiscal misjudgments or misuses for refining our character? What can we learn from our mistakes or unintended trials? Am I experiencing suffering because of something I need or because of something I want? Even in this hopeless situation, God calls us to remember him and to testify to who he is. When we are thankful in every context, even in suffering, we glorify him.

Principles for Preaching on Painful Finances

Preaching on Money Regularly

The seriousness of financial hardships should not be minimized. David King reports, "In my interviews with hundreds of Christian pastors and lay leaders, few disagree with the significance of the role our relationships with money plays in the faithful practice of individuals and institutions.

---

23. Adam J. Copeland, introduction to Copeland, *Beyond the Offering Plate*, xi.

Those same religious leaders, however, admit struggling mightily to integrate the stewardship of finances into a broader vision of faith formation."[24]

Preaching on money terrifies many. But consider the longitudinal study conducted by Maya Clayton, José Liñares-Zegarra, and John O. S. Wilson, who found a direct correlation between health and debt: "Higher household debt is linked to poorer general health. The results are also significant in extreme cases where households are among the most financially distressed (over-indebted). We also find a link between debt maturity and health. Long-term household debt reduces life expectancy and increases premature mortality."[25]

As a result, we might consider preaching a regular series on money at least once per year. A natural seasonal time period to preach on stewardship is from Thanksgiving to Christmas. The incurring of holiday debt is palpable in North America and around the globe. It is the time when people want to be generous with others (which is a positive trait); however, they give a surplus beyond their means. This overgiving leaves them in gross debt after the new year. It's conceivable that congregants have overspent on their Christmas gifts when the pastor notices that tithes and offerings are down in the first quarter of the following year.

When I served as a senior pastor, I preached a short stewardship series regularly, and occasionally in the weeks leading up to Christmas. Those who adhere to the church calendar would squirm at the thought of replacing Advent sermons with financial stewardship messages. Of course, not every sermon before Christmas should concern money. Yet, a sermon or two may be just what the church needs in order to help prevent grave misappropriations of personal funds and unwise choices with regard to personal and family finances. The pastor is responsible for shepherding the flock especially in this delicate area of discipleship.[26]

Preaching on Money and Human Dignity

How we treat others is often based on their perceived income bracket. This is no different in the church context. Eugene Peterson admits, "I

24. King, "Stewardship of Money and Finances," 33.
25. Maya Clayton, José Liñares-Zegarra, and John O. S. Wilson, "Can Debt Affect Your Health? Cross Country Evidence on the Debt–Health Nexus," *Social Science and Medicine* 130, no. 4 (2015): 51.
26. Satterlee, *Preaching and Stewardship*, 9.

love being an American. I love this place in which I have been placed—its language, its history, its energy. But I don't love 'the American way,' its culture and values. I don't love the rampant consumerism that treats God as a product to be marketed. I don't love the dehumanizing ways that turn men, women, and children into impersonal roles and causes and statistics. I don't love the competitive spirit that treats others as rivals and even as enemies."[27]

When I served as a pastor in Denver, Colorado, we had frequent visitors from among those who live outdoors. Since we were an affluent congregation, it was challenging for church members to interact with our guests as normal human beings. Certainly their pungent stench and tousled appearance were quite remarkable. Yet it saddened me that we as a congregation failed to show better hospitality to these downtrodden persons who are made in the image of God in the same way we would show hospitality to a person of status and wealth. The congregation felt uncomfortable, on edge, suspicious, even proud and superior, whenever such visitors entered the building.

There's something inherent about money that separates. As James, the apostle, makes plain, "Suppose a man comes into your meeting wearing a gold ring and fine clothes, and a poor man in filthy old clothes also comes in. If you show special attention to the man wearing fine clothes and say, 'Here's a good seat for you,' but say to the poor man, 'You stand there' or 'Sit on the floor by my feet,' have you not discriminated among yourselves and become judges with evil thoughts?" (James 2:2–4). Preaching, therefore, on money, human dignity, bias, favoritism, and prejudice may be challenging, but it invites us and our listeners into a new realm of discipleship that hasn't been readily exposed.

Preaching on Contentment Will Lead Eventually to Giving

Some Christians suffer from the infectious malady of affluenza, which has been defined as "extreme materialism and consumerism associated with the pursuit of wealth and success and resulting in a life of chronic dissatisfaction, debt, overwork, stress, and impaired relationships."[28] How

---

27. Eugene H. Peterson, *The Pastor: A Memoir* (New York: HarperCollins, 2011), 5–6.
28. "Affluenza," *Merriam-Webster*, accessed June 25, 2020, https://www.merriam-webster.com/dictionary/affluenza.

do we know this to be the case? Excessive borrowing is a prime indicator of a heart crazed by affluenza. The US government's economic philosophy is to borrow, borrow, and borrow more. In 2019, the federal debt of America stood at a mind-boggling $22 trillion.[29] As Americans have adopted the same "pay it back later" philosophy, many, if not all, of our congregants are in some form of debt: a hefty mortgage on a home or business, home equity loans for improvements, student loans, Christmas debt, and car payments, or splurging on vacations, eating out habitually, buying a boat, and much more. What would happen if we took an anonymous survey and asked our church members how much money they owe cumulatively?

Remember the powerful and sobering words of Paul to Timothy in 1 Timothy 6:6–10: "But godliness with contentment is great gain. For we brought nothing into the world, and we can take nothing out of it. But if we have food and clothing, we will be content with that. Those who want to get rich fall into temptation and a trap and into many foolish and harmful desires that plunge people into ruin and destruction. For the love of money is a root of all kinds of evil. Some people, eager for money, have wandered from the faith and pierced themselves with many griefs."

Money and finances can be a major source of grief and pain for our listeners. When the congregation is receptive to the Holy Spirit, however, and thereby more content with what they have, we can take greater liberty to preach more directly to their financial concerns. Rick Ezell believes that Christians want to give to God. He explains:

> Most believers have a desire to give, but many can't due to poor planning, excessive debt, improper spending habits and other financial pitfalls. These people need to be released from their bondage. They need a money make-over. They need to understand and practice sound financial principles so they can be in a position to give. Therefore, I almost always preach on giving in the context of money management. I share biblical principles:
>
> - God owns it all.
> - We are stewards of His resources.
> - Everything will be returned to Him.
> - We can't take it with us.

29. Chuck Bentley, "Ask Chuck: What to Do about America's Debt?," Crown Financial Ministries, March 8, 2019, https://www.crown.org/blog/ask-chuck-what-to-do-about-americas-debt.

- The first 10 percent is His.
- We need to have a financial plan.
- Live below your means.
- Save and invest for long-term needs.[30]

Once we train the saints to be grateful and content with what they already have, it will be easier to encourage giving to the kingdom. Preach gratitude and contentment first, before preaching giving.

Conclusion

Preaching on finances is both unpleasant and tricky. The wide spectrum of topics related to finances and pain cannot be fully covered in this chapter. At the least, we want to recognize that many parishioners suffer silently regarding their financial situations. Sometimes we would be completely alarmed by who's struggling financially. Pray and ask the Holy Spirit when and how to preach on economics and the Christian life. It is crucial to preach on money because money is a spiritual, discipleship issue. Exhibit pastoral empathy by permitting your listeners to grieve over financial mistakes and struggles. Then, as their focus draws closer to Christ and his kingdom, we can preach tough truths about money in a spirit of love and about its kaleidoscope of entrapments. The battle in the pulpit will not let up in the following chapter as we discuss preaching on painful health issues.

Discussion Questions

1. How do you personally struggle with finances and financial decisions?
2. What financial decisions in the past have been painful for you?
3. In what areas do you need to grow in financial wisdom and stewardship?
4. How can you assist your congregation in trusting God with your finances?

30. Rick Ezell, "Preaching and Money," Preaching.com, accessed June 25, 2020, https://www.preaching.com/articles/preaching-and-money.

"The Secret to Contentment"

Sermon on Philippians 4:10–20

> **HOMILETICAL IDEA:** The secret to contentment is being in love with God and giving to others, because God will provide for all your needs.

Being content with what we have is quite difficult.

During my childhood as the son of immigrants, my parents really struggled economically. I remember that when my stomach wanted a Big Mac, my parents always said to us, "We can't afford to take you to McDonald's. It's too expensive for us." For my friends, eating at McDonald's wasn't a luxury. They did it all the time. But for my parents, Mickey D's was a fortune.

So I learned early on that money was hard to come by for my family. But I remember that one day when I was thirteen my dad took me to Sport Mart and bought me my first pair of Nike Air basketball shoes. They cost about fifty dollars. We could never, ever have afforded that before, so I guess my parents were doing a little better financially at that time, or maybe my dad had scrimped and saved his hard-earned money to get me something really nice. Maybe it was because I had just made the seventh grade basketball team, and this was his way of telling me how proud he was of my accomplishment.

The only thing was that both of my brothers tagged along for the ride. In my dad's generosity, he told my brothers they could buy whatever Nike Air shoe they wanted. Rather than just being content and grateful with what my father had just bought me, I couldn't help but think two things. First, his generosity wasn't fair. I had to wait thirteen years to get my first pair of Nike Airs, and my brothers were getting them at the ages of ten and eight, respectively. Second, I thought, "What did they do to deserve Nike Air basketball shoes?" I just made the seventh grade basketball team.

I'd like to think that I've grown up since the age of thirteen. As time went on, I was thrilled when my brothers succeeded and did well. I didn't envy or resent them when they received financial help from my parents. Their success meant our success as a family. But no matter how blessed we are, there's something within each of us that makes it difficult to be content with what we get in life.

In contrast, God is calling our church to be externally focused. Our mission is to learn how to be content in this life. Sometimes life doesn't seem all that fair. In fact, sometimes God doesn't seem all that fair. The apostle Paul once wrote a letter to the Christians in Philippi. He taught them a profound lesson about how to become content with what we have. Let's turn there and see what we can learn from his letter. Turn with me to Philippians 4:10.

I. Be content with whatever you have, because God is the source of your contentment.

Paul writes in verse 10, "I rejoiced greatly in the Lord that at last you renewed your concern for me. Indeed, you were concerned, but you had no opportunity to show it."

The apostle Paul wrote this letter to the Philippians from the harsh confines of a tiny prison cell. He was thrown in jail for causing a public disturbance for the sake of Christ. At the time of his writing, Paul was awaiting his sentence and possible execution. The church at Philippi was a church in many respects just like ours, one that is trying to make an impact in the world for Jesus. Philippi was also just like Denver, a place near the mountainside.

Paul was a traveling missionary and preacher. He was called a tentmaker. He made his living making tents and selling them. That is the way he supported himself and his ministry. Once in a while, he needed the financial support of various churches, but that was the exception, not the rule. The church at Philippi was one such congregation that helped him out. In this final chapter, he's thanking them for showing concern even though they were going through financially difficult times. He's not thanking them because he wants more . . . look with me at verse 11.

Paul writes this letter to the Philippians from his jail cell. Now, I've not seen a jail cell in person, but in the movies and on TV it looks pretty bleak on the inside. All you have is a sunken mattress for a bed and a toilet nearby—if you're lucky. That's it. There's no seventy-inch state-of-the-art TV. There's no internet access. There's no refrigerator to store your beverages. There's nothing. And in this dire situation, Paul writes with all sincerity that he has learned to be content in all circumstances. Twenty-first-century prisons are luxurious compared to first-century prison cells.

What is the secret to contentment? How can we be satisfied with what we have?

People spend millions of dollars a year on pop psychology books that tell them how they can be more content and happy in this life. Psychology professor Barbara Fredrickson teaches at the University of North Carolina at Chapel Hill. She is convinced that in order to be happy in this life we need to tap into our positive emotions. She defines positive emotions as "joy, amusement, gratitude, pride, [and] contentment." She once conducted a study with one hundred undergraduate students and "found that people who also felt positive emotions—such as gratitude, a renewed sense of community, and an intense curiosity about world events—recovered more quickly from [their] emotional trauma [in their lives]." Positive thinking is a good thing. But it's not the path to a contented life. Our positive thinking comes and goes. It's fleeting. It changes like the direction of the wind.

Why are we not content with what we have? The world teaches us a distorted philosophy about material possessions: that we need "just a little bit more." Play this mental game with me: If I only had _____, then I'd be happy.

Dear church, the source of our contentment is not more money, more things, a more positive attitude, a more beautiful house, a faster car, better graphics, a better-looking spouse, a larger retirement investment. No! Paul says in verse 13 that the antidote to discontentment is a more fulfilling relationship with God our Creator.

He says, "I can do all things through him who strengthens me." Often this verse has been used out of context. Pastors will use it to say Jesus will give us the physical power to lift a car in an emergency situation or give me the mental strength to ace an exam. God will give me the ability to run faster, think more critically, speak more eloquently, make more money, or do anything in my imagination.

But that's not what Paul is saying, is it? We have to look at this verse within its context. He's telling us that the reason why he is able to be content with very little or much is his relationship with God Almighty. He's saying, "I can endure all things and all forms of suffering because I'm connected to God. He is the source of my contentment. My contentment is not based on my circumstances but simply on the fact that God loves me and I love him back." God is enough. Is God the source of your contentment? Without God, we can own the entire world and still be dissatisfied in life.

In an interview on the TV show *60 Minutes* in June 2005, then quarterback of the New England Patriots, Tom Brady, made this observation about his life:

> Tom Brady: Why do I have three Super Bowl rings, and still think there's something greater out there for me? I mean, maybe a lot of people would say, 'Hey man, this is what is.' I reached my goal, my dream, my life. Me, I think: God, it's gotta be more than this. I mean this can't be what it's all cracked up to be. I mean I've done it. I'm 27. And what else is there for me?
>
> Steve Kroft: What's the answer?
>
> Brady: I wish I knew. I wish I knew.[1]

Tom, we know! And we have the answer! Contentment is found in God alone, not in what we have, our title, or what we own. That is why Paul learned to be content with whatever he had, because God was the source of his contentment.

Second, we learn that . . .

II. God is pleased when we share with others during tough times.

Paul thanks the Philippians for the gift they gave him through the person of Epaphroditus. He explains specifically that he's not in need right now. In this time period, good orators, skilled in the art of communication, would travel around preaching the gospel in the name of Christ and asking

1. Tom Brady, interview by Steve Kroft, CBS News, November 4, 2005, https://www.cbsnews.com/news/transcript-tom-brady-part-3.

for financial gifts for self-gain, kind of like today's televangelists. Paul, however, wants to clarify that he's not one of these people.

Our second antidote to contentment in this life is to give our wealth away. Giving to others is our act of spiritual worship to the Lord. John Wesley, the founder of the Methodist denomination, once said that we should "make all we can, save all we can, and give all we can." It pleases God when we can be content with what we have so that we can give freely to others.

This is now quite dated, but I have a friend who once had a PDA, a personally distracting appliance—I mean personal digital assistant. Do you remember those? He had it for about six months and wanted a new one with color and better applications. With a big smile, he tried to give it to his wife saying, "Honey, look at this nice PDA. I'd like to give it to you." She responded, "Why do you want to give it to me? Don't you need it?" And he replied, "Yes, I need one, but I need a new one."

This is not the kind of giving that God is asking us to do. Rather, God calls us to give even sacrificially to those who need our help. He's blessed us not for the accumulation of our own wealth, but so that we can give to others. Those acts of giving will be remembered. Those acts of giving free us from the materialism that consumes all of us.

Lastly, the reason why we can be content in all things is that . . .

III. God will provide for all our needs.

The author of Hebrews says it this way: "Keep your lives free from the love of money and be content with what you have, because God has said, 'Never will I leave you; never will I forsake you'" (Heb. 13:5). We can give freely to others because God will provide for all our needs. The writer doesn't say that God will provide everything I want, but everything I need, for both this earthly life and the life to come.

On a personal level, I confess to you that I struggle with contentment. I'm human too. Sometimes I wish I could drive a fancy car, own the house with the picket fence, or have surplus to help my parents retire from their financial burdens. Sometimes I wish I had more to buy nice things for Sarah, Ryan, Evan, and Aidan. Sometimes I think, "God, I could be more influential for your kingdom working in a secular job and evangelizing those who don't know you and, by the way, also making a six-figure salary."

But do you know what, friends? Yes, I may not have a six-figure salary or own nice cars or own my own home. Yes, I may not be able to afford the fancy steak dinners or vacation in exotic places. But there has never been a time when God didn't provide for all my needs. I've never been hungry. I've never shivered because I didn't have warm clothing. I've never had to beg for money or for food. God has provided all that I need.

When I was in seminary, the church I served gave me a monthly check of $600.00: that's $7,200 per year. From that $7,200, I set aside my 10 percent to give to the church and 20 percent to pay my taxes to the government, leaving me with a whopping $420 per month. I used that money to pay my rent, food, and gas. Would I have enjoyed more money if I had it? Yes, absolutely. But, I have never been closer to God than at that time.

God promises us that when we give our life to God, when we give freely to others, he will take care of all our needs. Yes, I may not enjoy all the fancy things this world has to offer, but I'm happy overall. Why? The secret to contentment is being in love with God and giving to others, because God will provide for all our needs. The secret to contentment is being in love with God and giving to others, because God will provide for all our needs.

Conclusion

In order to become a missional church, we must learn to be content with what we have. Everyone at some point has made a poor financial decision: borrowing excessively—or even once—without considering the consequences, purchasing the latest gadget, going on that vacation that set us back a few thousand, buying a television, car, or home we couldn't afford, and more.

Here's this week's challenge. Can you not spend a single penny on yourself to buy something new and not eat out any meals for one week and see how much money that comes out to? Can you then take that money and give it to someone who really needs it? Maybe you could support an orphaned child in Africa or Asia. Maybe you could give that money to a homeless shelter. Maybe you can give that money to a faithful Christian organization. God wants you to trust him today, and not your finances.

Remember this week: the secret to contentment is being in love with God and giving to others, because God will provide for all your needs.

6

Painful Health Issues

In March 2013, I experienced the unexpected trauma of physical and mental suffering. Playing basketball one evening with college and seminary students, I was struck in the head at full velocity with a basketball. I didn't see the ball coming straight for my head. The fierce impact knocked my head back and made me black out temporarily. Due to my love for the game, however, I just kept playing. The next morning I was incredibly dizzy and fatigued the entire day. I presumed that the concussion symptoms and brain injury would just go away eventually, but they rudely persisted day after day. I was dizzy every waking moment of the day. I struggled to fall asleep at night because of the whirlwinds of motion that seemed to go on endlessly in my cranium. Unlike a person suffering from vertigo, which is a spinning or twirling sensation, I felt like my brain was being tossed up and down, side to side, and corner to corner in the sea of fluids confined in my skull. The wooziness could not be controlled or tamed.

A few months later, I went to see several medical specialists: an audiologist for hearing; an ear, nose, and throat doctor for imbalance; a neurologist for the dizziness; and an eye doctor for vision problems. From unscientific comments like "It's probably just stress" to "It should go away eventually," no physician could give a legitimate diagnosis other than wanting to pump me full of prescription drugs. The only doctor who could properly diagnose me was the glaucoma specialist who confirmed that I had undiagnosed moderate to severe glaucoma in both eyes (age thirty-six at the time of diagnosis), which is the reason why I didn't see the ball due to significant loss of peripheral vision.

Even today, over eight years later, I am still suffering from chronic dizziness, 24/7. You would never know just by looking at me. Every moment of the day I'm dizzy. It feels like my brain is a boat on the sea being tossed by the waves. The dizziness cannot be controlled or tamed. In addition, for over sixteen years I have suffered from moderate/severe tinnitus (ringing in the ears), contributing to poor sleep and at times poor concentration; ACL reconstruction and setbacks; stomach pains; a partial rotator cuff tear and a frozen shoulder; and a couple of other persistently nagging health issues. I admit that I'm tired every day as my energy is sapped like the bars on a cell phone battery from having to give full concentration to nearly every single task. I have continued to seek out medical consultation and countless treatments, only to be disappointed time and time again. After squandering scores of hours in hospital waiting rooms and thousands of dollars in co-pays and deductibles, disheartened and even staring depression in the face at times, I'm in a condition that some, like Sheldon Vanauken, would label "a severe mercy."[1] In other words, while the dizziness rages on, some might say that at least the doctors caught my glaucoma, or else I would probably be nearly blind today. Only God knows how many tears I have shed, asking for deliverance and healing for my prognosis. Yet for some divine reason, the time for healing hasn't arrived. It is only by God's grace that I continue to teach, preach, and write despite the encumbering nature of my condition.[2] People who haven't experienced physical and mental suffering will have difficulty comprehending the body's demise unless suffering rudely forces its way into their lives—God forbid.

No one expects to be born with physical or mental disabilities. Nor do people imagine or anticipate during childhood what types of health issues will strike them later in life, such as a terminal illness like cancer, a ravaging disease which close to 40 percent of Americans will suffer from at some point in their lifetime.[3] One of the most crushing forms of pain and suffering concerns health issues—both the physical and mental.

1. Sheldon Vanauken, *A Severe Mercy: A Story of Faith, Tragedy, and Triumph* (New York: HarperOne, 2009).
2. I recognize that this is an academic book, but would you please pray for me as I pray for you?
3. See "Cancer Stat Facts: Cancer of Any Site," National Cancer Institute, accessed August 3, 2020, https://seer.cancer.gov/statfacts/html/all.html.

How might a preacher encourage a congregation and individuals who are experiencing unbearable health concerns that linger on indefinitely and sometimes for a lifetime? Before personal bouts with physical health difficulties, my metrics for compassion and empathy for those struggling with physical and mental health issues were meager at best and nonexistent at worst. Until one plunges into the depths of bodily suffering, one cannot empathize and identify with how others feel as they trudge through life with daily pains.

Millions of Americans live with chronic pain, and health issues plague the members of our churches. New illnesses pop up every week or month. People are asking: "Why me, God?" "Is there any relief or healing for me?" This chapter speaks into how we can live as Christians in view of these physical hardships and care for others who experience these challenges. We will explore four broad forms of physical and mental health issues: chronic pain and autoimmune diseases, mental health, physical and mental disabilities, and terminal illnesses. While we should never promise a health-and-wealth gospel or miraculous healing, preachers can use sermons to encourage congregants undergoing physical and mental suffering.

Ruth Graham, the daughter of Billy Graham, says in her book *In Every Pew Sits a Broken Heart*, "You may be sitting unaware in church week after week with suffering people, even as friends and acquaintances sat beside me while I smiled and behaved as though I didn't have a care in the world."[4] Likewise, pastor Steve Norman shares, "Never underestimate the pain in the room."[5] There are physical and mental pains in your congregation today, and probably many of them remain hidden, private, unspoken. Some considerations for a mental grid on congregational health pains will be suggested in this chapter. In addition, as in the previous chapters, we will look at a Scripture text together and ask of it various questions in preparation for the sermon, and last, a couple of best practices for preaching on health issues will be discussed.

Imagine four quadrants to think about health issues in the congregation. The following table will offer a mental map for sermon preparation

---

4. Ruth Graham, *In Every Pew Sits a Broken Heart: Hope for the Hurting* (Grand Rapids: Zondervan, 2008), 13.

5. Steve Norman, "Preaching on Suffering in a 'Pain-Free' Culture," *Preaching Today*, August 2016, https://www.preachingtoday.com/skills/2016/august/preaching-on-suffering-in-pain-free-culture.html.

as you peruse the people worshiping in your sanctuary or worship center. Although you may not be able to speak to all four quadrants every week, you may choose one or two depending on the text and sermon topic. The people obviously may not be sitting in that section of the sanctuary, literally, but you get the picture.

Four Quadrants of Pain

1 Chronic pain and autoimmune diseases	2 Mental health
3 Disabilities	4 Terminal illness

Preaching and Chronic Pain and Autoimmune Diseases

Let's begin with the first quadrant (top left). Living with chronic pain and autoimmune diseases wearies the soul. The delight in daily life is sucked dry. It's utterly exhausting. There is little that is more discouraging than not knowing if or when your illness and pain will ever go away. The pervasiveness of such unrelieved physical maladies is staggering. Timothy Beavis notes, "Ninety million Americans had a chronic illness in 1987, and by 1998 it grew to 120 million. By 2030 it will probably be 171 million."[6] That means one in two congregants will be battling chronic illness such as rheumatoid arthritis, fibromyalgia, AIDS, nerve pain, neck and back pain, migraines and cluster headaches, and more. Benaroya Research Institute estimates that there are approximately eighty different kinds of autoimmune diseases that debilitate the lives of over 23 million Americans (including type 1 diabetes, multiple sclerosis, Crohn's disease and colitis,

6. Timothy Beavis, "Preaching in Pain: How Chronic Illness Impacts the Preacher's Ministry" (DMin thesis, Gordon-Conwell Theological Seminary, 2013), 1, citing Jeffrey H. Boyd, *Being Sick Well: Joyful Living Despite Chronic Illness* (Grand Rapids: Baker Books, 2005), 8.

lupus, celiac disease, various food allergies, shingles, liver disease, and heart disease, just to name a few).[7]

The two interrogatives most frequently employed by sufferers of chronic issues are why and when. *Why* did this happen to me, and *when* will it disappear? For the preacher, these interrogatives most likely cannot be answered satisfactorily, to the chagrin of our hearers. Replacing why and when is the interrogative *how*. Mary Yerkes says, "Their symptoms—like pain, fatigue, muscle aches and weakness, disturbances in vision, cognitive difficulty, intestinal distress and memory loss—aren't always visible to the naked eye. Harder still, friends, family and co-workers can't always recognize a sense of loss, loneliness and isolation. Despite the obstacles sufferers must overcome on a daily basis, experts agree that, yes, people living with chronic conditions can live full and meaningful lives, regardless of the severity of their condition."[8]

While easier said than done, how does the Christian pursue life and even thrive in spite of one's chronic pain and illnesses? One way to encourage our listeners is to remind them that they are not alone and that Bible characters similarly experienced a variety of chronic pains: the first mention in Scripture of pain entering the world is found in Genesis 3:16, where God says to Eve, "I will make your pains in childbearing very severe; with painful labor you will give birth to children." In the next verse, God associates physical pain with "painful toil" of producing crops through manual labor and the sweat of one's brow (v. 17). In a fascinating article, Stephen Mathew and Jeyaraj Pandian provide insight into a number of modern-day diagnoses for biblical characters in the Old Testament. They write in the abstract:

Interestingly, Goliath probably suffered from acromegaly. We propose autism as a diagnosis for Samson, which would precede the first known case of autism by centuries. Isaac was a diabetic, and he probably had autonomic neuropathy. [A] few verses from the books of I Samuel, Psalms, and Ezekiel reveal symptoms suggestive of stroke. Jacob suffered from sciatica, and the child of the Shunammite woman in II Kings had a subarachnoid

7. "Disease Information," Benaroya Research Institute, accessed June 25, 2020, https://www.benaroyaresearch.org/what-is-bri/disease-information.

8. Mary J. Yerkes, "Living with Chronic Pain and Illness," Focus on the Family, February 1, 2007, https://www.focusonthefamily.com/lifechallenges/emotional-health/living-with-chronic-pain-and-illness.

hemorrhage. These instances among others found in the Old Testament of the Bible offer newer insights on the history of current neurological diseases.[9]

Since the fall of humanity, bodily suffering has been the norm. If we were to attempt to provide a nonmedical reason for the why interrogative, perhaps more than any other reason, God allows chronic suffering so that we depend utterly on him. Jeremy Linneman, a pastor in Missouri, who has suffered from chronic pain since his teen years, writes: "I've realized it's become a crucial part of my daily dependence on God. . . . Chronic pain, like every type of suffering, is a form of brokenness that drives us to Christ. When the pain persists, there's simply nowhere else to go."[10] Meditating on the suffering of Christ can become a timely form of soul medication that serves as a spiritual and emotional balm. While evangelicals are wary of "positive thinking" gimmicks and "Christian pop psychology," exhibiting a positive attitude to nurture attitudinal shifts can be a vehicle for meaningful living when one faces debilitating hardships.[11]

My godly mother and father have lived with chronic pain and health concerns for decades: my mother has suffered from diabetes and dizziness for over forty-four years, and my father has endured excruciating back and nerve pain for over three decades. Even during the time of this writing, my father was diagnosed with cancer. Postsurgery, he is recovering well, by God's grace.[12] As they have slogged through these moments of suffering, I have never heard them complain about their conditions, though it's been ineffably challenging. If pressed, they may admit that "it's been a really rough day." Otherwise, their lips are sealed as they trust in God's sovereignty and mercy, which is renewed for them each and every morning. Somehow they rise above the situation, keeping their eyes fixed on God in Christ, even excelling joyfully in the Christian life.

9. Stephen K. Mathew and Jeyaraj D. Pandian, "Newer Insights to the Neurological Diseases among Biblical Characters in the Old Testament," *Annals of Indian Academy of Neurology* 13, no. 3 (July–Sept. 2010): 164–66.

10. Jeremy Linneman, "The Paradox of Chronic Pain," Gospel Coalition, December 7, 2015, https://www.thegospelcoalition.org/article/the-paradox-of-chronic-pain.

11. Nick Vujicic mentions the Harvard psychologist and philosopher William James, who promoted the attitudinal philosophy that "by changing our attitudes, we can change our lives." See Nick Vujicic, *Life without Limits: Inspiration for a Ridiculously Good Life* (New York: Doubleday, 2010), 91.

12. My children suffer from febrile seizures and numerous food allergies, forcing my wife to make almost all of our meals at home.

Preaching and Mental Health

The National Alliance on Mental Illness reports incredible findings with regard to the prevalence of mental illness in the United States:

- Approximately 1 in 5 adults in the US—43.8 million, or 18.5 percent—experiences mental illness in a given year.
- Approximately 1 in 25 adults in the US—9.8 million, or 4 percent—experiences a serious mental illness in a given year that substantially interferes with or limits one or more major life activities.
- Approximately 1 in 5 youth aged 13–18 (21.4 percent) experiences a severe mental disorder at some point during their life. For children aged 8–15, the estimate is 13 percent.
- 1.1 percent of adults in the US live with schizophrenia.
- 2.6 percent of adults in the US live with bipolar disorder.
- 6.9 percent of adults in the US—16 million—had at least one major depressive episode in the past year.
- 18.1 percent of adults in the US experienced an anxiety disorder such as posttraumatic stress disorder, obsessive-compulsive disorder, and specific phobias.
- Of the 20.2 million adults in the US who experienced a substance use disorder, 50.5 percent—10.2 million adults—had a co-occurring mental illness.[13]

Mental illness can often be a source of shame for all people—especially among Christians.[14] There's a stigma—particularly within certain pockets of ethnic cultures—associated with confessing that one is seeking professional help from a psychiatrist, psychologist, counselor, or mental health professional or that one is taking medication for depression, anxiety, or another related issue. And yet mental illnesses seem overly common, striking an inordinate number of people these days in

13. See "Mental Health by the Numbers," National Alliance on Mental Illness, last updated September 2019, https://www.nami.org/learn-more/mental-health-by-the-numbers; "Mental Illness," National Institute of Mental Health, last updated February 2019, http://www.nimh.nih.gov/health/statistics/prevalence/any-mental-illness-ami-among-adults.shtml.

14. For a pastoral perspective on mental illness, see Steve Bloem, *The Pastoral Handbook of Mental Illness: A Guide for Training and Reference* (Grand Rapids: Kregel, 2018).

our congregations. Think of who in your congregation today might be struggling with schizophrenia, bipolar disorder, anxiety and panic disorders, phobias, depression, trauma from domestic violence, suicidal thoughts, posttraumatic stress disorder (PTSD), and more.[15] Sadly, studies continue to reveal that mental illness is increasing especially among today's youth.[16] How might pastors respond to the mental health crisis in their preaching ministry, perhaps even for clergy who are facing the same battles?

There are no simple medical solutions for mental health concerns. Pharmaceutical companies claim the ability to heal but oftentimes only mask the problem by dispensing prescription drugs for nearly every condition. Sometimes prescription drugs provide temporary relief, but the side effects can be astounding and just as harmful to the body as the illness itself. However, spiritually speaking, what might be lying under the surface that we can discuss to assist struggling Christians suffering from mental health issues? Without overspiritualizing, how might Satan be involved in exacerbating the world's mental health decline?

If anything, rather than promoting denial, projection, or distraction techniques, the Bible encourages Christians to face our struggles and look to God in the form of lament. In Scripture, we find a number of Bible persons who suffered mentally and emotionally: Rachel, Rebekah, Hannah, David, Elijah, Jonah, Job, Moses, Jeremiah, Paul, and even Jesus himself experienced distressing trials. More than anything, our ailments and trials can draw us closer to God. We see this truth manifested in the lives of godly men and women in Scripture. As Lauren Winner explains, "That God is pressed up against *all* the corrosive shame in my life—not just the shame I feel about my body, but all my whatever-else shame, all the many pockets of curdling shame and regret I carry. While I feel cloaked with shame, God is tenderly stitching me a suit of clothes. The clothing is God's own self."[17]

---

15. See "Mental and Behavioral Health," Johns Hopkins Medicine, accessed June 25, 2020, https://www.hopkinsmedicine.org/health/mental-and-behavioral-health. Christopher A. Cook has suggested a positive way to cope with and even reach "positive outcomes" from PTSD. See Cook, "Posttraumatic Growth Development: Core Belief Disruption, Event Centrality, and Time since Trauma" (PhD diss., University of South Carolina, 2017), 2.

16. See "Teens & Young Adults," National Alliance on Mental Illness, accessed June 25, 2020, https://www.nami.org/find-support/teens-and-young-adults.

17. Lauren F. Winner, *Wearing God: Clothing, Laughter, Fire, and Other Overlooked Ways of Meeting God* (New York: HarperOne, 2015), 59–60.

Preaching and Disabilities

Physical disabilities are multifaceted in the world. People are born every day missing one or more organs, limbs, or digits or lacking one of the five major senses, such as being blind, deaf, or mute. They may have an illness or brain injury that renders them physically disabled in some capacity. A nonexhaustive list of physical disabilities includes spinal cord injury, spina bifida, cerebral palsy, cystic fibrosis, epilepsy, multiple sclerosis, muscular dystrophy, Tourette syndrome, dwarfism, Prader-Willi syndrome,[18] and more.[19] A Scripture verse that immediately enters our consciousness when we think of embodied disabilities is Exodus 4:11 where God inquires of Moses: "Who gave human beings their mouths? Who makes them deaf or mute? Who gives them sight or makes them blind? Is it not I, the LORD?" It's evident that the Lord is sovereign over all of creation—even in the handiwork of creating physical disabilities. This directly challenges many Christians' understanding of theodicy and God's goodness.

Nick Vujicic, an Australian author, immediately comes to mind as a Christian who has joyfully endured major physical disabilities.[20] In his book *Life without Limits*, Vujicic heroically documents his life of joyful struggle and obedience as one born without arms and legs, which most people take for granted. He writes, "I was born without any limbs, but I am not constrained by my circumstances. . . . What my family and I could never foresee was that my disability—my 'burden' could also be a blessing, offering me unique opportunities for reaching out to others, empathizing with them, understanding their pain, and offering them comfort."[21]

Similarly, Jen Bricker entered the world without legs and was consequently given up for adoption. For individuals like Nick and Jen, life is full of inconveniences as they live without the basic comforts and necessities of having limbs. Adopted by positively minded parents, Bricker writes, "Comfortable is easy, comfortable is safe. . . . But if I went through life

---

18. As an undergraduate student at Carleton College, I took a psychology course on intellectual disabilities and worked for a semester with someone with Prader-Willi syndrome (PWS). In short, PWS is a complex medical condition in which a person can overeat to the point of death because his or her stomach never feels full, among other anomalies.

19. "Types of Physical Disabilities," Aruma, accessed June 25, 2020, https://www.hwns.com .au/about-us/about-disability/types-of-disabilities/types-of-physical-disabilities.

20. Joni Eareckson Tada is another prime example of a person who has endured physical disability with an infectious spirit of joy.

21. Vujicic, *Life without Limits*, viii.

simply content to be comfortable, I never would have found performing. I never would have seen the world. I never would have gotten so close to God."[22] What would our lives be like if we were born into their situations? Would we still have a positive outlook on life and live it to the fullest?

For most Christians, even pastors, loving those with disabilities is foreign and unfamiliar territory. We tend to freeze in the presence of the disabled. Disability activist Robert Hensel once said, "There is no greater disability in society, than the inability to see a person as more." Mental disabilities are equally perplexing, such as those of persons with autism or of persons deemed "on the spectrum," those with Down syndrome, and others.[23] As a church leadership team, when did we last converse about how friendly or unfriendly our church is toward those with disabilities?[24]

Two theologians who have done remarkable scholarship in the area of disability theology who can assist our homiletical thinking and manners are John Swinton and Amos Yong.[25] In *Becoming Friends of Time: Disability, Timefullness, and Gentle Discipleship*, Swinton challenges readers to appreciate time and the time that every person is granted by God regardless of what physical and mental suffering they embody. The glaring truth, says Swinton, for all mortal beings is this: "Time draws our attention to uncontrollable change and death."[26] The challenge is how preachers present the time we now share and experience here on earth and how we recommend that our listeners make the most effective use of it regardless of our present bodily circumstances.[27] To encourage a positive mindset is easier said than done. Yet we can take stock in Swinton's critical observation

22. Jen Bricker, *Everything Is Possible: Finding the Faith and Courage to Follow Your Dreams* (Grand Rapids: Baker Books, 2016), 167.

23. See "Data & Statistics on Autism Spectrum Disorder," Centers for Disease Control and Prevention, last reviewed March 25, 2020, https://www.cdc.gov/ncbddd/autism/data.html.

24. Listen to this podcast for helpful information on disability in the church: "Is Your Church Disability Friendly?," *Influence Podcast*, https://podcasts.apple.com/us/podcast/165-is-your -church-disability-friendly/id1025266295?i=1000428082996.

25. See, e.g., John Swinton, *Finding Jesus in the Storm: The Spiritual Lives of Christians with Mental Health Challenges* (Grand Rapids: Eerdmans, 2020); Amos Yong, *The Bible, Disability, and the Church: A New Vision of the People of God* (Grand Rapids: Eerdmans, 2011); and Yong, *Theology and Down Syndrome: Reimagining Disability in Late Modernity* (Waco: Baylor University Press, 2007).

26. John Swinton, *Becoming Friends of Time: Disability, Timefullness, and Gentle Discipleship* (Waco: Baylor University Press, 2016), 167.

27. Swinton, *Becoming Friends of Time*, 207.

that in Christ "the barriers between so-called able-bodied people and so-called people with disabilities begin to crumble. . . . Within the body of Christ, *every body has a place*, and every body is recognized as a disciple with a call from Jesus and a vocation that the church needs if it is truly to be the body of Jesus. Such vocations stretch our ecclesial imaginations in powerful and deeply healing ways."[28] Similarly, Amos Yong, in *The Bible, Disability, and the Church*, applies a "hermeneutics of suspicion" and shares a more hope-filled perspective on disability: "Our goal here is to identify redemptive readings of the Christian Scriptures for people with disabilities. Again, in order to do so, we need to confront head on how surface readings of the New Testament have perpetuated discriminatory attitudes toward disabilities over time."[29] People with disabilities are not to be cast as spectators sitting on the sidelines of the Christian life. Rather, every person—including those with disabilities—are created in the *imago Dei* and have significant roles to play in the kingdom of God. Therefore, in our preaching, it is our joyful responsibility to point out how every member of the body of Christ can do his or her part.

Preaching and Terminal Illness

Death is the common enemy for all human beings. Whether we die in an accident, of natural causes, due to terminal illness, or even murder, everyone will eventually depart from the earth. In 2020, COVID-19, a disease caused by a novel coronavirus, spread like wildfire around the entire globe, not only forcing much of the world to shut down operations in businesses, restaurants, travel, schools, colleges and universities, sports, and more, but also rapidly causing thousands of fatalities.

While death is ubiquitous, we avoid thinking about it. Rabbi David Wolpe, in his national bestselling book *Making Loss Matter: Creating Meaning in Difficult Times*, shares how in high school he read Ernest Becker's book *The Denial of Death*, which "describes the strategies, good and bad, that we use to deny or evade the fact that we all one day will die."[30] Yet something about terminal illness makes death more unbearable

28. Swinton, *Becoming Friends of Time*, 208 (emphasis original).
29. Yong, *The Bible, Disability, and the Church*, 50.
30. Rabbi David Wolpe, *Making Loss Matter: Creating Meaning in Difficult Times* (New York: Riverhead, 1999), 1.

than it already is. Having a terminal illness is akin to an actual death sentence with merely a façade of optimism. In some cases, the terminal illness will go into remission, but it will at some point return for a final visit. Preaching on terminal illness and to those suffering with some form of cancer, therefore, may be the toughest topic with regard to health issues. How do we preach hope in the midst of agony, hopelessness, and impending death?

Although terminal illness has become one of the leading agents to take victims, something happens when cancer or another terminal illness strikes—a greater propensity to understand others. In Tony Hoagland's poignant essay "The Cure for Racism Is Cancer," he says, "In fact, it seems as if the whole world has cancer. With relief and dismay you'll realize, *I'm not special. Everybody here has cancer.* The withered old Jewish lefty newspaper editor. The Latino landscape contractor with the stone-roughened hands. The tough lesbian with the bleached-blond crew cut and the black leather jacket. And you will be cushioned and bolstered by the sheer number and variety of your fellows. . . . You are all simply cancer citizens, bargaining for more life. . . . And because of this, perhaps, our hearts soften."[31] C. S. Lewis says, "Pain insists on being attended to. God whispers to us in our pleasures, speaks in our conscience, but shouts in our pain: it is His megaphone to rouse a deaf world."[32] Perhaps it is only through dire measures, like terminal illness, that God gets our attention and enables us to see others as he sees them.

How can anyone say with absolute certainty and confidence why terminal illness strikes a person? Why does God heal some and choose not to heal others? The simple answer is, we don't know. David Wolpe continues: "We search for an answer to the riddle of 'why' because we want control. Give us a way to make sure that we will not lose again. But God gives this privilege to no one."[33] We have no control over terminal illness. Yet, as Joni Eareckson Tada shares, "Suffering reminds us where our true strength lies."[34] Our strength comes from the Lord and from the promises in his Word.

31. Tony Hoagland, "The Cure for Racism Is Cancer," *The Sun*, September 2018, https://www.thesunmagazine.org/issues/513/the-cure-for-racism-is-cancer.

32. C. S. Lewis, *The Problem of Pain* (New York: HarperCollins, 1996), 91.

33. Wolpe, *Making Loss Matter*, 9.

34. Joni Eareckson Tada, *A Place of Healing: Wrestling with the Mysteries of Suffering, Pain, and God's Sovereignty* (Colorado Springs: David C. Cook, 2010), 82.

Preaching on Painful Health Issues

How will we preach an effective sermon on painful health issues? Employing our range of questions, let's focus on a Bible passage and work our way through the process of preaching on health concerns.

1. Which Passage Will I Preach On?

A natural Scripture passage related to health issues—in particular, physical disability—is the narrative of Peter and John found in Acts 3:1–10, where they go to daily prayer at the temple. They encounter a man lame from birth who sits and begs near the temple gate. The story is in many ways remarkable because of the disciples' reaction to this man. This will be the text for our upcoming sermon this Sunday.

2. What Type of Pain/Suffering Is Revealed in the Text?

The primary form of pain is physical suffering. Imagine being lame from birth—never having used one's own two feet to walk and move around. You must rely on other people every single day to bring you to and from the temple to ask for spare change and be a panhandler. In fact, verse 2 says the lame man was being transported to the temple as the story begins. Not only does this man suffer physically in his inability to walk; we must also consider the mental and psychological anguish incurred because of the shame of his condition and perhaps even the insults he heard daily as people walked by.

3. How Does the Bible Character or Biblical Author Deal with the Pain?

We are not privy to personal details concerning how the lame man has dealt with his physical disability and emotional pain every moment of his life. This disability has been his entire existence. This is all his memory knows. This is the only thing people see: his disability. He can't walk or work, so the only form of financial provision comes from begging at the temple gate called Beautiful. When he sees Peter and John, he does what he's done instinctively for all of these years, which is to ask for money (Acts 3:3).

4. How Does This Pain in the Text Relate to Our Listeners' Pain?

As mentioned throughout this chapter, the possible number of physical and mental disabilities and struggles is incalculable. Look at your church membership roster and pray about what types of pain currently circulate within the congregation. The pain and suffering in their lives may well include several or all of the quadrants mentioned above. The more direct route would be to address a couple or a few of the physical hardships currently experienced by our listeners.

5. What Does This Pain Say about God and His Allowance of Pain?

It's clear from various passages in Scripture that God not only permits physical and mental suffering but also is the one who ordains such things to happen. The short answer from God is that he can do whatever he wants with every person on the planet. In Peter Kreeft's *Making Sense out of Suffering*, he notes that "if the most important thing in life [*summum bonum*] is reconciliation with God, union with God, conformity to God, then any price is worth paying to attain that end, if necessary."[35] This necessity would include God's allowance for physical pain and suffering in the world.

6. How Does God / Jesus / the Holy Spirit Help Us in Our Suffering?

We are prone as human beings to seek the immediate relief of physical suffering. Whereas the lame man sees only his physical limitations and needs, and therefore asks for temporary relief in the form of money, God shows up through Peter and John to deliver a more eternally valuable gift. In this particular instance, Peter tells the man, "Silver or gold I do not have, but what I do have I give you. In the name of Jesus Christ of Nazareth, walk" (Acts 3:6). The lame man receives not only physical healing but, most critically, the salvation of his soul, as evidenced by his praising God (vv. 8–9).[36]

The challenge in this text is that, as we know well, God does not always physically heal people. At the same time, we can trust that God can and will be present with the sufferer and lead him or her to himself salvifically. In this example, God helps the lame man by bringing him to the exact location where this providential meeting occurs between him and the two disciples. God provides not what the man wants but what he needs—by

---

35. Peter Kreeft, *Making Sense out of Suffering* (Ann Arbor, MI: Servant, 1986), 169.
36. David F. Watson, "Luke-Acts," in *The Bible and Disability: A Commentary*, ed. Sarah J. Melcher, Mikeal C. Parsons, and Amos Yong (Waco: Baylor University Press, 2017), 324.

his mercy and grace restoring the man's legs and, most importantly, saving him spiritually.

Over twenty years ago, my uncle succumbed to lung cancer. We, as a family, prayed incessantly for his physical healing, but God had a different plan for his life. Ultimately, the suffering of lung cancer caused him to see his need for God more clearly and led him to accept Christ as his Lord and Savior before leaving this world. Prior to his terminal illness, he wanted little to do with Christ. How does God help us in our physical suffering? Sometimes he helps us by providing anything in our lives—even the hardship of lung cancer—that will draw us closer to him.

7. How Can Our Preaching Show Care and Empathy?

It's easy to preach a delayed-gratification type of sermon when addressing physical hardship. Just hold on a little longer, for one day you will enter an eternal paradise free from tears and pain (Rev. 21:4). As true as this assurance is, it must be coupled with earthly empathy today. Sometimes words that demonstrate care and empathy can be of some help, such as "This is really hard," "I'm so sorry that you are experiencing this much pain," "We are praying for you," "Tell us what you can eat and we'll gladly drop it off."[37] Much of the time, words are mere platitudes to the one dying of terminal illness or suffering an entire lifetime with a disability. "When there are no words, let there be no words."[38] This is a primary opportunity to bring a sense of dignity and honor to the individual. Caring for them physically and being present emotionally, even just to hold their hand, can be welcome gestures of love. Once we care for the person physically and emotionally, then we can issue words of eternal promises, hope, and comfort.

8. How Can We Share This Pain in Christian Community?

There are many typical ways to offer assistance to those undergoing physical and mental hardships. Traditionally, we try to pick each other up by saying something positive. Yet those words of supposed construction might become counterintuitively the very words of destruction in sufferers'

---

37. Kate Bowler provides a number of helpful responses to suffering in her book *Everything Happens for a Reason: And Other Lies I've Loved* (New York: Random House, 2018).

38. Sarah Beckman, *Alongside: A Practical Guide for Loving Your Neighbor in Their Time of Trial* (New York: Morgan James, 2017), 197.

ears. This is where borrowing from the words attributed to Francis of Assisi might come in handy: "Preach the gospel at all times, and if necessary use words." Rather than telling people what we think they want to hear or need to hear, appropriate actions and behaviors toward others may be the best way of sharing the pain of health issues within the community of God's people.

Sarah Beckman's *Alongside: A Practical Guide for Loving Your Neighbor in Their Time of Trial* is a helpful resource on living out the gospel for those who are hurting. Some of the ways she encourages individuals, families, and congregations to get involved are offering specific help, being present, loving with food, doing without asking, listening well, giving good gifts, praying diligently, making them laugh, collaborating with others, and more. John Swinton agrees: "If theology is for the purposes of love, propositional knowledge should not be separated from embodied practice."[39]

9. How Will God Use Our Suffering to Transform Us and Bring Himself Glory?

As I established elsewhere, pain and suffering can be tools that God uses to transform and mature believers and return all glory to himself. People commonly react to health problems in one of two ways. Edward Brian Grassley writes, "Spiritual maturity is God's work. . . . Faith is also the central spiritual issue for the person who suffers: will I cleave to God in the midst of suffering, or will I allow the suffering to embitter me and alienate me from God?"[40] The true test of a person's spiritual maturity is whether he or she will praise and glorify God even if God refrains from healing on this side of eternity. We can encourage our listeners to do as Paul instructed the Corinthians to do, "for we live by faith, not by sight [or another disability or illness]" (2 Cor. 5:7).

Preaching Principles for Painful Health Issues

Preach Regularly on a Theology and Celebration of Weakness

While the world preaches about its strengths, we Christians preach about our weaknesses. Peter Scazzero explains: "Why does God do this

---

39. Swinton, *Becoming Friends of Time*, 6.
40. Edward Brian Grassley, "The Role of Suffering in the Development of Spiritual Maturity" (DMin thesis, Gordon-Conwell Theological Seminary, 2000), 84.

[permit suffering]? He releases the curse in order to drive us to our knees and to seek him, to recognize our need for a Savior (Gal. 3:21–25). The problem is instead of being broken by the thorns and thistles of life and thus coming to Christ, we either flee, fight, or hide. . . . Everyone is broken, damaged, cracked, and imperfect. It is a common thread of all humanity—even for those who deny its reality in their life."[41] We can appreciate the apostle Paul's self-understanding of weakness and brokenness in 2 Corinthians 12:10 when he reflects on his limitations in order that Christ may be exalted in his life. He says, "That is why, for Christ's sake, I delight in weaknesses, in insults, in hardships, in persecutions, in difficulties. For when I am weak, then I am strong." The strength comes not from oneself or one's life but from Christ alone. The countercultural sermon is necessary here to remind our listeners that it's perfectly acceptable to admit one's mortality and one's limitations and even weaknesses.

What would happen in our congregations if we cultivated vulnerable church cultures that confessed weaknesses? Scazzero explains in *The Emotionally Healthy Church* that there are two different types of churches: one kind that is proud and defensive and the other that is broken and vulnerable. For example, the proud and defensive church member says, "I am guarded and protective about my imperfections and flaws," whereas a broken and vulnerable person confesses, "I am transparent and weak; I disclose myself to appropriate others." Or the proud and defensive member says, "I often hold grudges and rarely ask forgiveness," whereas a broken and vulnerable person says, "I don't hold people in debt to me, and am able to ask others for forgiveness as needed."[42] While there is no universal governing principle that demands we must always be broken and vulnerable before others, Scazzero notes the importance of having a posture of brokenness and vulnerability to increase one's emotional health.

Correct Bad Theologies

Due to our pursuit of theological answers, people have come up with rather poor and extreme theologies of suffering. Kerry Wynn, in her

41. Peter Scazzero, *The Emotionally Healthy Church: A Strategy for Discipleship That Actually Changes Lives* (Grand Rapids: Zondervan, 2010), 116–17.

42. Scazzero, *Emotionally Healthy Church*, 118–19.

essay "Johannine Healings and the Otherness of Disability," explains: "The two most common assumptions in popular theology that marginalize people with disabilities are 1) disability is caused by sin, and 2) if one has enough faith, one will be healed."[43] Everyone is seeking an answer and offering reasons. Kate Bowler, the Duke professor and stage 4 colon cancer sufferer mentioned in chapter 2, writes, "In a spiritual world in which healing is a divine right, illness is a symptom of unconfessed sin—a symptom of a lack of forgiveness, unfaithfulness, unexamined attitudes, or careless words. A suffering believer is a puzzle to be solved. What had caused this to happen?"[44] We, as a human race, seek answers and solutions to problems of various stripes. We're not satisfied with not knowing the answer to the nagging question "Why?" or "Why me?" We even become syncretistic unintentionally when we associate and even blend Christianity with Buddhist tenets like karma. "God is getting me back for what I did in high school or college or during my marriage!"

The binary dimensions of grace and judgment play out starkly when dealing with how we understand physical or mental suffering. Lenny Luchetti offers the following theological observation: "The preacher who is convinced of the impassibility of God, his apatheia, will stress divine sovereignty, transcendence, power, and justice. The preacher who views God as passible will emphasize divine love, mercy, and, yes, empathy. Perhaps the goal is to emphasize both sides without neglecting either in our preaching."[45] Teeter-tottering, most preachers fall on one side of the fence or the other. While it is dissatisfactory to many, we must be content sometimes with the nonanswer that only God knows why and how people suffer. Consider for a moment the absolute craziness and sinful outbreaks that would happen in this world if everyone knew the exact day and moment they were going to die! We can only imagine the sins and sinful nature that would erupt on all of humanity. We must let God be God and respond with preaching his comfort as the only lasting remedy and substitute (see 2 Cor. 1:3–11).

43. Kerry Wynn, "Johannine Healings and the Otherness of Disability," *Perspectives in Religious Studies* 34 (2007): 61, cited by Jaime Clark-Soles, "Disability and the Bible," *Christian Citizen*, February 21, 2018, https://christiancitizen.us/disability-and-the-bible.

44. Bowler, *Everything Happens for a Reason*, 15.

45. Lenny Luchetti, *Preaching with Empathy: Crafting Sermons in a Callous Culture* (Nashville: Abingdon, 2018), 24.

Respond with Praise to God

Finally, if we are to handle suffering gracefully, there is no substitute for a life of joyful praise. Timothy Keller says, "There's nothing more important than to be equipped to face evil and suffering, because it is absolutely coming. It is inevitable. . . . Faith in Jesus Christ gives you the resources to face suffering so that instead of withering you or shrinking you or crushing you, it will actually enhance you and deepen you and grow you."[46]

It's humanly absurd to think that God still sought praise from Job despite his immense suffering. And yet, no matter the circumstances of our lives, God is jealous for his glory, honor, and praise. That paradox includes moments of elation and even soul-crushing trials and bodily impairments. God still expects glory from his people. Well-known author and speaker Joni Eareckson Tada, a quadriplegic for over fifty years, writes, "I pray that my pain might be removed, that it might cease; but more so, I pray for the strength to bear it, the grace to benefit from it, and the devotion to offer it up to God as a sacrifice of praise."[47] May this Christlike attitude be true of us as well, no matter our mental and physical condition.

Conclusion

Physical and mental health issues are a by-product of living in a post-Edenic society. There is no human control over how we are born into the world and what problems will befall us in life. Our listeners are grieving. They experience myriad mental and physical adversities. They want and don't want to hear God's voice all at the same time. It's a perplexing phenomenon to preach on health issues. And yet the challenge and opportunity afforded to today's preacher is somehow, through confidence in God's all-surpassing truth, to guide our listeners to respond to various trials by being transformed into the image of Christ, to cultivate spiritual maturity and depth, and to give praise and glory to God. Not everyone chooses to grow deeper, so we encourage all believers but recognize that only a portion will choose joyfulness in spite of their pain. I close with

46. See Timothy Keller's book advertisement, "Walking with God through Pain and Suffering, Timothy Keller," YouTube video, 1:44, September 12, 2013, https://youtu.be/y53u6iFR6gQ.
47. Tada, *Place of Healing*, 35.

the indelible words of Horatio Spafford, who, despite incredibly painful circumstances, wrote:

> Tho' Satan should buffet, tho' trials should come,
> Let this blest assurance control,
> That Christ has regarded my helpless estate,
> And hath shed his own blood for my soul.
>
> *Refrain*: It is well, it is well with my soul.[48]

The answer to every trial goes back to the basics of the Christian life. We are nothing without Christ, and we have everything as long as we have him. Only when Christ alone is our true source of satisfaction can we also cry out like Spafford, "It is well with my soul."

Discussion Questions

1. What types of health issues exist among the people in your congregation?
2. What is their attitude toward physical, mental, chronic, and even terminal suffering?
3. How do you encourage them to press on in the Christian life despite these challenges?
4. In what ways could you more intentionally use the pulpit to foster hope and peace in uncertain times?

48. See the website dedicated to this hymn: "It Is Well with My Soul"—Spafford Hymn, https://www.spaffordhymn.com.

"Panhandling for True Satisfaction"[1]

Sermon on Acts 3:1–10

> **HOMILETICAL IDEA:** Spiritually speaking, we're all panhandlers looking for the satisfaction that only Christ can give.

Being asked for spare change by a person on the street corner can often make for an awkward situation. Do we look them in the eyes or do we gaze off into the distance? Do we read their sign for help or do we choose to ignore it? Do we extend them some cash or do we withhold it? These and more questions may race through our heads during those thirty seconds we're stopped at the red light.

As I look back on my past experiences with panhandlers, I confess that my giving has been erratic. If I'm in a good mood or the person's signage is humorous or heartbreaking, I will open the window and lovingly hand the person a dollar or two. On the other hand, if I'm having a less than stellar day or I've lost any semblance of compassion, I'll divert my eyes from the person; I won't read their plea for assistance; I won't give them a nickel or dime. Being asked for spare change is often burdensome.

You may recall that once-promising story about a local news reporter in Columbus, Ohio, who met Ted Williams. No, I'm not talking about the Boston Red Sox Hall of Famer. This Williams became a media sensation overnight, known as "the man with the golden voice." His video footage went viral on YouTube, with over 18 million hits. He eventually was offered a job with the Cleveland Cavaliers basketball team as an announcer

---

1. Matthew D. Kim, "Panhandling for True Satisfaction," *Preaching Today*, April 2013, https://www.preachingtoday.com/sermons/sermons/2013/april/panhandling-for-true-satisfaction.html. Used by permission.

and was considered for other radio broadcasting positions. But, sadly, his former ways got the better of him, and he lost his way.

As we travel through life, we meet all types of people who need our help. But what if what they're asking for is not all that they need? In Acts 3:1–10, Peter and John are making their way to the temple for afternoon prayer when they are stopped by a panhandler looking for a handout. What can we learn from this story as we think about the people that God sends our way?

I. We want to satisfy physical needs.

In verse 1, Peter and John were walking to the temple for daily prayer, as usual. Luke shares that they were greeted by a man who was lame from birth. Every day the people in this man's close network carried him to the temple gate so he could beg for money. Imagine being this lame man, who had never walked on his own two legs. Every single day he relied on others—twenty-four hours a day, seven days a week.

Years ago, my brothers and I wanted to bring our aging grandmother from her nursing home to our parents' home for the annual Kim family Thanksgiving dinner. The difficulty was that grandma could no longer walk—her legs were limp and lifeless. We would need to carry our grandmother and carefully place her in the back seat of the car. Then once we arrived at home, we would have to carry her into the house and sit her down on the living room couch. Grandma looked so weak and frail. She was skin and bones, so we thought this would be an easy task. But when we lifted her, she was heavier than she appeared. She was heavy not because she was overweight but because the lower part of her body was completely inactive. She couldn't control her legs. They were dead weight, like dense tree branches. We loved our grandmother dearly and wanted her to be present at Thanksgiving supper. We were able to make this effort once a year so she could spend some time with the entire family.

The friends or family of this man with a disability loved him so much that they were willing to wake up every morning and transport him on their backs to the temple. Imagine for a moment being a friend or family member of someone with special needs. Some of you probably already are. When I was in college, I volunteered for two years at Laura Baker School, an educational facility that specialized in helping students with special needs and developmental disabilities. Each week I witnessed the toils of individuals with disabilities struggling to do daily activities we take for granted. Some of them couldn't put on their own shoes or even lift a fork to their mouth. This was their lot in life. And this was also the lot of the man in Acts 3.

Notice the physical descriptions that Luke includes in his narrative. This man was lame from the moment he was born. His physical body needed to be carried every day to the temple gate called Beautiful—another physical description. Bible scholars are uncertain where this so-called beautiful gate was located on the temple grounds, but we do know that this gate led into the temple, which meant heavy foot traffic and potential charitable givers.

Then, in verse 3, the man sees Peter and John about to enter the temple, so he asks them for money. When we go through difficult situations, often the only thing that we can think about is meeting our immediate physical needs. Our minds gravitate toward how we can satisfy our physical bodies: our stomachs, our looks, or something else. Obviously, the man in Acts 3 struggled to find work. His body couldn't perform manual labor because of his disability. He was overlooked because of his physical appearance. So the only thing he could think to do was ask for change from those passing by.

There's nothing wrong with the man's request. In fact, that's what any person in his situation would do. That's what we would do, too. We all would stretch out our hands and ask for some change. But the truth is, we need a different kind of change. In his book *Just Generosity*, ethics professor Ron Sider asks this profound question: "How would I feel if I were a poor person living in the richest nation on earth and knew my comfortable neighbors simply did not care enough to offer me real opportunity?"[2]

Ron Sider is asking Christians to think outside the box. Yes, we are commanded by God to care for the poor and meet their physical needs. We remember Jesus's powerful parable about the sheep and the goats in Matthew 25. The people that Jesus considered the sheep truly cared for those in need by feeding them, by relieving their thirst, by providing shelter, by giving them clothes to wear, by tending to the ill, and by visiting prisoners. The king in Jesus's parable says, "Truly I tell you, whatever you did for one of the least of these brothers and sisters of mine, you did for

---

2. Ron Sider, *Just Generosity: A New Vision for Overcoming Poverty in America*, 2nd ed. (Grand Rapids: Baker Books, 2007), 31.

me" (v. 40). Jesus commands the people of God, you and me, to care for the least of these as if we were caring for Jesus himself.

But as we continue reading in Acts 3, there's greater depth to the story than simply emptying the change from one's pockets. In fact, Peter and John are going to offer this man change that will alter his life forever. We want to merely satisfy our physical needs and leave it at that, but true satisfaction is found in Jesus.

II. Satisfaction is found in Jesus.

Verse 4 says, "Peter looked straight at him, as did John. Then Peter said, 'Look at us!'" The disabled man is distracted and does not give Peter and John his full attention. So Peter commands the man to look at him. It's like when I'm trying to get the attention of my sons, especially when they're watching TV. They can probably sense that my eyes are fixed on them and I want their attention. But they're often so engrossed in what they're watching that what Dad wants right now is not all that important. So I have to raise my voice a little and say, "Look at me!"

In verse 5, you can picture this man people-watching and studying the crowd to figure out which temple worshiper might stop and give him some money. He's people-watched before. He knows who'll care to stop and who won't. After Peter gets his attention, the man reaches out his hand, hoping that Peter and John might pull out some coins—preferably the shiny kind.

What must be going through the man's mind at this moment in verse 6 as he's completely healed? Here is a person who from birth has never been able to take a step. His mother and father never had the joy of witnessing his first steps when he was an infant. But years later, Peter takes his right hand and pulls him up to his feet. He can feel his feet and ankles get stronger by the second. He jumps to his feet and begins to walk. Little does he know that his miraculous story of healing will be recorded in the Bible.

The man thought he needed something monetary to meet his physical needs, but Peter and John granted him a special gift that changed his life forever. As we study the Bible's account of miraculous healings, we know that when the healer speaks those precious words, "In the name of Jesus Christ of Nazareth," what the recipient receives is not only physical but spiritual restoration and healing. And that's what this man with profound disabilities experienced as well.

Just a moment ago, the man's feet and ankles were dead and lifeless. He was immobile. But as Jesus's name entered the halls of his ears, he received new life in his legs and feet, and, more importantly, in his soul. Continue reading with me the second half of verse 8: "Then he went with them into the temple courts, walking and jumping, and praising God."

This man needed far more than spare change. He needed Jesus and the healing that only Jesus could provide for his body and soul. What do you think you need right now? You may not be reaching out your hand for spare change, but you probably require change of some sort in your life.

All of us are disabled in some way. We are in need. We're lame spiritually because we don't love Christ and serve him wholeheartedly. Some of us in this room are stretching out our hands, hoping that God might give us love in the form of a spouse, a marriage partner. We want a husband or a wife who we think will satisfy us. Some of us are reaching out for a new job or a promotion we think will grant us happiness. Some of us are hoping to receive the gift of a child we think will give us greater satisfaction. Although none of these things is necessarily wrong, God has something greater in store for our lives.

We are like the man in this story, who thought he knew what he needed. He wanted some dimes and quarters to get him through the day. He had little hope. He had little vision. He had little expectations. Instead of asking for a fishing net, he was happy to get a bite of leftover salmon. The human heart seeks satisfaction in anything and everything but Jesus Christ. Yet he's exactly what we need.

What are we seeking in this life to bring us satisfaction? Some of the physical and mental issues that we're dealing with are excruciatingly difficult! Are we struggling with our physical health? Do we live every moment with chronic pain? Do we have diabetes or MS or vision problems? Do we have a terminal illness? Are we battling mental illness? Are we caring for a loved one with Alzheimer's or dementia? These are challenging conditions that often don't have solutions or remedies or an expiration date. Are we seeking satisfaction through worldly success, through wealth, through careers, through status, through fancy homes and fancy cars, by living out our dreams vicariously through our children, or in hearing the praise of people? Put frankly, in the midst of such trials, is Jesus enough for us?

By God's grace and mercy, this man is healed. Notice the response of the man after being healed by God in body and soul. At the beginning of the story, all this man wanted was to satisfy his physical need through money, but he soon discovered that he really needed Jesus. After receiving the name of Jesus in his life, his immediate reaction was to sing praise to God.

III. Satisfaction is found in bringing God glory.

In verses 9 and 10, in his utter astonishment and excitement, the man could have left Peter and John behind in the dust and run off with his newly found freedom after being miraculously healed by them. But instead, this man with disabilities chose to walk with them into the temple for all the worshipers to witness what God had just done in his life through the healing and saving power of Jesus's name.

Those who had come for afternoon prayer that day saw this man walking and praising God. Luke reminds us for a second time that this was indeed the same man they saw every single day panhandling outside the temple gate called Beautiful. This same man was now walking, jumping in the air, and praising God. And the entire temple was brimming with wonder and astonishment at what they had just witnessed.

What can we learn from this man's story? We want to satisfy physical needs, but satisfaction is found in Jesus and in bringing God glory. You can imagine all the people in the temple praising God as a result of the transformation that took place in this man's life. The man's witness brought praise to God, contagious praise. So often in this life, what we want is not what we really need.

In her article "Satisfaction in the Savior," a young Christian woman named Cantiese Burrell tells a story about her friend and his remarkable family. At dinner, he and his siblings finished their plates, headed over to their dad's side of the table, and began eating off his plate. They did this ritual every evening: "These children had all eaten, but none of them were satisfied until they could eat something from their father's plate. In the same manner, God is our heavenly Father and no matter what we have eaten or what we have been drinking of this world, satisfaction only comes when we eat from his plate. In Christ Jesus, God has prepared a spiritual plate for all to take part and eat from. Jesus is the source and the sustainer of life."[3]

3. Cantiese Burrell, "Satisfaction in the Savior," RHEMA Bible Training Center newsletter, March–April 1998, https://www.rdricketts.com/trust/cantiese.html.

Conclusion

Will you praise God today even if he does not bring earthly satisfaction or healing? I'm not suggesting that this is easy by any means. Life is full of heartache and brokenness. Yet, as I think back on my life, I have been most satisfied when I was head-over-heels in love with Jesus Christ, when Jesus alone brought me satisfaction. The greatest moments of satisfaction also came when, in some small way, my life has brought God praise. Like the man in Acts 3, perhaps we've been focusing on the wrong things to bring us satisfaction. Only Jesus and living for him can truly satisfy every longing in our hearts.

7

Painful Losses

On November 8, 2015, I woke up to over twenty missed calls from my youngest brother, Dennis, who lives on the West Coast. He asked me to return his call as soon as possible no matter what time. I felt in my gut that something terrible had happened. But I never fathomed what I would hear next. "Matt, I don't know how to say this but Tim [our middle brother] died in an accident in Manila." "No, that's impossible," was my response in utter disbelief and numbness. My heart was pounding. I must have repeated myself at least ten times. "It's a mistake. They must have identified the wrong person. No, not Tim! That's not possible." The conversation spun around viciously in circles of incredulity.

To condense a very long story, Dennis and I traveled to the Philippines, where Tim had been working as a successful international marketing manager.[1] Putting the clues together like special agents on a CSI episode for nearly a week, we concluded that without a doubt Tim had been targeted for his money and brutally murdered at his apartment complex—his body thrown at some point from the twenty-third floor (i.e., double floors, so the fall was nearly five hundred feet). The police report said it was an accident. But this was clearly no accident. A fake wallet was even planted in his back pocket (with corner-cut credit cards), further stoking the flaming evidence of foul play. He was celebrating his thirty-sixth birthday on the

---

1. Tim modeled the life of the good Samaritan, and his selfless way of life will serve as an example of Christlikeness in our memories.

night of his premature death. We pursued justice from every angle, only to have Tim's case closed within a few weeks due to multilayered corruption in the Philippines. The tragic loss of Tim has shattered our hearts. Full stop. But we press forward in life with hope in Christ that one day we will be reunited with Tim when the new heavens and earth join together. Loss is tragic, horrific, and gut-wrenching, and time does not heal all wounds—unlike what the old cliché suggests. A flurry of tears trickle down my cheeks today as I write this chapter on loss.

Listeners live with losses of all kinds: death of grandparents, parents, a spouse, children, siblings, relatives; loss of jobs; loss of promotions; loss of retirement savings; loss of homes; loss of respect and status; loss of a marriage; miscarriage; infertility; and more. Loss is crushing, and everyone will experience it in some shape or form—over and over again. How can we bring the hope of the gospel into such experiences and feelings of loss? This chapter addresses various forms of loss and demonstrates how to preach with greater empathy and hope. All loss in this world can be generally demarcated into three categories: loss of identity and status, loss of possessions and property, and loss of people.

Loss of Identity and Status

Loss is devastating, whether expected or not. A first type of loss relates to identity and status. One common example would be the involuntary loss of a job or the inability to find gainful employment. Getting demoted in one's profession may similarly invoke a feeling that one has lost one's status. Some may unexpectedly lose a job and gain a disability as a result of a tragic injury or accident, fighting in military combat, or even terrorist attacks. Such was the case for Jeff Bauman, who cheered on his girlfriend at the 2013 Boston Marathon and lost both of his legs as one of the now infamous backpacks exploded at his feet. He says, "I know exactly when my life changed: when I looked into the face of Tamerlan Tsarnaev."[2] We can lose our identity through dementia or Alzheimer's or another mental illness or brain injury. We lose our identity when our identity is wrapped up in a relationship, a job, a profession, a position, or a familial role like that of husband, wife, son, or daughter.

2. Jeff Bauman, *Stronger* (New York: Grand Central, 2014), 3.

Many immigrants and refugees suffer from the loss of identity as they emigrate from or evacuate their home countries, where they received professional training as doctors, lawyers, engineers, or business professionals, only to come to North America to find "a better life" and work as janitors, convenience store clerks, and other positions of menial labor due to language limitations and cultural barriers. I invite you especially to sit down with your parishioners who are immigrants and refugees and hear their stories of what they sacrificed in order to come to the United States and Canada. Loss of identity and status can be immense sources of shame and grief.

Loss of Possessions and Property

A second form of loss involves possessions and property. The stuff of life. From wildfires in California to hurricanes in Houston and New Orleans to tornadoes in Tulsa, the loss of possessions and property eradicates and decimates individual lives and families. In summer 2014, our new cul-de-sac on the North Shore of Boston experienced the devastation of arson as three teenagers lit up two unfinished homes in our circle. All eleven homes in our circle were damaged to varying degrees (requiring the replacement of windows, doors, roof shingles, and vinyl siding, which looked like melted ice cream). The fire burned halfway through the home immediately next door to us. God in an act of mercy miraculously prevented our home from burning to a crisp. In the blink of an eye, we can lose our homes, cars, savings, IRAs, 401(k)s, and other retirement and equity assets.

Kathleen Nielson writes, "We spend our lives trying to keep things. To keep things safe. To keep things from being spoiled. And not just things such as money and houses and clothes and food—all that is hard enough. . . . We spend a lot of energy trying to keep many things. Ultimately, we can't."[3] It's no wonder that Jesus commands us, "Do not store up for yourselves treasures on earth, where moths and vermin destroy, and where thieves break in and steal. But store up for yourselves treasures in heaven, where moths and vermin do not destroy, and where thieves do not break in and steal. For where your treasure is, there your heart will be also" (Matt. 6:19–21).

3. Kathleen Nielson, "Born Again to a Living Hope," in *Resurrection Life in a World of Suffering: 1 Peter*, ed. D. A. Carson and Kathleen Nielson (Wheaton: Crossway, 2018), 48.

Loss of People

As mentioned above, the most destructive of all losses is of course the loss of human life. The loss of the unborn or the stillborn, miscarriages, infertility, aborted babies, loss of family members—parents and grandparents, spouses, children, siblings—loss of dear friends, and more: nothing hurts more than losing someone we love. We also lose people through broken relationships, the subject of our next chapter. The finality of death is numbing, to say the least. Michael Hebb's *Let's Talk about Death (over Dinner)* locates the strong penchant we have as human beings to avoid conversations about death. Hebb observes, "In all our striving, we fail to bring death into the conversation, and yet our mortality is the fulcrum of all personal transformation. We don't think about improving our lives in the context of death, and we don't talk about improving our deaths."[4] How do we preach in such a way as to bring comfort to the millions of couples who experience miscarriage or infertility and whose emotions abruptly waver "from overflowing to desolate, elated to despondent, fleshly to inanimate, and vibrant to monochromatic"?[5] What can we say to minister to those whose loved one has chosen suicide as the final escape or to help prevent someone from thinking that suicide is the only last resort?[6]

Years ago in California, I attended the funeral of a distant relative of my wife. He had been young by any standard—only in his thirties. His mother, not a believer, wailed uncontrollably like I had never witnessed before. At the interment, she actually climbed on top of the casket not wanting to release her son from this earth. It was one of the most painful moments I had ever witnessed—a person grieving without Christian hope. For professed believers in Christ, death must be different—albeit raw and painful nevertheless. When we preach as those who place faith in the person and work of Jesus Christ, we educate and encourage our

---

4. Michael Hebb, *Let's Talk about Death (over Dinner): An Invitation and Guide to Life's Most Important Conversation* (New York: De Capo, 2018), 5.

5. Matthew Arbo, *Walking through Infertility: Biblical, Theological, and Moral Counsel for Those Who Are Struggling* (Wheaton: Crossway, 2018), 98.

6. Three valuable resources to guide our thinking on the topic of suicide are Al Hsu, *Grieving a Suicide: A Loved One's Search for Comfort, Answers, and Hope* (Downers Grove, IL: InterVarsity, 2017); Karen Mason, *Preventing Suicide: A Handbook for Pastors, Chaplains and Pastoral Counselors* (Downers Grove, IL: InterVarsity, 2014); and Scott M. Gibson and Karen Mason, *Preaching Hope in Darkness: Help for Pastors in Addressing Suicide from the Pulpit* (Bellingham, WA: Lexham, 2020).

congregants to view the loss of life as Paul encourages the believers in
1 Corinthians 15:55: "Where, O death, is your victory? Where, O death,
is your sting?" Perhaps an image that we can liken this to is a bee whose
stinger is removed. The bee lands on us—we can feel it—but it now has
nothing that can harm us. I will speak of this more in the conclusion of this
chapter. What might it look like for us to put together a sermon on loss?

Preaching on Painful Losses

Painful losses require heartfelt sermons that forthrightly exert the truth in
Scripture coupled with empathy and compassion. Imagine with me that
our upcoming sermon passage on pain is 2 Corinthians 1:3–11.

1. Which Passage Will I Preach On?

Second Corinthians provides firsthand personal testimony of Paul's
sufferings. It is commonly referred to as the most vulnerable of all his
epistles. He says in 2 Corinthians 11:30, "If I must boast, I will boast of
the things that show my weakness." I chose 2 Corinthians 1:3–11 because
of what it conveys about God and who he is in the midst of afflictions,
especially as Paul acknowledges the universal nature of God's comfort for
all forms of suffering in 1:3. Preaching on loss commonly addresses the
individual and his or her circumstances. What we want to demonstrate in
our sermon is that God is bigger than our trials because of his manifesta-
tions of compassion and comfort—even though these trials are admittedly
severe at times.

2. What Type of Pain/Suffering Is Revealed in the Text?

Paul speaks more broadly about universal afflictions, but he does begin
to open up specifically about his own trials endured in Asia Minor beginning in 2 Corinthians 1:8. We do not have conclusive knowledge of what
these hardships involved exactly.[7] What we do know is that they were so
severe that Paul writes, "We were under great pressure, far beyond our
ability to endure, so that we despaired of life itself. Indeed, we felt we had

---

7. Colin G. Kruse, *2 Corinthians*, Tyndale New Testament Commentaries (Downers Grove,
IL: IVP Academic, 2015), 91.

received the sentence of death" (vv. 8–9). Other trials are elaborated on in 6:3–13 and 11:16–33, including incarceration, flogging, beatings, stoning, shipwreck, and numerous threats to his very life (11:23–26).

3. How Does the Bible Character or Biblical Author Deal with the Pain?

The first—rather paradoxical—thing that Paul encourages the believers to do is to praise God for being the God of all comfort and compassion (2 Cor. 1:3). It is a countercultural command and goes against human nature. When things go south in our lives, the last thing that comes to mind is to praise and glorify God. Instead, what wants to come out of our mouths is cursing. Paul's instruction, we presume, indicates how he dealt with his own suffering, pain, and trials. We don't envision Paul as being a hypocrite here. He's not telling the Corinthians to practice only what he preaches but fails to embody right now.

As in the letter to the Philippians, Paul channels his energy toward God, who alone can bring lasting comfort. Mark A. Seifrid notes how Paul does not suffer alone, but "uses it as an opportunity to invite the Corinthians to work with God for him in prayer. In that way, they too shall render thanks to God for him. The God who delivered him once in Asia shall do so again through their prayer."[8] Unlike many Christians today who burrow inward during challenging seasons, Paul exhibits his outward nature at all times. Aída Besançon Spencer describes Paul in this way: "The apostle Paul is a theologian, learned in doctrine, and a pastor who loves and desires the best for his people. Not a loner, he works with co-workers."[9] He employs his suffering as a way to advance the gospel and ultimately to glorify God, because "many will give thanks on [Paul's] behalf for the gracious favor granted [to Paul] in answer to the prayers of many" (2 Cor. 1:11).

4. How Does This Pain in the Text Relate to Our Listeners' Pain?

The possible painful scenarios of loss represented in our congregation are familiar to us. Again, as we focus on loss, we may gingerly raise to consciousness pain that our listeners have repressed or are battling today. During my years as a pastor, the congregation desired to hear sermons

8. Mark A. Seifrid, *The Second Letter to the Corinthians*, Pillar New Testament Commentary (Grand Rapids: Eerdmans, 2014), 33.
9. Aída Besançon Spencer, *2 Corinthians*, People's Bible Commentary (Oxford: BRF, 2001), 13.

specifically about mothers and fathers on Mother's Day and Father's Day. The double-edged sword of God's Word swung around the sanctuary, because these particular holidays often bring the painful past to the surface: past experiences of parental abuse, neglect, violence, or the tragedy of miscarriages and infertility for would-be mothers and fathers. With pastoral wisdom and sensitivity, we can speak to the pain in the room. And perhaps one of the most effective ways to accomplish this is to disclose our own suffering as preachers. How are we in pain or how have we experienced pain in our history?

Prior to writing this book, I began a common practice of sharing my pain from the pulpit when the Scripture text and situation called for it. Opening up about my own physical afflictions and losing my brother have become conduits for promoting congregational openness, especially for listeners who have often bottled up their pain. Sometimes, as congregants leave the sanctuary at the conclusion of the service, I greet lines of people who share how thankful they were that I could be so genuine, raw, and transparent from the pulpit. They often whisper in my ear how they wish more pastors could be vulnerable so that they could reciprocate and share their own pains. I share this not as self-congratulations to boast about my preaching ability. Rather, it's confirmation that we can disclose our wounds wisely from the pulpit and share our suffering with our hearers.

5. What Does This Pain Say about God and His Allowance of Pain?

Throughout Scripture, it's clear that God permits pain and suffering (e.g., Job and others). Notice that God is no respecter of persons when he permits afflictions. Anyone is fair game. Yet if someone could be exempt from suffering, from our finite human perspective, it would be the apostle Paul. A Christian stalwart of the faith, Paul champions the gospel to the Jewish and gentile worlds. And yet, as is clearly documented in 2 Corinthians, the book of Acts, and other epistles, suffering and pain did not evade him. What God accomplishes with Paul's afflictions is that he enables Paul to utilize pain as a source of fuel to boast about Christ and his own weakness (2 Cor. 11:30).

6. How Does God / Jesus / the Holy Spirit Help Us in Our Suffering?

The verse that stands out with regard to God's assistance in the midst of our struggles is 2 Corinthians 1:4. As Aída Besançon Spencer explains that God's love, unlike human love, is never exhausted: "God is the one consoling us (v. 4). God is the one who, not just once but continually, stands at our side defending us and helping us."[10] Specifically, God's ability to console us is an ongoing, ceaseless type of consolation. David Garland says, "Paul's use of the *paraklēsis* word group ('comfort,' 'consolation,' 'appeal') predominates in 2 Corinthians (twenty-nine out of fifty-nine instances in the New Testament). . . . Comfort relates to encouragement, help, exhortation. God's comfort strengthens weak knees and sustains sagging spirits so that one faces the troubles of life with unbending resolve and unending assurance."[11]

It might be helpful to illustrate to our listeners that God's comfort and consolation are like a silo of your favorite crop at the local farm fully stocked and available at all times. God provides access to this silo anytime we are in need. The best part of this silo is that it is omnipresent—a silo on wheels, which comes to us rather than us having to travel to it. The problem for many Christians is not that God is not available. Rather, the issue is that we, in our hearts, are unavailable to God to receive his comfort and consolation. When trials come, we typically run from God. By encouraging our listeners to go to God in any affliction, we remind them of God's bountiful provision, which emboldens us to handle any situation that comes our way as his disciples.

7. How Can Our Preaching Show Care and Empathy?

Our natural tendency is to express consolation through our use of words. This is a well-meaning and kind gesture, when done appropriately and gently. We want to tap into Hallmark's database of flowery language in their greeting cards. Yet, in most if not all cases, words are meaningless when someone has suffered a devastating loss. Life becomes a shell as we become despondent. So, then, what is a preacher to do—whose vocation is to communicate words of truth to fragile listeners?

Instead of offering words of consolation, what if we provided more space in the sermon for the simplicity of silence and silent grieving? Give listeners time in the message to mourn, to lift their hands to God in sweet

10. Spencer, *2 Corinthians*, 30.
11. David E. Garland, *2 Corinthians*, New American Commentary 29 (Nashville: Broadman & Holman, 1999), 60.

surrender, to invite his presence to comfort and console the brokenhearted disciple as only he can, to admit the futility of their own efforts to comfort themselves. Although preachers can be terrified of silence, it may have positive benefits when we're addressing losses of myriad kinds. The next time you preach on loss, make concerted, intentional room for silence and silent lament. Ask your listeners how they felt when sermonic space was given for God to speak through the power of the Holy Spirit.

8. How Can We Share This Pain in Christian Community?

The universality of pain should not be underestimated. Well-known Christian writer Philip Yancey says that "pain plays as a kind of background static to many lives."[12] Loss is part of that static for many Christians, if not all. Paul's encouragement or admonishment in this passage is for the Christian to share the comfort that he or she has experienced from God with others in community. We don't hoard the blessing of consolation; as Paul writes in the second part of 2 Corinthians 1:4, ". . . so that we can comfort those in any trouble with the comfort we ourselves have received from God."

As we create a congregational culture of vulnerability (see chapter 2), it will become easier to share our losses with others. This is why it's so critical for the pastor to act as an agent of openness and brokenness. We can be the impetus of change to combat loneliness and isolationism. Satan desires that all Christians will feel alone and abandoned by God and by others. As part of the worship service, ask the congregation to break into twos or threes to share and pray together for their loss(es). At first, this act will seem quite awkward and contrived, particularly if such honesty is taboo or novel to many. This aversion to group sharing is especially nerve-wracking for introverts. Over time, however, as freedom trumps self-consciousness, prayers among God's people will foster friendship and greater concern within the body of Christ, so that believers' faith moves beyond Sunday worship into the rest of the week. We can invite the congregation to learn how to become active listeners rather than merely conversationalists who do all of the (one-directional) conversing. When someone encounters unspeakable loss once, and especially if more than

12. Philip Yancey, *The Question That Never Goes Away: Why?* (Grand Rapids: Zondervan, 2013), 17.

once, it changes the person. It changes how they view life, view God, and view others. Life becomes stained, like when mustard dribbles on a white dress. Taking time to listen to others' painful stories accomplishes many things, among them empowering the person who vulnerably shares and equipping the listener with greater empathy.

9. How Will God Use Our Suffering to Transform Us and Bring Himself Glory?

Something happens to people when they experience loss. In many ways, it humbles them. It also changes the way they view others and view life. Mayhem in life cannot help but engender maturation. How could someone who lives a privileged life ever understand someone whose possessions fit into a shopping cart? How could someone who has never lost a loved one resonate with a couple whose toddler dies in a car accident? The person who experiences some form of loss can empathize with others who have lost something or someone.

On paper, I have lived a life of privilege. Growing up in suburban Chicago in a middle-class family whose parents sacrificed everything for their kids, I have been extraordinarily blessed by God. Our parents moved so that we could attend a first-rate high school. I went by God's grace to a top-notch liberal arts college and later received the finest of theological educations at Gordon-Conwell Theological Seminary and the University of Edinburgh in Scotland. I have seen magnificent parts of the world firsthand in Africa, Asia, and Europe. I didn't experience the doldrums of extended singleness, as I married young at the age of twenty-five to one of the most beautiful, intelligent, kindhearted of Christian women. I have been blessed with three beautiful, healthy sons. I'm a published author and teach at a reputable seminary.

When I preached on suffering before ever having experienced suffering, I would often receive dubious looks from listeners. I'm sure some were thinking, "What could you possibly know about suffering? Your life is perfect." Now that I share with others about my physical trials and my brother's murder, however, people no longer look at me that way. They don't look at me that way because I no longer look at them in that way— that peculiar, polished, privileged way, not weathered by true suffering. Suffering changes us. It forces us to slow down. It makes us see the world through another's vantage point. We increase in empathy. It raises thoughts and questions that we never had before our trials. It helps us understand others better. It generally produces "softer" pastors.

Before I lost Tim, empathy was simply a foreign word to me, even theoretical. Now I can say that it's a way of life. Loss has forever changed the way I see others. Loss has forced me to sit with others in their pain. Before, I didn't have any patience for others. I had better things to do than to sit and listen to them dole out their pain. Now, loss has enabled me to have more of the heart of God. Ultimately, our losses glorify God because we depend on him and begin to resemble him more. God lost everything when he lost his Son, Jesus Christ, and yet he simultaneously gained back his children.

Principles for Preaching on Painful Losses

Preaching Feed-Forward Sermons

Receiving sermon feedback is both a blessing and a curse. How many times have we heard listeners say, "Nice sermon, pastor!" as they walk out of the sanctuary? It feels good temporarily to hear positive statements about our preaching, but they are not necessarily constructive. What does "nice" really mean? Similarly unhelpful is, "Not your best sermon, pastor!" If we want genuine feedback, we need to find people who can speak detailed truth into our lives about our strengths and weaknesses as preachers in order to mature. Just as sermon feedback is beneficial for all preachers, feed-forward is a vital tool for preaching as well.[13]

One of the most helpful tools for preaching on pain, especially losses, comes from feed-forward groups who can assist us in anticipating what types of loss exists in the congregation. Imagine the following: you assemble a small sample of four to six members (what some may call a "preaching team") who represent different genders, ethnicities, cultures, vocations, generations, and life stages, and the group meets together on a weeknight prior to the sermon to speak freely about the types of painful losses represented in their lives and the lives of your congregants. Think about all the knowledge we could acquire by listening to our people talk about the pain in their lives. Allow them to shape your congregational

---

13. Ken Shigematsu, "Hitting Your Creative Peak," *Preaching Today*, June 2015, https://www.preachingtoday.com/skills/2015/june/hitting-your-creative-peak.html.

exegesis as well by asking thoughtful questions about how they understand and interpret the text—what Stuart Murray has coined "congregational hermeneutics."[14] Although we may not directly include every detail shared in the focus group—nor should we—feed-forward groups give us a better sense of the level and varieties of pain among our listeners as group synergy takes its course.

Preaching about Loss in an Age of Excess

Several paradoxes exist in the Christian life as modeled and prescribed by Christ.[15] Jesus said, "The last will be first, and the first will be last" (Matt. 20:16). He also said, "It is more blessed to give than to receive" (Acts 20:35). And he explained that loss is gain, saying, "For whoever wants to save their life will lose it, but whoever loses their life for me will find it. What good will it be for someone to gain the whole world, yet forfeit their soul?" (Matt. 16:25–26). Even Paul got in the act of paradox when he said, "For when I am weak, then I am strong" (2 Cor. 12:10), when he described himself as "having nothing, yet possessing everything" (6:10), and in other statements.

The culture in which we live perpetually promotes the worldview of "gain as gain" by regarding excess as the primary way to define whether someone is successful. For instance, once a neighbor in our cul-de-sac bought a boat, others decided that they needed one too. However, the beautiful boat just sat idly in their driveway, never to touch the water, even after several years. J. Ellsworth Kalas notes in *Preaching in an Age of Distraction*, "So who are these people to whom we preach? For one thing, they are people who subscribe naturally and deeply to the doctrine of abundance. . . . It's difficult for us to keep our bearings in a time when excess is considered not only normal but commendable."[16] Though I am not masochistic, championing human suffering through losses, preaching regularly on loss may not be a bad approach for combatting worldly

---

14. Stuart Murray, *Biblical Interpretation in the Anabaptist Tradition* (Kitchener, ON: Pandora, 2000), cited by Andrew P. Rogers, *Congregational Hermeneutics: How Do We Read?* (New York: Routledge, 2016), 5.

15. See Brandon Hilgemann, "4 Paradoxes of the Christian Life," Pro Preacher, January 31, 2018, https://www.propreacher.com/paradox-of-the-christian-life.

16. J. Ellsworth Kalas, *Preaching in an Age of Distraction* (Downers Grove, IL: InterVarsity, 2014), 54–55.

definitions of success and for purging Christians of cultural misappropriations that have become stumbling blocks to their spiritual maturity. If we fail to temper the culture's messages of what is valued, by our silence we argue that culture is right, and as a result, culture ultimately wins. Perhaps we can build into our preaching calendars regular one-off sermons or sermon series that speak about loss in constructive ways that build our character and mold us into beings who are being sanctified and who resemble more and more our Creator God.

Preaching on Death, and Not Just at Funerals

As with preaching on loss, it may be a commendable practice to preach more about death, and not just at funerals. Perhaps, like me, you can remember fewer than five sermons you have heard on death except for funeral services. As mentioned in the previous chapter, our aversion to thinking about death prevents us from dealing with its reality. Nobody wants to die. It's the aftermath of the fall. Yet to not mention it from the pulpit on occasion from a biblical perspective is to fail to ground ourselves with an eternal perspective on life itself.[17] We don't know when it will be our time, so we and our listeners must be prepared at all times.

In a sermon entitled "Death Is Not the End of Our Story," from 2 Corinthians 5:1–5, Ray Pritchard opens with this: "Of all the fears that plague the heart of man, none is greater than the fear of death. It is our greatest fear, the sum of all other fears. We are afraid to die. We are afraid of what happens when we die. Death is the fundamental human problem." The sermon is sobering, as Pritchard shares a number of stark statistics about the reality and regularity of death. For instance, "Worldwide, there are approximately 56,600,600 deaths each year. That works out to 4.7 million per month, 155,000 per day, 6,500 per hour, 107 per minute, and 1.8 per second." He even goes into some detail about how fragile the human body is:

> Our bodies are like tents. They wear out, they sag, they expand, they wrinkle, the joints get creaky, the arteries harden, gravity pulls everything

17. See J. Todd Billings, *The End of the Christian Life: How Embracing Our Mortality Frees Us to Truly Live* (Grand Rapids: Brazos, 2020).

downward, the heart slows down, the eyes grow dim, the teeth fall out, the back is stooped, and the arms grow weary. Our bones break, our muscles weaken. The body bulges in the wrong places. We brag about our strength but a tiny microbe can kill us. Sooner or later we grow old and our bodies begin to break down. Eventually they stop working altogether. No amount of Vitamin C or Siberian Ginseng can change that fact. At best, we can only slow down the aging process; we cannot delay it forever.[18]

Yet the sermon does not simply point out the finiteness of humankind. That would be rather depressing. Pritchard, instead, emphasizes the eternal destination of those who put their faith in Christ alone. He reminds the listeners of the power of the resurrection. He reminds the hearers that they will receive new bodies not affected by the scars of sin. He reminds the congregation that "death is not the end of our story" for Christians. The sermon is a powerful reminder that refocuses listeners on what the purpose of life is and how they should live in light of their future glory. We need to hear about death and loss on Sunday morning. From time to time, the preacher feeds the flock a balanced diet by sharing an encouraging message about death from the pulpit.

Preaching God's Comfort and Consolation in Community

Lastly, preaching on loss requires a recommitment to the importance of communal life among the body of Christ. The passage in Acts 2:42–47 describing the early church gives us a glimpse into how the church functions when it's at its best. It is a selfless community that sacrificially and tangibly cares about others and their struggles. The more sermons are individualistic, the more we perpetuate the Lone Ranger syndrome among our congregants. Part of our joy and responsibility as preachers is to reenergize the church about the indispensable nature of the church. In other words, we must preach on ecclesiology and why the church matters.[19] Although we can be busy as pastors with many important tasks, we must never forget that one of our principal responsibilities is to care for and

18. Ray Pritchard, "Death Is Not the End of Our Story," Keep Believing Ministries, September 30, 2010, https://www.keepbelieving.com/sermon/death-is-not-the-end-of-our-story.

19. Two helpful volumes on the purpose and function of the church are Terry L. Cross, *The People of God's Presence: An Introduction to Ecclesiology* (Grand Rapids: Baker Academic, 2019); and Scott W. Sunquist, *Why Church? An Introduction* (Downers Grove, IL: InterVarsity, 2019).

shepherd God's people and model true community. Lee Eclov reinforces the importance of preachers serving the pastoral function of presence, particularly by showing concern for individual people: "One-on-one pastoral care is every pastor's inefficient imperative. It invariably seems we could get more done if we were left alone to study or plan, or if we could be with a group of our people all at once to teach or worship or just eat together. There is this powerful instinct to always shepherd the flock in bunches, in herds, because it seems patently obvious we'd get more done. But efficiency is a poor pastoral master."[20]

Word gets around quickly as to whether we are spending time with people. When I first began my ministry as a senior pastor, the leadership requested that I spend a lot of time on my preaching and teaching ministries. So, being an introvert, I happily obliged their request by hibernating in my study. Though I preached "solid sermons," they later complained that they never saw me around. Ministry requires pulpit time and people time. Imbalance will lead to ineffective preaching and ineffective discipleship. People cannot grow unless they eat the Word rightly, but they need to also receive pastoral feeding from our ministry of presence. As we model for the church what true community looks like, they will see that it's actually quite contagious. We want to be there especially before, during, and after loss.

Conclusion

I share about an amazing couple in my church in a sermon entitled "No Other Gospel," from Galatians 1:6–10:

> Peter and Grace were faithful members of my church. Their youngest son, who was 1.5 at the time, was diagnosed with a rare genetic immune disorder called HLH. It's a disease where the body attacks itself. In the final stages eventually organs begin to fail. Jonah was getting treatments throughout the summer, and he was preparing to receive a bone-marrow transplant, which

---

20. Lee Eclov, "Pastoring the One When You'd Rather Pastor the Ninety-Nine: Personal Attention Is a Minister's Inefficient Imperative," *Christianity Today*, April 23, 2019, https://www.christianitytoday.com/pastors/2019/april-web-exclusives/pastoring-one-when-youd-rather-pastor-ninety-nine.html.

is the only hope to defeat HLH. In November 2010, his health deteriorated rapidly and on December 21st HLH took Jonah's life.

In the week leading up to his passing, I remember sitting with Peter in the hospital. He still had hope that God would save Jonah's life. But on the day of Jonah's death, Peter felt a strong conviction that this was indeed the end. Jonah died that afternoon. After Peter held Jonah in his arms and kissed his face, he laid him on the hospital bed and began to play his favorite song by Casting Crowns, "Praise You in This Storm." He and Grace raised their arms to the heavens as they sang this song to the Lord. The attending nurse and I stood in the hallway speechless as we watched Peter and Grace worship God.[21]

After I returned from Manila with the horrific knowledge of Tim's murder, the first person I called—other than my family—was Peter. I knew that he was the one person in my life who would understand my pain of loss. I told him what had happened. After listening to me, he said, "Pastor Matt, I will never stop praying for you. This tragedy will only make you stronger as a person and as a pastor." In the days and weeks going forward, Peter sent me texts of Scripture verses reminding me of God's love and power to comfort me. In its best form, this is the church. Church members are there for each other in times of loss and adversity. Peter and Grace were able to comfort me "with the comfort they had received from God." They and their continued ministry to me have been a healing balm for my troubled soul.

Nothing can bring Tim back to life, back to our family. We miss him so much, and we will always miss him. And yet God has provided another brother for me in the person of Peter. He will never replace Tim, but he will always be a brother to me. Painful losses are exactly that: painful. However, God provides comfort at times in the form of other people who have similarly endured great trials. When we lose members of our biological family, God provides us with the consoling gift of spiritual family—brothers and sisters in Christ—who can share in our grief and even bring comfort. Painful losses require pastoral, empathetic preaching, but also and equally importantly, one's pastoral presence.

21. Matthew D. Kim, "No Other Gospel," *Journal of the Evangelical Homiletics Society* 13, no. 1 (March 2013): 48.

Discussion Questions

1. What types of loss are your congregants currently experiencing?

2. How have these forms of loss perhaps deterred them from growing in discipleship?

3. Are there ongoing ways that you minister to the people who have experienced loss?

4. Beyond the pulpit, what can your congregation do to assist those who have experienced loss amid their pain and suffering?

"Successful Suffering"[1]

Sermon on 2 Corinthians 1:3–11

> **HOMILETICAL IDEA:** Comfort each other with the hope that you have received from the God of all comfort.

One of my callings in life is to be a cheerleader of fellow Christians. So let's do something a little differently today and begin with a cheer. If you're able, please stand with me and repeat each letter after me as if you're cheering on your favorite team in their stadium. Ready, okay!

Give me an S.
Give me a U.
Give me a C.
Give me a C.
Give me an E.
Give me an S.
Give me an S.

What's that spell? What's that spell? What's that spell? "SUCCESS!"

Success—that's what many of us strive for. Success—that's what the world values. We remember winners, not losers. We remember gold medal Olympians like Michael Phelps and Usain Bolt. We remember tennis champions like Serena Williams and Steffi Graf. We remember basketball greats like Michael Jordan and the late Kobe Bryant. We don't remember the 10,000-plus Olympians who failed to receive a medal. We don't remember

---

1. See Matthew D. Kim, "Successful Suffering," *Preaching Today*, October 2017, https://www.preachingtoday.com/sermons/sermons/2017/october/successful-suffering.html. Adapted and used by permission.

runners-up! We remember champions, valedictorians, CEOs, celebrities, the rich and the famous, those at the top—not those on the bottom.

We live and breathe in a culture that celebrates success. And sometimes, if we're honest, even in the church what we secretly value is success over faithfulness. I was thinking about the most recent National Preaching Conference, held here on our campus this fall. What if we advertised Pastor George as the headliner: a rural pastor in a small town in Texas whom nobody has ever heard of but who has faithfully served his congregation of 127 members for twenty years? Would anyone still sign up for the conference? It's a sobering thought, isn't it?

We love winners. We scorn losers. We love success. But how do we feel about that other word that also begins with an *s*? It begins with the first two letters in "success," but then it takes a drastic turn: S-U-F-F-E-R. "Suffer." Ugh. We don't like that word very much. We often speak to each other about our successes, but how often do we share our sufferings?

The truth is that many, if not all, of us are suffering. My wife took counseling classes at Denver Seminary while I was a pastor in Denver. In one of her classes, the professor told her a profound truth: "People's pain is people's pain."[2] Everyone has pain in their lives, whether we consider that particular pain painful or not. Some of us are suffering physically, spiritually, emotionally, relationally, financially, and the list goes on and on.

What did the apostle Paul have to say on the subject of suffering? As we know from Acts 18, Paul spent one and a half years in Corinth, teaching them God's Word. His time there was not without conflict and suffering. Paul writes his second letter to the Corinthians from Macedonia and begins with his usual greeting in verses 1 and 2. Then he starts up in verse 3.

I. Praise the God of all comfort.

God comforts us in all of our troubles. Paul's first words are, "Praise be to the God and Father of our Lord Jesus Christ, the Father of compassion and the God of all comfort" (v. 3). Isn't it strange that Paul would begin his letter with a message of comfort? To begin with comfort would naturally mean there was some type of suffering, trial, or difficulty in his

---

2. I write about this in greater detail in Matthew D. Kim, *Preaching with Cultural Intelligence: Understanding the People Who Hear Our Sermons* (Grand Rapids: Baker Academic, 2017), 59.

life and in the lives of the Corinthians. And he begins by praising God for who God is. He is the God of all comfort.

The repetition of the word "all" here is not unintentional. Paul uses the Greek word *pas* three times to emphasize "all." The word "all," which is *pas* in Greek, means "all" whether it's in English, in Korean—*mo dun*—or in German—*alles*. It still means all! All means all! God does not bring comfort only in certain arbitrary situations. Rather, Paul reminds us that in all of our troubles, God is still the God of all comfort.

What kind of comfort are we talking about? Comfort means encouragement, assurance, and strength. In these several verses, Paul uses the word for "comfort" eight times. The word has less to do with a short-term relief of sadness and much more to do with finding lasting encouragement, strength, and assurance in God alone. As Bible scholar David Garland says, "God's comfort strengthens weak knees and sustains sagging spirits so that one faces the troubles of life with unbending resolve and unending assurance."[3] The comfort that God provides for the people of God is one of courage and strength.

Why did Paul need such comfort? He reminds us in verses 8 and 9. [Read 2 Cor. 1:8–9.] He continues in 2 Corinthians 11, starting at verse 23b. [Read 2 Cor. 11:23b–28.] What kinds of suffering are you enduring today? In what ways do you need God's comfort?

How are you suffering today? Financially, physically, relationally, emotionally, spiritually, psychologically—or perhaps someone you love is suffering. Will you take a moment to think about your suffering?

Some of us may think we are exempt from suffering. If anyone should be exempt from suffering, certainly it would be the Lord Jesus, as well as Paul. Paul had every human right to be exonerated from suffering. He planted several churches and produced countless converts and disciples. He wrote half of the New Testament. Acts 19:11–12 tells us that "God did extraordinary miracles through Paul, so that even handkerchiefs and aprons that had touched him were taken to the sick, and their illnesses were cured and the evil spirits left them."

If we're honest, sometimes we believe God should exempt us from suffering as well—especially those who have offered their lives in full-time service to God. But the truth is that none of us is exempt from suffering.

---

3. David E. Garland, *2 Corinthians*, New American Commentary 29 (Nashville: Broadman & Holman, 1999), 60.

I think of Joni Eareckson Tada, the well-known Christian author and speaker who became paralyzed in a diving accident in her late teens. I think of Nabeel Qureshi—a *New York Times* bestselling author and a convert from Islam—who worked with Ravi Zacharias International Ministries and wrote several apologetics books on how we can reach Muslims for Christ. Qureshi was diagnosed with stage 4 stomach cancer in his early thirties and died soon thereafter. We wonder why. Why him? Surely someone like him should have been exempt from suffering. He was someone with so much potential to bridge relationships between Christians and Muslims.

I think even of myself. If I can be transparent for a moment, I used to think I should be exempt from suffering. I've given my life for the Lord. I've relinquished many treasures in this life to serve God. And yet suffering has come to me as well.

I had various sufferings in pastoral ministry, but nothing out of the ordinary. But after transitioning here to Gordon-Conwell, I suffered a concussion playing basketball, and the dizziness still has not gone away, more than eight years later. Every day, for close to 3,000 days, I have woken up every morning and have gone to bed each night dizzy, with my brain feeling like it's floating up and down and side to side, tossed by the waves in the ocean. In seeking to find out what was wrong with me, the doctors later diagnosed me with glaucoma, which potentially, at some point later on in my life, may take my vision.

But nothing prepared me for what happened on November 7, 2015. My younger brother Tim, who was living and working in the Philippines, had been brutally murdered. Nothing prepared me for the suffering of seeing his dead body lying in a casket in Manila. There's not a day that goes by that I don't think about him and weep: Why, God? Why did you allow them to take his life? He was celebrating his thirty-sixth birthday on the night he was murdered. He had so much future ahead of him. Why, God?

Although many of you have suffered various other trials and are suffering specific afflictions, Paul reminds us that we are to praise God because God is the God of all comfort. Yes, God can even comfort me in Tim's death and in every form of human suffering.

Can you praise God today for his comfort even in the midst of suffering?

II. Put your hope in God and receive his comfort.

Not only does Paul praise God for being the God of all comfort, but he encourages the Corinthians to put their hope in this God. Just as Christ suffered, Paul suffered greatly in his ministry—but his hope and comfort in God were greater than his suffering.

There is great suffering, but there is even greater comfort that comes from Christ. The Greek word in verse 5 for "overflows" or "abounds" relates to the idea of profit and surplus. One commentator explains that in this ancient culture, the locals used this word in reference to a financial balance sheet with two columns. One side represented the sufferings of Christ, and the other represented comfort through Christ. The commentator says, "Ministering in this present evil age brings [Paul] a surplus of suffering that becomes almost unbearable. But the consolation column also shows a surplus, and it more than balances the suffering."[4] Paul suffered. We are suffering. And the comfort we have in Christ is greater than the suffering we are experiencing now.

In any circumstance, we can receive Christ's comfort. In verse 6, Paul reminds readers that he is suffering on account of not only their comfort but also their salvation, since he was the instrument to bring them the gospel. This comfort they have received will produce in them endurance, because they will, like Paul, suffer the same things. But as we know, the Corinthians didn't want to suffer, and they lived in a culture of comfort and affluence.

But God's comfort comes from Christ's sufferings, and we must receive this comfort. In verse 7, Paul's hope comes from sharing in Christ's sufferings and sharing his comfort, which means we must receive this comfort. In your place of suffering, have you received God's comfort? Since suffering and comfort go hand in hand, in verse 4 we are encouraged to receive suffering as well as the comfort God provides. Suffering is inevitable, but will we receive God's comfort?

In the Old Testament narratives, King David received his comfort from God. David was a man on the run. He had countless enemies, including King Saul. Even his own son tried to kill him. David suffered greatly, and you may remember 1 Samuel 30:6: "But David found strength [or, in other words, comfort] in the LORD his God." In the same way, Paul

4. Garland, *2 Corinthians*, 65.

reminds us to receive God's comfort, his strength, his encouragement, and his hope.

Often we put our hope in others, first seeking comfort from them. But people can say the strangest and most hurtful things when we are suffering. After my brother was murdered, my mom—who is a people person—called others to try to receive comfort from them. One of her close friends said to her, "Why don't you just get over it?" In times of loss, you may have heard or even said phrases like "I know he's in a better place" or "It was God's plan." I've been guilty of uttering similar well-meaning words. But as much as we want others to validate our suffering and comfort us, the greatest comfort and hope come from the Lord.

Others may seek comfort in temporal pleasures. In her book *Counterfeit Comforts*, Robia Scott says that many people seek temporary relief and comfort in things or activities like shopping, becoming a workaholic, watching television, and—my personal favorite—bingeing on ice cream. But, Paul says, only God can give us the kind of comfort we really need.

Hope and comfort come from God. In his suffering, Paul was reminded that "this happened that we might not rely on ourselves but on God, who raises the dead" (v. 9). There is no greater hope than God raising Christ Jesus from the dead. Paul continues: "He has delivered us from such a deadly peril, and he will deliver us again. On him we have set our hope that he will continue to deliver us" (v. 10). If God can raise Jesus from the dead, surely he has the power to comfort us in all of our suffering.

III. Comfort each other with the hope you have received from the God of all comfort.

In suffering, Paul reminds the Corinthians to praise God, who is the God of all comfort. Second, he reminds them to put their hope in God, who is the God of all comfort, and to receive that comfort.

Finally, the suffering and comfort do not start and end with us. There is a relational aspect to this comfort and an invitation to comfort others who are suffering. Comfort does not end with us; rather, we are to comfort others. We are called to comfort others. But how?

First, comfort comes by prayer, as seen in verse 11: ". . . as you help us by your prayers." Christians are called to pray together and lift each other up in times of suffering. But as we see in verse 4, suffering Christians also receive comfort from others who have suffered: "[God] comforts us in all our troubles, so that we can comfort those in any trouble with the comfort we ourselves receive from God."

Some of the first people I called after Tim's passing were Peter and Grace, because I knew they would understand my suffering. Peter and Grace were a couple I ministered to when I was in Colorado. Their third child was diagnosed at one and a half years of age with a rare genetic disorder called HLH, which ultimately caused all of his organs to fail. Six months after the diagnosis, he died, just before his second birthday. Not long ago, Grace's younger brother was driving on the highway when he suffered a massive heart attack and died. Peter and Grace know what it means to suffer.

As I called Peter, he comforted me with hope in the God of all comfort. He quoted me Scripture verses regarding God's faithfulness and character. He consoled me by reminding me who God is. He shared with me how God worked in his life through his suffering and how God comforted him. In the following weeks, he continued to text me Bible verses to comfort me. He told me he would continue to pray for me. Although I ministered to them in their time of suffering, they in turn ministered to me in mine. Paul is right. Yes, only God can give true comfort, but sometimes he uses others to be his channel of comfort.

Conclusion

Ultimately, all this suffering and all this comfort lead to thanksgiving in verse 11, as the people of God see fellow Christians comforting each other. My prayer for us today is that this will be a community that celebrates not just our successes but our sufferings. Can we be a community that can be real with each other? Can we share our sufferings with each other and intercede for each other? Many people here in this room and across our campuses are hurting in different ways. Paul wants to remind us of a simple truth, and it's this: comfort each other with the hope you have received from the God of all comfort. Will we do that? Comfort each other with the hope you have received from the God of all comfort.

8

Painful Relationships

All relationships—whether sacred bonds or mere acquaintances—don't have as much value as they used to. This nonchalance toward others has contributed to an increasingly lonely society. For some it's even become a nuisance to have friends. The General Social Survey reports that when people were asked about the number of friends they had, the highest percentage replied with "zero," with men struggling more than women to keep and maintain friendships.[1] The void of friendship has become so catastrophic that in 2018 the United Kingdom actually created a new government position for a minister of loneliness.[2] The digital, social-media world in which we live has squashed human interaction, with many settling for virtual communication through written texts on a screen rather than meeting face-to-face or even hearing a living, breathing person's voice over the phone. For instance, when was the last time you called someone to wish them a happy birthday and heard their voice on the other end? Most of the time, we resort to sending a text message or a generic,

1. Markham Heid, "You Asked: How Many Friends Do I Need?," *Time*, March 18, 2015, http://time.com/3748090/friends-social-health. See also Miller McPherson, Lynn Smith-Lovin, and Matthew E. Brashears, "Social Isolation in America: Changes in Core Discussion Networks over Two Decades," *American Sociological Review* 71, no. 3 (2006): 353–75, https://journals .sagepub.com/doi/abs/10.1177/000312240607100301.
2. See Carey Nieuwhof, "Overcoming the New Leadership Epidemic—Isolation and Loneliness," Carey Nieuwhof, accessed August 6, 2020, https://careynieuwhof.com/overcoming-the -new-leadership-epidemic-isolation-and-loneliness.

two-second message on social media with a few obligatory emojis and exclamation points.

In her book *Friending*, Lynne Baab observes, "The new communication technologies of the past two or three decades have shrunk our world. People far away are present to us with an immediacy that was unimaginable only thirty years ago."[3] However, the fragility, brokenness, lack of intimacy, and even absence of human relationships—whether familial or otherwise—is astounding in our day. As others have already articulated, we are more virtually connected and yet more starved for human interactions and bonds than ever before.[4] Baab continues, "They [writers] believe we have exchanged meaningful and intimate face-to-face friendships for impersonal, superficial online connections. People can't talk to each other with any depth these days, they assert, and as a result relationships are impoverished."[5]

How is your congregation doing with regard to relationships? Similarly, pastors are not exempt from this conversation. How are we doing with our friendships and relationships?[6] God has created us as social beings to be in relationship and community with one another. As we know well, not all relationships flourish. In fact, many congregants are suffering from fragile and fractured relationships with grandparents, parents, stepparents, a spouse, children, friends, neighbors, coworkers, bosses, church members, and others. Our relationships with others are also divided on a number of different levels, including race, ethnicity, socioeconomics, gender, beliefs, political views, interests, hobbies, agendas, and more. This chapter names and articulates a few ways forward in addressing these painful relationships from the pulpit and beyond. Three primary relational categories to be discussed here are broader familial relationships, the unique husband-and-wife relationship, and other interpersonal relationships.

---

3. Lynne M. Baab, *Friending: Real Relationships in a Virtual World* (Downers Grove, IL: InterVarsity, 2011), 11.

4. See Nieuwhof, "Overcoming the New Leadership Epidemic."

5. Baab, *Friending*, 11.

6. Pastors are alone and lonely. One study states: "Over 70% of pastors experience loneliness and have no close friends they trust with personal matters." "Seventy Percent of Pastors Are Lonely," Stand Strong Ministries, accessed June 25, 2020, https://www.standstrongministries .org/articles/seventy-percent-of-pastors-are-lonely. Barna Group and Pepperdine University engaged in a major research project, "How Healthy Are Pastors' Relationships?," Barna, February 15, 2017, https://www.barna.com/research/healthy-pastors-relationships.

Familial Relationships

One of the most important kinds of relationship other than our vertical relationship with God is our relationships within our nuclear families. The Bible has a lot to say about family interactions and dynamics. Sadly, much of that biblical discussion regards pain in the family, dealing with strained and even broken family bonds. Even the first family serves as a prime example of strained family relationships. Cain and Abel, the sons of Adam and Eve, are received differently by God upon presenting their offering in Genesis 4. Abel's offering of firstfruits was well received and pleasing to God, but Cain's gift didn't measure up and was deemed "less than." From sibling rivalry (and even murder in this case) to parent/child relations, to relations with in-laws and more, the family is a central theme in Scripture.

Fast-forward two thousand years and many families are still holding on by a thread. Families are rather complex systems if we use the language of family systems theory.[7] One or more persons' dilemma, struggle, conflict, or problem has an impact on the entire family. The parts affect the whole. When things are going well, we like to boast about it on social media with an obligatory snazzy photo. However, when our family struggles to have and retain meaningful familial ties, we care not to admit it, especially to other church members, out of fear of becoming the object of unwanted fellowship hall gossip.

Signs of brokenness in the home are something we want to prevent others from seeing, fearing we will become a public spectacle. Russell Moore notes in his book *The Storm-Tossed Family*, "As part of a family, it is almost impossible to maintain the image of ourselves we so carefully construct for the world, and for our own sense of meaning."[8] For families tossed by the inevitable waves, Moore astutely observes, "The only safe harbor for a storm-tossed family is a nail-scarred home."[9] Stated differently, part of our struggle in keeping a Christian family together is that our home may not be Christ-centered and cross-centered. In the midst of the busyness of work, overtime, homework, reports,

7. See R. Robert Creech, *Family Systems and Congregational Life: A Map for Ministry* (Grand Rapids: Baker Academic, 2019).

8. Russell D. Moore, *The Storm-Tossed Family: How the Cross Reshapes the Home* (Nashville: B&H, 2018), loc. 144 of 507, Kindle.

9. Moore, *Storm-Tossed Family*, loc. 112 of 507, Kindle.

papers, exams, sports, extracurricular activities, music lessons, clubs, community service, and more, there is no time or energy for Jesus and for participating in the life of the local church. In many parts of the country, the soccer and football fields or the baseball diamond has replaced the sanctuary as the destination families hop in the car and go to on Sunday mornings. The preacher's responsibility is not simply to preach an annual sermon series on staying together as a family through holidays, fun, relaxation, and respite, although these are important; more vitally, the preacher must urge members to become a family of faith that together as a unit dies to itself and its desires in order to advance the gospel. Families must be gospel-centered, Christ-centered, cross-centered.

Marriage, Domestic Violence, and Sexual Abuse[10]

Marriage, for some pastors, may be a somewhat consistent sermon topic on the preaching calendar. Due to the private nature of what a marriage constitutes, however, it is increasingly difficult to preach on marriage without the sermon hurting someone or making them feel excluded somehow.[11] Successful marriages, strained marriages, broken marriages, sexless marriages, separation, divorce, emotional and sexual affairs leading to adultery, remarriage, cohabitation, widows and widowers, singles, blended families, and so many other marital scenarios are represented every Sunday.[12] How can we preach effective sermons on the marriage relationship? The traditional wedding sermon from Genesis 1:27–28, 1 Corinthians 13, or Ephesians 5 may be the only time we hear or preach a sermon specifically

10. Beth Swagman provides helpful definitions: "Physical violence against a female is called wife abuse, spousal abuse, or wife battering. Physical violence against a male is husband abuse or spousal abuse. Sexual violence against a female spouse may be called marital rape. Psychological violence primarily using words or threats is verbal battering. Psychological violence using nonverbal communication, gestures, and mind games is psychological battering. Individuals who commit acts of domestic violence are called offenders, batterers, assailants, perpetrators, and abusers." See Swagman, *Responding to Domestic Violence: A Resource for Christian Leaders* (Grand Rapids: CRC Publications, 2002), 14.

11. Bob Russell makes this and other helpful points in his article "The Ever-More-Difficult Marriage Sermon," *Christianity Today*, October 1, 1997, https://www.christianitytoday.com/pastors/1997/fall/7l4060.html.

12. For a helpful resource on affairs and adultery, see Dave Carder, *Anatomy of an Affair: How Affairs, Attractions, and Addictions Develop, and How to Guard Your Marriage against Them* (Chicago: Moody, 2017).

on marriage. Some principles for preaching on marriage will be suggested at the end of this chapter.

Every October, which is National Domestic Violence Awareness Month, preachers have the opportunity to address the painful issue of domestic violence and abuse, offering counsel and comfort to those who suffer from it (often silently) and perhaps even confronting perpetrators and offenders.[13] LifeWay Research reports that pastors seldom preach about domestic violence (with 1,000 surveyed senior pastors). Forty-two percent said that they rarely or never preach on this important topic, and 22 percent reported that they preach about it once a year.[14] Bob Smietana writes, "For many Protestant pastors, domestic violence is the pro-life issue they almost never talk about."[15] By failing to address domestic violence from the pulpit, preachers ignore the many who are grieving silently because they are being abused verbally, physically, and sexually and their very lives are in danger. However, the gospel speaks into this critical issue, and the pulpit can be a safe and even necessary place to let hearers know that domestic violence goes against God's standards for a marriage and all other relationships. Lindsey and Justin Holcomb report that "every nine seconds a woman in the United States is assaulted or beaten."[16] The topic of domestic violence disturbs and disrupts the congregation, but the Bible speaks truth into these situations as well.

Another related and significant topic that preachers can regularly build into the preaching calendar concerns sexual harassment, abuse, assault, and rape.[17] The #MeToo movement reveals the oft-hidden sexual brokenness of so many members of society, including pastors.[18] Tarana Burke,

13. A number of helpful books are available on this topic, including Anne Marie Miller, *Healing Together: A Guide to Supporting Sexual Abuse Survivors* (Grand Rapids: Zondervan Reflective, 2019); Elaine A. Heath, *Healing the Wounds of Sexual Abuse: Reading the Bible with Survivors* (Grand Rapids: Brazos, 2019); and Heather Davediuk Gingrich, *Restoring the Shattered Self: A Christian Counselor's Guide to Complex Trauma*, 2nd ed. (Downers Grove, IL: InterVarsity, 2020).

14. Bob Smietana, "Pastors Seldom Preach about Domestic Violence," LifeWay Research, June 27, 2014, https://lifewayresearch.com/2014/06/27/pastors-seldom-preach-about-domestic-violence.

15. Smietana, "Pastors Seldom Preach about Domestic Violence."

16. Lindsey A. Holcomb and Justin S. Holcomb, *Is It My Fault? Hope and Healing for Those Suffering Domestic Violence* (Chicago: Moody, 2014), 13.

17. See, e.g., Elaine Storkey, *Scars across Humanity: Understanding and Overcoming Violence against Women* (Downers Grove, IL: IVP Academic, 2018); and Rachael Denhollander, *What Is a Girl Worth? My Story of Breaking the Silence and Exposing the Truth about Larry Nassar and USA Gymnastics* (Carol Stream, IL: Tyndale Momentum, 2019).

18. Ruth Everhart, *The #MeToo Reckoning: Facing the Church's Complicity in Sexual Abuse and Misconduct* (Downers Grove, IL: InterVarsity, 2020).

the founder of the #MeToo movement, seeks to exhibit and cultivate a culture that consistently shows empathy for victims and survivors rather than just highlighting the instigators and predators. In an article about the movement and Burke's work with it, Ashley Lee writes:

> Empower survivors by empathizing with them. Try to understand what this life is like; try to put yourself in this place where you've had this experience. I know sometimes people are like, "I want to do something more, I want to go out and volunteer, I want to write a check." That's great, but it's important that people have empathy for survivors, because these are the people who will be jurors on trials, who will influence public opinion about policy. We have to make sure that those people really understand what it is we hold with us.[19]

Although preaching on sexual abuse, violence, rape, and other sexual matters makes listeners uncomfortable, the preacher's silence on these critical topics demonstrates silent condoning and a laissez-faire perspective on sinful, destructive sexual behavior and attitudes. For the sake of victims and survivors but also for the sake of perpetrators and sexual predators, the preacher today cannot be silent on this subject. As the United Nations Secretary Ban Ki-moon once pledged, "But there is one universal truth, applicable to all countries, cultures and communities: violence against women is never acceptable, never excusable, never tolerable."[20] God's Word must confront the perpetrators of such violence head-on. God's Word must challenge and convict their sin and lead them to repentance and complete surrender to his will.

Other Interpersonal Relationships

The Bible speaks often about relationships and friendships. We must distinguish between friendships and working relationships. Whereas the biblical principles regarding the two types of interpersonal connections

19. Ashley Lee, "Tarana Burke Debuts Powerful #MeToo PSAs Spotlighting Sexual Violence Survivors," *Los Angeles Times*, January 28, 2019, https://www.latimes.com/entertainment/la-et-metoo-movement-tarana-burke-psa-20190128-htmlstory.html.
20. "We 'Cannot Wait' to End Violence against Women—Secretary-General Ban," UN News, February 25, 2008, https://news.un.org/en/story/2008/02/250192-we-cannot-wait-end-violence-against-women-secretary-general-ban.

are similar, the pain created by difficult friendships and that created by
working relationships differ greatly. Proverbs 18:24 provides an example
of how intimate friendships can become: "One who has unreliable friends
soon comes to ruin, but there is a friend who sticks closer than a brother
[or sister]." What often destroys friendships and other interpersonal relationships are common divisive characteristics such as conflict, betrayal,
gossip, pride, and jealousy. For instance, in the New Testament, Paul encourages the Romans, "Live in harmony with one another. Do not be
proud, but be willing to associate with people of low position. Do not be
conceited" (Rom. 12:16). When we have relational breakdowns, we can
attribute them at times to pride, arrogance, conceit—that is, the opposite
of being humble.

Rifts in relationships also develop when we lose sight of a person's
imago Dei qualities for any length of time. Every person on the planet
possesses some good qualities and some negative ones as well. The good
characteristics are "godly" in that they reflect a good God who bestows
such positive traits on people. The damaging, sinful characteristics in
people are obviously a result and by-product of the fall. When people hurt
us, it is often because of unresolved issues in their past: lingering hurts suffered at the hands of people whom they have not forgiven and with whom
they have not reconciled, personal hang-ups, and other festering pains.

There are many sayings that reflect the ongoing effects of the inability to
properly address and be healed from one's relational pains—for example,
"Hurt people hurt people" and "Bullies bully because they were bullied."
As I mentioned in the sample sermon in chapter 7, a helpful life lesson my
wife taught me about empathy came from one of her counseling professors
at Denver Seminary who said, "People's pain is people's pain."[21] Stated
another way, everyone has pain, whether we validate it or not. This phrase
corrects our natural tendency to minimize others' pain. This pain can often
be one or more major traumas in life that spill over into every other sphere.
For example, a child of divorce never sees life the same again in terms of
relational integrity. A child growing up in an alcoholic's or drug abuser's
home never experiences stability and shalom. A child who experiences
verbal, physical, or sexual abuse from parents, relatives, or even siblings

---

21. I write about this in greater detail in Matthew D. Kim, *Preaching with Cultural Intelligence: Understanding the People Who Hear Our Sermons* (Grand Rapids: Baker Academic,
2017), 59.

cannot relate to those in authority in the same way that others can who have not experienced such trauma. And on and on it goes. This pain does not go away on its own. Often it continues into adulthood, and for some even for a lifetime. Andrea Brandt explains, "Trauma generates emotions, and unless we process these emotions at the time the trauma occurs, they become stuck in our mind and body. . . . The healthy flow and processing of distressing emotions, such as anger, sadness, shame, and fear, is essential to healing from childhood trauma as an adult."[22]

When we seek to empathize, however, we can visualize or imagine what it would be like to live with and encounter the pain of others. As pastors, there are usually a few members with whom we have difficulty relating to and loving. We can become easily flustered by their idiosyncrasies and unlovable peculiarities, especially those that damage relationships within the church. Yet when we hear stories about how they grew up and what they went through, we begin to put ourselves in their shoes, envisioning what our lives would be like today if we had faced their same trials. We can learn much about others simply by listening to their stories. Once we hear their stories of pain and loss, we begin to have grace for them, we begin to pray for them, we begin to demonstrate care for them, and we even begin to truly love them. Although knowledge does not automatically and magically lead to forgiveness or greater empathy, it can contribute to the process. When relationships break down in Christian community, between friends, and even at work, it's often because we lack compassion for others.

There are raw contributors to relational collapses like gossip, betrayal, and jealousy that destroy friendships and work relationships as well. For example, David and Jonathan's friendship in the Old Testament and Saul's jealousy show us how relationships can be unearthed by destructive qualities. Although nothing in Scripture indicates that Saul and David were friends per se, we see the effects of relationship deterioration as Saul becomes increasingly jealous of David's success.

Preaching on painful relationships, forgiveness, restoration, and compassion is difficult. Conversations on these topics are emotionally charged, and they require a delicate four-step dance of (1) proclaiming the truth;

22. Andrea Brandt, "9 Steps to Healing Childhood Trauma as an Adult," *Psychology Today*, April 2, 2018, https://www.psychologytoday.com/us/blog/mindful-anger/201804/9-steps-healing-childhood-trauma-adult.

(2) acknowledging the reality of that truth's challenges; (3) allowing people to grieve, mourn, and lament; and (4) preaching Christ's ability to overcome our inability to forgive and to reconcile relationships. Since many people struggle with broken relationships at any given moment, the pulpit can be a place to raise these tensions and speak life-giving, biblical wisdom on how our listeners can deal with their relational pains.

Preaching on Painful Relationships

We can choose from several scriptural pathways when connecting the sermon to relationships. Which one we choose for a given sermon really depends on whether the sermon falls within a series on an entire Bible book or whether it's in a topical series. If the former, then the pathway we choose should emerge organically from the passage. If the latter, a helpful approach might be to deliver a sermon series on Bible characters who successfully or unsuccessfully maintained friendships and relationships. Some Bible relationships (including friendships and ministry partnerships) that immediately come to mind include Abraham and Lot (Gen. 13), Moses and Aaron (Exod. 3–4), Jonathan and David (1 Sam. 20), Elijah and Elisha (2 Kings 2), Ruth and Naomi (Ruth 1–4), Daniel and his three friends (Dan. 3), Job and his three friends (Job), Paul and John Mark (Acts 15), Paul and Barnabas (Acts 15:35–41), Paul and Timothy, and Euodia and Syntyche (Phil. 4).

1. Which Passage Will I Preach On?

For this particular sermon on painful relationships, let's zoom in on a story from the book of Ruth. This type of message could be preached on a special day like Mother's Day or on a different occasion. Specifically, we will focus in on Ruth and Naomi's relationship and explore what a positive mother-in-law/daughter-in-law relationship can aspire to be. For good reason, in-law relations are often joked about as being difficult. We can show our listeners what types of attitudes and actions can engender a mutually beneficial and symbiotic familial relationship.

2. What Type of Pain/Suffering Is Revealed in the Text?

Naomi, Ruth's mother-in-law, suffers Job-like pain (Ruth 1). Her husband, Elimelech, dies. Ten years later, Naomi's two sons, Mahlon and

Kilion, also pass away, leaving behind their Moabitess wives, Orpah and Ruth. There's also a severe famine in the land, to boot, causing Naomi and her daughters-in-law to return to Judah, which means she must leave behind her entire community, family, and friends. The compilation of tragedies even robs her of her own identity (prompting her to change her name from Naomi to Mara [v. 20]). Naomi feels abandoned by God: "It is more bitter for me than for you, because the Lord's hand has turned against me!" (v. 13). Orpah, the older daughter-in-law, decides to return to Moab. The suffering and pain caused by three significant deaths, and even abandonment, crush Naomi's soul. In addition, we cannot forget or minimize Ruth's unspeakable pain in losing her own husband, Kilion.

3. How Does the Bible Character or Biblical Author Deal with the Pain?

Naomi expresses her pain by weeping (Ruth 1:9) and weeping some more (v. 14). She acknowledges the reality and finality of her suffering, feeling the loss of her two grown, adult sons especially keenly (vv. 12–13). She feels the natural human tendency to internalize her sense of having been betrayed and abandoned and even of being the victim of God's vengeance (v. 13). At least that is how she feels at the moment. Upon her return to Bethlehem, Naomi responds to her name (which means *pleasantness* in Hebrew) in the following way: "Call me Mara [meaning "bitter" or "sorrow"], because the Almighty has made my life very bitter" (v. 20). She continues: "I went away full, but the Lord has brought me back empty. Why call me Naomi? The Lord has afflicted me; the Almighty has brought misfortune upon me" (v. 21). When one experiences the crushing loss of death and abandonment—especially from multiple people—it's quite common to feel animosity toward God. Notice, however, that Ruth's attitude is God-centric.

4. How Does This Pain in the Text Relate to Our Listeners' Pain?

The pain of death has already been taken up in the previous chapter, on loss. Therefore, we will not go into depth regarding the suffering of losing loved ones. Rather, we want to explore the loss created by Orpah's departure. Abandonment—whether emotionally or physically—is a common experience for many listeners. Abandonment may be caused by death, divorce, separation, adoption, workaholism, a negligent parent or guardian, drugs and other addictions, and many other factors. In our specific text, the immediate context is a relationship between in-laws: a mother-in-law and a daughter-in-law (Naomi and Orpah). In-law relationships are quite complex—as those who are married can attest. The biblical author does not provide details about what their relationship was like, because the primary narrative concerns Naomi and Ruth. We are not privy to Orpah's rationale for leaving her mother-in-law behind. It could be simple pragmatics, as Naomi tells her to leave since Naomi can't bear another child while Orpah waits for another husband. Perhaps Naomi and Orpah didn't get along. We can imagine, however, that some or even many in-law relationships can be a source of pain for our listeners and for many different reasons.

5. What Does This Pain Say about God and His Allowance of Pain?

Only God's sovereignty can explain why certain people endure hardships so grave that other people might cry out, "That's not fair!" There is no simple explanation. We simply don't know. Naomi's pain is quite remarkable: losing a husband, losing two sons to death, losing a daughter-in-law, and even losing community and her identity. The pastor's temptation is to try to speak up for God when God is silent. When tragedy strikes, we desperately want, like Job, to hear God defend himself. Why, God? Why me? Yet in our displeasure and anger toward God, we are quick to forget that God suffers as well, and often on account of his people. Michele Novotni and Randy Petersen remind us, "Why is God suffering? Because he has put his heart in the hands of his creatures and they have broken it."[23]

We may be disappointed by God, but how much more might God be disappointed with us? For divine reasons, we cannot possibly attempt to communicate definitive explanations for God's permittance of suffering in our lives or in the lives of others. When observing painful relationships, though, the key is to remember that we cannot change other people. We can only change our own attitude and how we respond to others—as I will highlight soon in the response of Ruth. What we can say is that God does allow various pains in the lives of people and that he will be there for us in the midst of that pain.

23. Michele Novotni and Randy Petersen, *Angry with God* (Colorado Springs: Pinion, 2001), 108.

6. How Does God / Jesus / the Holy Spirit Help Us in Our Suffering?

It's clear from hindsight that God has not abandoned Naomi—even though it really does feel like that to her. In the heat of the moment, many of us would feel similarly and would, like Naomi, question God's goodness and be vexed at his audacity in allowing so much pain. Yet God does show up. He shows up in the person of Ruth. Ruth's tenacity in loving Naomi and staying with her in spite of all that has happened proves God's feet in walking beside Naomi through suffering. Ruth could have said her goodbyes just like Orpah did. There was nothing morally, culturally, or even religiously obligating her to stay with Naomi. Ruth's striking statement in verses 16–17 would be an encouragement to any downtrodden person: "Don't urge me to leave you or to turn back from you. Where you go I will go, and where you stay I will stay. Your people will be my people and your God my God. Where you die I will die, and there I will be buried. May the LORD deal with me, be it ever so severely, if even death separates you and me." God's comfort is expressed bodily and relationally through Ruth. Without Ruth, we can assume that Naomi's life would have ended up bitter. With Ruth, her future had hope, as we know from the rest of the story.

7. How Can Our Preaching Show Care and Empathy?

Painful relationships are quite complex, because multiple factors contribute to the decline of a relationship. Particularly, abandonment in any form can be traumatic and have destructive consequences for listeners. Here are two areas to demonstrate sensitivity. First, recognize that abandonment issues are often connected to and projected onto God and how we view him. How many of our congregants equate difficulty in loving God the heavenly Father with strained or nonexistent relationships with earthly fathers? The narratives of similar dynamics will permeate the congregation. Second, speaking too quickly about forgiveness and reconciliation appears to defend the other person as well as denigrate one's right to feel pain and to lament the broken relationship. Since we know our congregations well, we can make that determination as to whether we should acknowledge these two areas of pain mentioned above or not. After the service, the preacher can invite listeners to come forward and share their pain of abandonment and other relational dilemmas with the preacher and other trusted leaders in the church in order to receive prayer and consultation (with trained counseling professionals). Giving permission (after the service or in another setting) to lament and vent one's frustrations can be a helpful tool to express one's trauma as well.

8. How Can We Share This Pain in Christian Community?

I have found pastorally that one of the most effective ways of helping hurting people with regard to relationships is through trusted small groups and accountability partnerships. When someone shares vulnerably his or her pain, the last thing we want to do is to ignore or forget to follow up, which reinforces the pain of abandonment. Loving and trustworthy small groups and accountability friendships provide immediate and long-term care for people who are hurting relationally. First, these relationships give the hurting person an opportunity to verbalize his or her pain. Second, they present moments for the small group to pray for that individual in the moment, throughout the week, and into the future. Third, these relationships offer friendship and community that the person desperately requires. In certain cases, we must refer to professional and licensed counselors to assist with long-term trauma. But in most cases, being present with others will assuage some of the suffering. What Ruth does in this narrative is to commit herself to the person, in this case her mother-in-law, Naomi. Nothing except for death will break the two apart. That is what Christian community is all about. We are a committed, spiritual family that surrounds and embraces those who are suffering. When one hurts, everyone hurts.

9. How Will God Use Our Suffering to Transform Us and Bring Himself Glory?

With the death of Elimelech and her two sons, Naomi is rendered "helpless" by society's patriarchal standards. However, upon their return to Bethlehem, Naomi and Ruth experience the favor of God through Ruth's relationship with Boaz, her kinsman-redeemer, and their eventual marriage. Later, Naomi receives the blessing of offspring and of becoming a grandmother to Ruth and Boaz's son (Ruth 4:17). It's apparent that nothing can replace her husband, Elimelech, and two sons, Mahlon and Kilion. This is a crushing pain that one can fully comprehend only through personal experience. Naomi must go on living with the pain of their passing. However, God in many ways "normalizes" Naomi's life through Ruth, who represents the picture of God's *hesed* love, loyalty, and faithfulness in this story.

As Naomi reexperiences the profound love and faithfulness of God through Boaz, her outlook on God and on life is restored (Ruth 2:20). Her negative attitude toward God takes a 180-degree turn as she remembers that God is indeed faithful and that he hasn't abandoned her. She says to Ruth, "He has not stopped showing his kindness to the living and the dead." Eventually, the entire community recognizes God's faithfulness to Naomi, and they even praise him: "Praise be to the Lord, who this day has not left you without a guardian-redeemer. May he become famous throughout Israel" (4:14). Through her suffering, God proves to Naomi his steadfast love and provision for her even though her pain is real and extraordinary. God provides Boaz, a kinsman-redeemer who will take care of her, her daughter-in-law, and her grandson. Her mourning has turned to dancing. Imagine what her life would have been like if she had remained in poverty and without the hope of future generations. In the same way, even in the most challenging of circumstances, we must remember to preach that God takes care of his people (in personalized and contextualized ways) and that he is loyal and faithful to provide.

Principles for Preaching on Painful Relationships

Preaching on Covenantal Sacrifice

Mutually beneficial friendships and other relationships require sacrifice. The writer of Ecclesiastes, Solomon, said, "Two are better than one, because they have a good return for their labor: If either of them falls down, one can help the other up. But pity anyone who falls and has no one to help them up" (Eccles. 4:9–10). Lifting the other up requires sacrifice. Without sacrifice, friendships and other relationships cannot succeed. Today, the crisis of friendship exists because people generally do not want to sacrifice for others.

David and Jonathan's friendship is a prime example of covenantal sacrifice—that is, making a covenant of friendship with another person. First Samuel 18:4 says, "Jonathan took off the robe he was wearing and gave it to David, along with his tunic, and even his sword, his bow and his belt." The statement or covenant made by the extravagant gift is shocking. R. D. Bergen explains: "The fact that Jonathan gave David the garb and armaments originally reserved for the heir to Saul's throne clearly possesses symbolic and thematic significance."[24] In other words, nothing was too precious for Jonathan to share with David. But material gifts are not the only way a person can sacrifice to show commitment to a relationship; relationships often suffer when one or more persons are unwilling to give time, energy, and other nonmaterial resources. Sermons on covenants and giving generously to others may be themes worth preaching about with regard to painful relationships. This is one of the reasons why "the love dare"—a forty-day challenge for married couples to express various gifts of love to one another—became so effective at healing broken marriages.[25] Although such activities are never foolproof, active demonstrations of love can be the catalyst for restoring and healing marriages, families, and friendships.

Preaching on Conflict and Unity

Many relationships fracture due to some form of conflict. Since many people flee from conflict, it would be valuable for congregations to hear on occasion about handling conflict in biblical, God-honoring ways. Classic examples in Scripture regarding tension-filled church relations are found in Acts 15:35–41, which narrates Paul and Barnabas's dispute about John Mark, and in Philippians 4:2, which refers to the mysterious tussle between Euodia and Syntyche. The common refrain when conflict arises is that "one person must yield to the other" or that "both parties must compromise to make things work." As a pastor, I came to realize that many Christians in the congregation did not have a biblically grounded rubric for addressing conflict.

As we venture on in the twenty-first century, I would be remiss if I failed to address racial and ethnic conflicts and divisions, which arise even in denominational and local church settings. The deep fragmentation along racial lines across much if not all of Christianity is heartbreaking. The

24. R. D. Bergen, *1, 2 Samuel*, New American Commentary 7 (Nashville: Broadman & Holman, 1996), 199–200.

25. Alex Kendrick and Stephen Kendrick, *The Love Dare* (Nashville: B&H, 2013).

general principle is that any minority must submit to the authority of the majority culture. Critical mass rules. Yet what do we do when we've been hurt by others, particularly in minority-versus-majority relationships? God can and will use painful relationships to transform us in some positive way. Bryan Loritts shares vulnerably:

> It has been said if you want to find your purpose take inventory of your pain! Oh yes, I've found that to be true in my own life. I am often asked how I came to be so passionate about the multiethnic church and seeing races come together. I always respond by saying that purpose was birthed out of a deep pain, the pain of being called a nigger in Bible College. I know many social workers who give their lives to help the abused and marginalized because in their story there was abuse and neglect. You want to know your purpose? Take inventory of your pain. Don't waste your pain. Your pain has a purpose![26]

The number of pages required to sufficiently address racial and ethnic conflicts far surpasses my allotted space here. Preaching to people in pain demands thoughtful consideration, preparation, and communication on an elephant in the worship sanctuary and fellowship halls—Christianity and racial division. A host of other topics are noteworthy for prompting conflict as well, including refugees and immigrants, abortion, politics, creation care, sexual orientation, the LGBTQ community, same-sex marriage, vaccinations, #MeToo, Black Lives Matter, and much more. As pastor-shepherds, we are responsible for knowing the inner workings of our people and for winsomely and boldly communicating God's Word, including hard truths that listeners need to hear from God's perspective rather than the culture's.

Preaching on Forgiveness and Reconciliation

It's not easy to forgive others. It's easier to tell others to forgive people who have hurt them. There, I've said it. That is the simple, hard truth. Whether we are Christians or not, forgiveness and reconciliation are two

---

26. Bryan Loritts, "Don't Waste Your Pain—Ruth 1," Bryan Loritts, August 9, 2018, https://mark-oshman-k3j3.squarespace.com/bryanloritts/2018/8/9/dont-waste-your-pain-ruth-1. Loritts also takes on race relations in evangelical Christianity head-on in *Insider Outsider: My Journey as a Stranger in White Evangelicalism and My Hope for Us All* (Grand Rapids: Zondervan, 2018).

of the most excruciating things for humans to do. How can we forgive when the thistles of pain run so deep? Craig Groeschel, speaking of how he felt upon learning that a trusted "friend" had molested his younger sister, confessed, "To say that I wanted Max to die and burn in hell doesn't even begin to convey how much I wanted him to suffer. Although the words *rage*, *hate*, and *revenge* come to mind when I think about Max, the English language simply doesn't have a word for what I felt."[27] Similarly, to be completely transparent, I have clung desperately to the so-called friend of "unforgiveness" toward the Filipinos who murdered my younger brother Tim. I still cringe every time I meet Filipinos or Filipino Americans or hear something about the Philippines. I see them and my heart sinks to the floor. "Do I really believe what I preach and tell others to preach about?" Forgiveness is so difficult. Lord, have mercy on me, a sinner!

In his article "Seeing My Son's Murderer," Robert Smith Jr.'s testimony of his journey through pain and suffering is quite heart-wrenching, inspiring, and humbling. On October 30, 2010, Smith's son, Antonio Maurice Smith, who worked at a restaurant, was shot and murdered in an attempted robbery. Smith writes, "Though the wound to my heart is still open, I have forgiven Tony's murderer [after nearly two years]. . . . Soon by God's grace I will see the young man whose face was the last face our son saw before standing in the presence of the Lord. I will offer the young man the forgiveness that Christ offers to me and to all who will believe."[28] What is more, Smith has even befriended this man who murdered his son, and has helped to bring him to the Lord.

Conclusion

Painful relationships are brought to wholeness via forgiveness and reconciliation—which are difficult topics for certain. When the text or situation calls for it, the pastor-shepherd gently prods the people to forgive and reconcile for their own benefit. As I write, I'm working on the same

27. Craig Groeschel, "When You Believe in God but Won't Forgive," Faith Gateway, February 1, 2019, https://www.faithgateway.com/believe-forgive.

28. Robert Smith Jr., "Seeing My Son's Murderer: Did I Really Believe What I Preach?," *Christianity Today*, January 1, 2015, https://www.christianitytoday.com/pastors/2015/winter /seeing-my-sons-murderer.html.

process for my own soul. I am asking God to help me forgive the people who murdered my brother and "got away with it." Since horizontal relationships are significant to God, they ought to matter to God's people as well. We can help our listeners by preaching on painful relationships regularly so that they too may receive healing and find hope.

Discussion Questions

1. Take an inventory of all the various forms of painful relationships in your congregation. What are one or two dominant relationship strains that might be addressed in an upcoming sermon series this year?
2. Do you have any fractured relationships in your life that need to be mended?
3. How can you push for greater unity in your congregation?
4. Who might the people in your congregation need to build and rebuild relationships with in the coming year?

"Honoring Mom as Honoring God"

Sermon on Ruth 1–4

> **HOMILETICAL IDEA:** Let's honor God every day by honoring our mom in every way.

When I was growing up, one of my favorite television shows was *The Brady Bunch*, which I watched in reruns. As you may know, this sitcom featured a blended family. The father in the show was Mike Brady, a widower who had three sons: Greg, Peter, and Bobby. He eventually married Carol, who had three daughters: Marcia, Jan, and Cindy. The story is about their new life and the joys and challenges of bringing these two very different families together. In every episode, some kind of conflict needed to be resolved by the end of the thirty-minute program. In life, we encounter serious problems—sometimes in the family—and obviously most family issues are not resolved in less than thirty minutes. The most painful areas of our lives often concern our own family.

I. As a family, we face famines.

In the Bible story we just read from Ruth 1, we see a picture of a family unit. Of course, it's different from the fictional Brady family. Here, there is a father, Elimelech, and a mother, Naomi. They have two sons named Mahlon and Kilion. However, the problem that this family faces has nothing to do with whether Marcia can get a date for Friday night or whether Bobby can fix his bicycle. The problems for this family are exponentially more significant. Its members are starving due to a famine.

So Elimelech and Naomi decide to relocate their two boys from Judah to Moab. It's not going to be an easy move. There's no U-Haul or Penske truck at their disposal. But they know they must do this in order to survive. Upon their arrival in Moab, things start to get worse. The father, Elimelech, suddenly dies. Mahlon and Kilion both get married, but within ten years they also pass away, leaving behind their mother, Naomi, and their wives, Orpah and Ruth.

As we all know, today is Mother's Day. Over the years, I've decided to learn more about these special national and international holidays, especially since I have to preach about them every year. So I did some searching. How and when did Mother's Day originate, and what was its original intention?

Anna Jarvis of Philadelphia in 1908 asked her church to remember and celebrate her late mother. Jarvis's mother herself had wanted to see an annual day of observance established when people would remember their mothers. After a two-year letter-writing campaign led by Anna Jarvis, in 1914 Congress passed a law to reserve the second Sunday of May as Mother's Day. Since then, Americans have taken Mother's Day quite seriously.[1]

Mother's Day is simply a day when we honor our mothers. We thank them for bringing us into the world. We thank them for their acts of kindness to us. Text on the website www.dayformothers.com reads: "Celebrated every year, Mother's Day is an occasion when individuals express their love and respect that they have for their mother. It's time to pamper her for all she has done for us over the years. On Mother's Day you can tell your Mom that she will always be important to you all and that you will continue to love her forever."[2] Of course, we also must mention that not all of us had or have positive memories and close relationships with our mother. For some of us, thinking about our mother causes much pain, whether she has passed away or whether the relationship remains strained.

Here, in this story, Naomi represents not simply a mother but a mother-in-law. Her being a mother-in-law may bring to mind another kind of stress and grief, as we may not always get along with our mother-in-law. We can respond to mothers and mothers-in-law in either of two ways.

1. See Olivia B. Waxman, "The Surprisingly Sad Origins of Mother's Day," *Time*, updated April 25, 2018, https://time.com/4771354/mothers-day-history-origins.
2. See Day for Mothers website, accessed August 6, 2020, www.dayformothers.com.

II. As a family, we always have a choice in how we respond to difficulties.

In verse 6, Naomi, Orpah, and Ruth, a mother-in-law with her two daughters-in-law, start out for Naomi's homeland after hearing that there is again food there. In verse 8, Naomi gives both Orpah and Ruth a choice.

Read with me starting at verse 8: "Then Naomi said to her two daughters-in-law, 'Go back, each of you, to your mother's home. May the LORD show you kindness, as you have shown kindness to your dead husbands and to me. May the LORD grant that each of you will find rest in the home of another husband.' Then she kissed them goodbye and they wept aloud."

As they are going along, Naomi tells her daughters-in-law to leave her, find new husbands, and start their lives over in a new place. Naomi is giving them a way out. In the ancient world, if a woman lost her son, the daughter-in-law did not necessarily have to stay and live with her mother-in-law. Now, we are not told what kind of mother-in-law Naomi was. We don't know if she was the controlling, possessive type who could not let her sons go. We don't know if she was a gentle, kind woman who loved her daughters-in-law just like her own sons.

Initially, both daughters claim that they will stay and not leave her. Naomi then goes on to explain her ancient custom. If they go back with her to Judah, there is little or no chance that they will be able to marry again because she will not be able to produce more sons. But if they leave now, they will probably be able to marry and continue their lives. And this is where Orpah and Ruth need to make a decision.

Verse 14 reads, "At this they wept aloud again. Then Orpah kissed her mother-in-law goodbye, but Ruth clung to her." We always have a choice. Although it probably pained both of them, Orpah says "See ya" to Naomi, whereas Ruth decides to stay indefinitely with Naomi. Now, is there anything wrong with Orpah's decision? No, absolutely not. It was the most logical thing to do. If she wanted to marry again and bear kids in the future, she would need to take this opportunity to leave Naomi now. What would you do? If given the choice, perhaps some or many of us would have done what Orpah does.

Yet, for some reason, Ruth demonstrates great self-sacrifice and kindness toward her mother-in-law and clings to her. In the Old Testament there is a single Hebrew word that means love, kindness, loyalty, faithfulness, constancy, and commitment: the word *hesed*. Ruth responds with *hesed* to Naomi's difficult situation.

III. As a family, we can respond with *hesed* love.

Ruth says in verses 16 and 17, "Don't urge me to leave you or to turn back from you. Where you go I will go, and where you stay I will stay. Your people will be my people and your God my God. Where you die I will die, and there I will be buried. May the LORD deal with me, be it ever so severely, if even death separates you and me." In the most basic terms, Ruth gives Naomi the "death look." It's like Gary Coleman's character Arnold on the popular TV show *Different Strokes*, when he would say sternly to his older brother: "Whatcha talkin' 'bout, Willis?" Ruth is saying to Naomi here: "Whatcha talkin' 'bout, Naomi?" At that point, Naomi backs off and agrees.

Isn't this the response that any parent would want from his or her child? Even though the parent knows it's good for the child to move on with life, they hold that iota of hope that the child will stay with them. Naomi's world has been completely shattered. She lost her husband and her two sons, and now Orpah has left too. In her world, to not have a husband or sons meant that she would not be able to provide for herself. In that moment, Ruth honored her mother-in-law. That's what Mother's Day is about. We want to honor our mothers as we honor God.

There is a common phrase in Asian culture that my dad told me: "Love always goes down, it rarely goes up." This means it's more natural for a parent to show acts of love and kindness to his or her children than the other way around. It's easier for an older sibling to show love for a younger than vice versa. Most of the time this statement is true.

But here Ruth shows us that love can go upward. Ruth is going countercultural here. She goes against the cultural norms. Ruth lived in the time of the judges, about which we know that "in those days Israel had no king; everyone did as they saw fit" (Judg. 17:6). Ruth does not do what's best for her; instead, she takes it upon herself to sacrifice her own future for her mother-in-law. She gives up her chance for a husband and for security. Yet if you read further in the book of Ruth, you learn that Ruth finds another husband in the person of Boaz. Although Ruth sacrifices her future for a time, she trusts in the Lord. She knows that God wants her to follow Naomi, and she obeys God. God honors Ruth by providing Boaz. This doesn't mean that God always promises a this-for-that relationship. Yet it's important still that we respond with *hesed* love regardless of what's in it for us.

Ruth's act of *hesed* brings honor and joy to Naomi and changes her completely. At the beginning of the book of Ruth, Naomi is crushed and embittered. Naomi means "beautiful" and "gentle." Yet in 1:20, she says, "Don't call me Naomi. . . . Call me Mara, because the Almighty has made my life very bitter." The name Mara means bitterness. In a moment of selflessness, Ruth restores Naomi's name.

What happens next will surprise us . . .

Conclusion

Let's turn now to the end of the story, in Ruth 4:13–17. It says:

> So Boaz took Ruth and she became his wife. When he made love to her, the Lord enabled her to conceive, and she gave birth to a son. The women said to Naomi: "Praise be to the Lord, who this day has not left you without a guardian-redeemer. May he become famous throughout Israel! He will renew your life and sustain you in your old age. For your daughter-in-law, who loves you and who is better to you than seven sons, has given him birth." Then Naomi took the child in her arms and cared for him. The women living there said, "Naomi has a son!" And they named him Obed. He was the father of Jesse, the father of David.

Through Ruth, God brings honor and joy to Naomi by bringing about Ruth's marriage to Boaz and giving the couple offspring. Because of Ruth's desire to honor her mother-in-law, we see the generations leading up to the birth of our Savior, Jesus Christ.

Yes, Ruth brings her mother-in-law delight in this moment. But the truth is, Ruth does this throughout the entire book. She seeks to honor Naomi at all times. Mother's Day is a day to celebrate our mother and mother-in-law. But the truth is, we can choose to honor them every single day. This doesn't mean we must honor them in dramatic ways, as Ruth honored her mother-in-law. But when we honor our mother, we are in many ways honoring God. This is the principle of the fifth of the Ten Commandments, which requires us to honor our father and mother. How we treat our mother reflects how we treat God.

Some mothers and future mothers may be thinking, "Yes, thank you very much, Pastor Matt, now I have a biblical example to share with my kids, proving that they must obey me and do what I say forever." Well, no, that's not what God is saying here. Our children don't always have to stay near us and live with us.

The story of Ruth is a clear example of the honor, love, kindness, and *hesed* we can show our mother and mother-in-law. Today is a difficult day for some. Maybe our mothers have passed away. Maybe we have no relationship or a strained relationship with our mothers. For others, mothers and mothers-in-law can be difficult and even frustrate us regularly. But remember this: Let's honor God every day by honoring our mom in every way.

Here are some suggestions on how to do this:

1. Let's pray for them daily.
2. Let's call them frequently.
3. Let's send them cards of appreciation.
4. Let's listen to their suggestions before reacting in anger.
5. Let's take them out for a meal or cook them a meal.
6. Let's care for them when they need help.
7. Let's visit their grave if they are no longer with us.

Let's honor God every day by honoring our mom in every way.

9

Painful Sins

Sins germinate in the darkest recesses of the mind and heart. They hide from others and thrive in the shadows. They get temporarily lost behind smiling Sunday faces. Tommy struggles with a pornography addiction. Joyce is a compulsive gambler. Lenny is living in the deceit of adultery. Samantha is illegally embezzling funds from her hedge fund company. Lance is clandestinely enjoying a same-sex relationship. Nancy can't stop gossiping and slandering against her coworkers. Bill continues to numb his pain with hard liquor every night. Alex is unable to forgive someone who has hurt him. Liza can't let go of the shame and pain of aborting a baby seven years ago. The list of sins and suffering that comes from such sins—whether public or private—embodied in any congregation goes on and on. Are there sins in your life that you can't seem to let go of? That's a rhetorical question.

Many idioms seek to communicate the power of sin over people. For instance, we might call sin the "monkey on our backs," "our demons," or even "just harmless vices." Regardless of one's convenient imagery to describe sin, every single person battles sins regularly. Certain sins haunt us more than others. Sometimes we convey gradations of sin. In Jerry Bridges's *Respectable Sins*, he mentions a certain category of sins that Christians often deem "respectable" or "tolerable," such as ungodliness, anxiety and frustration, discontentment, unthankfulness, pride, selfishness, lack of self-control, impatience and irritability, anger, judgmentalism, envy, jealousy, sins of the tongue, and worldliness.[1] "First-class" sins having a choke hold on our spiritual lives include sexual sins, murder, assault, abuse, adultery, addictions, homosexual behavior, same-sex marriage, felonies and misdemeanors, and crimes against humanity.

Although Jesus tells the woman caught in adultery and us to "go now and leave your life of sin" (John 8:11), the troubling truth is that the power of sin still holds us captive. Sins are confounding sources of unarticulated pain and shame. Satan is vigilant in discouraging Christians about past and current struggles with sin. He wants us to suffer silently and feel powerless against sin, feel numb to it, and even to privately cherish and revel in our sin. Our listeners (and we) vacillate between victories over and relapse into particular sins. How can preachers address sin in their sermons and even share some personal struggles with the congregation as well? This chapter helps pastors see the value in citing personal and corporate sins in the congregation and recommends ways to overcome them by the power of the Holy Spirit.

A Past Decision or Action

I once guest-preached at a friend's church. During the sermon at some point, I had mentioned that it's important how we choose to live our lives and that God will hold us accountable for every thought and deed (as Paul says in Rom. 14:12, "So then, each of us will give an account of ourselves to God"). After the service, a younger woman sat down next to me in the pew. She was visibly upset. Her first words were, "I thought God forgave our sins and didn't remember them. Why did you say that we are held accountable for things in the past?" Just a few curt sentences later, she verbalized her pain of having an abortion some time ago. This moment was something she wanted to forget, but my sermon brought to the surface her past sin and suffering. Of course, it was not my intention to cause sermonic pain for this sweet lady. What this postsermon moment taught me is that the pain of past sin is real and that it's quite challenging to forgive ourselves for our past sins, actions, and behaviors.

Our memories are powerful, just as they are complex and even selective. In *As I Recall*, Casey Tygrett asks, "*Why do we remember some things and*

1. Jerry Bridges, *Respectable Sins: Confronting the Sins We Tolerate* (Colorado Springs: NavPress, 2007).

not others? Why do we hold memories from nearly thirty-five years ago in the vault, while a conversation from thirty-five minutes ago might slip into oblivion?"[2] As I ruminate further about the discussion mentioned above, I've been struggling with these questions as they pertain to preaching on sin, particularly sins in our personal histories: Is it our responsibility as preachers to consciously or subconsciously remind listeners of their past sins and failures—to bring up "old stuff"—or is it to help them forget about their past and not cause former pains to rise to the memory's surface? When past sins are brought to listeners' consciousness, is it the work of the Holy Spirit to encourage them to repent and find healing from those sins rather than to avoid the thought of them? Is it the Spirit's desire that we preach on past sins so that those in recovery can celebrate their victories? How can we preach about sin effectively, productively, and constructively when it feels awkward and messy? Is it even possible to preach on sin without producing some form of unintended pain in our hearers? Should that even be our sermonic pursuit? We'll try to address some of these questions in our principles section at the end of the chapter.

In addition to abortion, other past sins may linger on and stymie our congregants' spiritual maturity and discipleship. It could be an unwise past relationship, a dissolved marriage, an emotional or sexual affair, a violent chiding of our children, abortion(s), a slew of unethical decisions at work, and a host of others. As we build relationships with our people, they will begin to open up their secret memory banks to us—even baring their souls. Past sins are one type of pain in our listeners' lives. A second form of painful sins is habitual, presently recurring sins and addictions.

Habitual, Addictive Sins

An equally complex form of painful sin is habitual sins and addictions. They are the types of sins about which we shamefully tell God yet again, "Please forgive me. I'll never do it again." Even that same day or the next, the same sin lurks to devour us, and we succumb to it again and again. Do we have a habitual sin or addiction that we can't seem to overcome? It could range from any form of sexual sin and addiction to gambling to

2. Casey Tygrett, *As I Recall: Discovering the Place of Memories in Our Spiritual Life* (Downers Grove, IL: InterVarsity, 2019), 3 (emphasis original).

drug and alcohol abuse to eating disorders (anorexia or bulimia) to lying and stealing to slandering and gossiping, and more. Chuck DeGroat observes, "Pastors have stunning rates of narcissism and porn usage, and many fear their shadow side will destroy their ministry, so they become adept at hiding. Sin-and-lust-management strategies don't work. Self-help strategies are Band-Aids on soul wounds. Until we risk moving our true selves from the shadows to the light, the unaddressed dramas within will continue to wield unconscious control over us."[3] The first step is to bring our habitual, addictive sins to the light of Christ and expose them to the light of trusted others.

When I was a youthful youth pastor, I was naïve enough to think that people weren't *that* bad or *that* sinful. Twenty years later into serving God, I am not surprised any longer by anyone's sin. The very nature of sin is that it is "that bad" and that people can do horrific, unspeakable things—even people we never thought capable. That is why Jesus paid the penalty for all forms of sin, no matter how "trivial" or "heinous." Sometimes, in pastorates, we find widespread, secretive sins that span congregations. For instance, in one church that I served, several congregants struggled with gambling addictions. Whether it was going straight to the casinos after a long day of work or playing Texas Hold'em in their dining rooms for sizable pots of cash, gambling was an unspoken addictive sin in the congregation.

Two moments brought these sins to my consciousness. The first was a phone call from one of my parishioners asking me to meet up. During our meal together, he confessed to me that he had been struggling with a gambling addiction. Another providential encounter occurred when I went to a church member's home for dinner and was surprised to find a host of congregants there drinking together and playing cards for sums of money. I had heard anecdotally that others in the church were struggling with gambling as well. Uncertain of what I should do, I contacted the late Kenneth Swetland, former dean, professor, and chaplain at Gordon-Conwell Theological Seminary. He had never heard of such a widespread and peculiar church problem. Eventually, in due course, I decided after

---

3. Chuck DeGroat, "Pastor, Why Are You Hiding?," *Christianity Today*, January 15, 2019, https://www.christianitytoday.com/pastors/2019/january-web-exclusives/pastor-why-are-you -hiding.html. See also Chuck DeGroat, *When Narcissism Comes to Church: Healing Your Community from Emotional and Spiritual Abuse* (Downers Grove, IL: InterVarsity, 2020).

prayer to preach a sermon on the dangers of gambling. I saw the tops of several heads during that message. It's an uncomfortable but necessary pastoral responsibility to unearth the hidden sins of individuals and congregations for the edification of the entire church.

A Relapse into Sin

A final relevant topic with regard to preaching on painful sins is any type of relapse into sinful thoughts and actions. Finding freedom from one's sins—a freedom gained by God's grace alone—is a remarkable feeling. When one relapses, however, the pain is devastating. We feel dirty, ashamed, empty, guilt-ridden, lost, heartbroken, numb, embarrassed, even worthless. Relapse into sin is the agenda of the Enemy. It's Satan's way of separating us from God on account of our shame. Tim Chester shares, "For years I wondered whether I'd ever overcome certain sins. While I can't claim to have conquered sin—no one ever can do so in this life—here are truths that have led to change in my life and in the lives of others."[4] Thus, the saying goes, "We are all works in progress." Sanctification is indeed a lifelong battle. Yet the power of the gospel is that we *can* change and *can* be transformed into the image of Christ.

When we Christians relapse into sin, we tend to believe the lie that our current suffering is a direct result of that sin. In other words, we are getting what our sins deserve. As Kent Richmond writes, "The notion that suffering is the means God chooses to punish persons for sin remains influential in the minds of many in the church. . . . Furthermore, when suffering is seen as a punishment for sin, it often produces guilt in the most undeserving persons, if it has not already led to an outright rejection of God."[5] Rather, Richmond suggests, a better alternative is to view suffering, at times, as a way for God to test a disciple. In particular, the suffering has a clear objective, such as being "the way in which God brings us to obedience, enabling us to learn to live in accordance with the divine will."[6]

4. Tim Chester, *You Can Change: God's Transforming Power for Our Sinful Behavior and Negative Emotions* (Wheaton: Crossway, 2010), 9.
5. Kent D. Richmond, *Preaching to Sufferers: God and the Problem of Pain* (Nashville: Abingdon, 1988), 46, 49.
6. Richmond, *Preaching to Sufferers*, 52.

Scripture is replete with imagery concerning the spiritual warfare against the devil that comes with the territory of being a Christ-follower. For example, Jesus warns in John 10:10, "The thief comes only to steal and kill and destroy." Paul writes to the believers in Ephesians 6:11, "Put on the full armor of God, so that you can take your stand against the devil's schemes." Peter admonishes the elders, "Be alert and of sober mind. Your enemy the devil prowls around like a roaring lion looking for someone to devour" (1 Pet. 5:8). James professes to the Jewish diaspora in James 4:7, "Submit yourselves, then, to God. Resist the devil, and he will flee from you." Letting our guard down allows Satan to attack us in our vulnerable areas. In our preaching, we can regularly remind our listeners of this spiritual battle that all believers are engaged in. We are naturally prone to wander from God.

Jeffrey Arthurs points preachers to the importance of our reminding function as pastors: "By remembering we renew our minds and strengthen ourselves in the Lord. By doing so, we keep ourselves in the love of God."[7] Relapse into sin can and has happened to us all in some shape or form as members of a sinful world. Yet we can remind our people and ourselves that God has already, according to Timothy Keller, crushed "our most powerful enemies—sin, guilt, and death itself—without destroying us";[8] or we can, in the words of Paul, regularly proclaim our victory—that we are all "more than conquerors" (Rom. 8:37) in Christ Jesus.

Preaching on Painful Sins

Giving in to the so-called pleasures and temptations of sin such as the seven deadly sins[9]—lust, gluttony, avarice, sloth, wrath, envy, pride—breaking one or more of the Ten Commandments or any other sin (according to one article, the Bible names approximately 125 distinct sins)[10] engenders shame and pain, especially when those sins are running rampant in the

---

7. Jeffrey D. Arthurs, *Preaching as Reminding: Stirring Memory in an Age of Forgetfulness* (Downers Grove, IL: IVP Academic, 2017), 41.

8. Timothy Keller, *Preaching: Communicating Faith in an Age of Skepticism* (New York: Viking, 2015), 19.

9. See Rebecca Konyndyk DeYoung, *Glittering Vices: A New Look at the Seven Deadly Sins and Their Remedies*, 2nd ed. (Grand Rapids: Brazos, 2020).

10. Jack Wellman, "A List of Sins from the Bible," Patheos.com, September 8, 2014, https://www.patheos.com/blogs/christiancrier/2014/09/08/a-list-of-sins-from-the-bible.

life of the believer. Preaching on painful sins is troubling because every human struggles with sin (to each his or her own). No other sermon topic forces the preacher to look into his or her spiritual mirror. This internal self-examination, no doubt, may discourage preachers as they prepare the sermon for a given week, knowing full well their own shortcomings and besetting sins. Commonly, we hear or preach sermons related to lust, envy, or gossip. The preacher's temptation is to stay away from difficult texts on sin so as to not cause discomfort in the pews. To be faithful to Scripture, preaching on painful sins is a necessity—no matter which specific sins the text addresses.

1. Which Passage Will I Preach On?

How we preach on painful sins will depend on whether this is a one-off sermon, part of a larger topical series, or part of a series on a whole book of the Bible. No matter how we choose to preach the message or sermon series, we will want to avoid strict moralism or mere behavior modification. At the same time, preachers ought to challenge the besetting sins that stymie one's sanctification. The potential danger of erring on the side of moralistic or legalistic preaching should not excuse the preacher from combatting sins from the pulpit. Scripture contains many stories whose characters illustrate what sin looks like: Adam and Eve (eating the forbidden fruit), Cain and Abel (Cain murdering his brother), Moses (murdering the Egyptian and striking the rock), David (committing adultery and murder), Solomon (marrying wives who worshiped foreign gods), Ananias and Sapphira (lying to the Holy Spirit), and many others. While all sins are disturbing and damaging to our relationship with God and humankind, there may be no greater earthly sin than denying Christ—especially three times. For our case study, let's explore the reinstatement of Peter found in John 21. In many ways, this passage serves as an umbrella for the grand issue of sin.

2. What Type of Pain/Suffering Is Revealed in the Text?

The selected passage is often referred to as "Peter's reinstatement" to ministry. It follows the epic failure of his denial of Christ—three times. As we know from Scripture, there is completely unforgivable sin: blaspheming the Holy Spirit, as Jesus warns sternly, "And so I tell you, every kind of sin and slander can be forgiven, but blasphemy against the Spirit will not be forgiven" (Matt. 12:31). Peter's sin of denying Christ, the Savior, is not an insignificant sin. It's a crushing sin, especially for the one who committed it. While all sins are upsetting, we can surmise that Peter had a rough time dealing with the aftermath. While John mentions no details specifically about the state of Peter's emotions, we can assume that Peter suffered because of his failing Christ at a critical moment, wallowing in his own disappointment and shame and perhaps even embarrassment.

3. How Does the Bible Character or Biblical Author Deal with the Pain?

When we pick up the story in John 21:15, the closing chapter of the Gospel, Jesus has just fed the disciples breakfast with yet another miraculous, magnificent surplus of fish (v. 6), a sizable catch of 153 large fish, in fact (v. 11). Peter is the one who drags the fish onto the shore (v. 11). We know from other Gospel writers that Peter "wept bitterly" after denying Christ (Matt. 26:75; Luke 22:62). Yet how he dealt with this pain and shame afterwards is unknown. Obviously, he went back to his old occupation of fishing (John 21:3). Peter's reinstatement here in John 21 reflects a narratival symmetry of sorts with regard to the narrative of his denial. Both moments include a fire scene and a series of inquiries that put into question Peter's identity and relationship with Jesus. Ben Witherington writes, "John has the threefold restoration take place in a setting similar to where the threefold denial did. It's like revisiting the scene of the crime, only this time getting it right."[11] It must have been an awkward, even humbling experience as Jesus directly asked him three times whether he loved him or not. John records that Peter was even "grieved" by the third time. Jesus was, of course, justified in his thrice-repeated question. Peter's three different responses to Jesus's question "Do you love me?" have been much speculated about. The underlying theme is that Jesus wants Peter back in ministry service, even after Peter committed such a sin.

4. How Does This Pain in the Text Relate to Our Listeners' Pain?

For listeners, the sin of denying Christ brings to consciousness either literally denying Christ, renouncing the faith, or letting him down in some

---

11. Ben Witherington III, *What Have They Done with Jesus? Beyond Strange Theories and Bad History—Why We Can Trust the Bible* (New York: HarperOne, 2006), 73.

significant way by means of being shackled to specific sins or a sinful lifestyle. The question for many is, "How can I possibly serve God when I have sinned or continue to sin in this particular way?" For ordained clergy and ministers of the gospel, this is a nuanced question that deserves requisite time to ensure that the one who has been disqualified from the pastoral office has fully repented and been restored, if at all possible and even warranted. The evil one wants all listeners—sinners saved by God's grace—to feel like they can never be forgiven or be able to worship or serve God again in any capacity. Sadly, this is the state of many Christians who experience such defeat, condemnation, guilt, and shame over their sin without a pathway to forgiveness, recovery, and hope.

5. What Does This Pain Say about God and His Allowance of Pain?

Jesus's loving but piercing inquiries for Peter are to be expected. His pastoral approach in asking Peter questions allows Peter to confess with his own lips and hear with his own ears his love for Christ. Each time Peter hears, "Do you love me?," he's reminded of his sin of denying Christ. Our culture today, even our church culture, can diminish the significance of sin. Simply praying the Sinner's Prayer as the be-all and end-all for dealing with sin has cheapened and mitigated the extent to which our sin hurts a perfect, righteous, and holy God.

The truth is that we should feel terrible about our sin. It should grieve us deeply and we should mourn over it. When our culture devalues the seriousness of sin, it needs to hear the plain words of Paul in Romans 6:23: "The wages of sin is death." He doesn't say, "The wages of sin is feeling bad for two minutes and moving on with your day." Kevin DeYoung notes, "When we sin we should feel bad, we should be embarrassed, we should hang our heads in shame. . . . So go ahead, take a chance and let yourself feel bad for the bad stuff you've done. Own it. Admit it. Turn from it. Then run to Christ."[12] Every time we fail to obey God, our response should be to weep bitterly as Peter does over his sin of denying his Savior and Lord, three times. God desires for his children to weep about, mourn over, and even to despise sin. He will allow us to feel the pain and shame of sin (often through its inevitable consequences and even public humiliation).

---

12. Kevin DeYoung, "We Are Supposed to Feel Bad about Stuff," Gospel Coalition, March 12, 2019, https://www.thegospelcoalition.org/blogs/kevin-deyoung/supposed-feel-bad-stuff.

Moreover, for Peter, God even permits his future suffering, including becoming a martyr for Christ, as indicated by Jesus in verses 18 and 19. Even so, Jesus says, "Follow me," knowing that Peter will never be abandoned.

6. How Does God / Jesus / the Holy Spirit Help Us in Our Suffering?

When I read this narrative of reinstatement, my mind quickly goes back to verse 14, where John explains, "This was now the third time Jesus appeared to his disciples after he was raised from the dead." Chronologically, then, we can presume that Jesus saw Peter potentially up to two times before this moment of reinstatement occurred. This shows that Jesus didn't provide an immediate resolution and proclaim that Peter was received back into ministry right away. It's taken some time. Peter has sat with his own disappointment, failure, embarrassment, pain, and shame. Perhaps the worst thing Jesus could have done for Peter was to reinstate him the first time he saw him after the resurrection. When we sin, we need to sit with its effects and consequences.

It's apropos that the resurrected Jesus physically comes to the water, where he had initially called Peter to follow him. He goes there this time to demonstrate his love and care for Peter (and the other disciples), and he finds Peter struggling with locating the fish. Perhaps, using our imaginations, we could conjecture that Peter's inability to find fish is a metaphor for his current spiritual condition. Jesus cares for the disciples' sustenance and nourishes their famished stomachs first. It's clear from the passage that Peter was hungry. He was the one who told the other disciples that he was going fishing. When they all finish eating breakfast, Jesus approaches Simon Peter about his larger spiritual issue. He longs to restore the broken relationship. As he had done many times in the past, Jesus seeks out the sinner and calls him to repentance and restoration. Jesus does the same in people's lives today.

7. How Can Our Preaching Show Care and Empathy?

There's a delicate balance in preaching between license to sin and legalism. Preachers tend to err on one side or the other. In our fear of upsetting the masses, we can avoid preaching about sin altogether or at least diminish its ubiquity and impact in the lives of believers. Another type of preacher harangues the listeners every Sunday with a litany of sins, making the sermon a weekly diatribe that names all the concrete and subtle ways God's people have failed him. To love the people in proclamation means at times to do as Jesus did here in this text from John 21. It involves a gentle reminder, a prophetic but tender word to the listener, "Yes, you sinned. You messed up. You did something evil in the eyes of God. But there is still hope for you."

To preach on sin effectively in our world today, we need to preach on sin using a loving, firm, and affectionate tone. We might even begin the sermon by telling the listeners how much God loves them and about the shepherding love that we, as pastors, have for them as well. It can be easier for people to hear rebuke and correction when it is prefaced with a clear acknowledgment of one's pastoral embracement. We may even admit (using our spiritual discernment) how difficult it is to break free from patterns of sin and how we ourselves battle the sinful nature in varying forms. Wagging our finger only hurts the process. Preaching on sin is necessary because the biblical text so often addresses it directly. Knowing how our congregants will receive God's truth requires pastoral sensitivity to say the right words in the right way at the right time. It also involves much prayer and assistance from the Holy Spirit.

8. How Can We Share This Pain in Christian Community?

As stated in the introduction, sin wants to be hidden and not exposed. Chris Nye writes in *Distant God*, "The last thing we feel like doing in our misdoings and sinning is to seek God. And yet, from the very first sin, we see a God who pursues us even as we are disobeying Him. This is, after all, the entire arc of Scripture's metanarrative in Christ."[13] The pulpit is one means of helping listeners see a God who pursues them so that they will confess, repent, and find restoration from sin. Thus, preaching is an important medium. But it's not all. What we want to do concurrently is to create a congregational culture where worshipers find freedom to share with others what they are going through detrimentally, relating to one another in their common sinful condition. This spirit of nonjudgmentalism and confession of sins can organically take place in the form of small group ministry. We can admit when we have "denied Christ" in all sorts of ways, whether literally or figuratively. We deny Christ every time we

---

13. Chris Nye, *Distant God: Why He Feels Far Away . . . And What We Can Do about It* (Chicago: Moody, 2016), 33.

fail to acknowledge him or testify to the truth of biblical claims in the world. We deny Christ when we allow the culture to define and dictate the standards for morality. We deny Christ when we are ashamed of him when we pray publicly. And more. We deny Christ whenever we sin. This pain and shame of sin can be readily confessed and disclosed within a trusted body of believers or even to one trusted person.

It can similarly occur in trusted programs like Celebrate Recovery (which Rick Warren began at Saddleback Church), where all are welcome to open up about their hidden sins, no matter what stripe or variety. "Celebrate Recovery is a Christ-centered, 12 step recovery program for anyone struggling with hurt, pain or addiction of any kind. Celebrate Recovery is a safe place to find community and freedom from the issues that are controlling our life."[14] The testimonies that have come from participants in Celebrate Recovery cause many tears to flow. Challengingly, attending these types of gatherings carries its own stigma, especially for those serving in full-time ministry. However, I was once part of a larger congregation where even the pastors actively attended Celebrate Recovery because everyone is dealing with some type of pain, hurt, or addiction in his or her life. The issue is not that nobody sins. Rather, the foundational problem is that not all can admit that they are sinners and need assistance to overcome their sins. What might happen in the local church if entire church communities worked together to overcome sin, pain, and grief collectively? It might just pique the curiosity of an unbelieving world and even set it on fire for Jesus and the gospel.

9. How Will God Use Our Suffering to Transform Us and Bring Himself Glory?

Peter's reinstatement is a powerful story of God's transformative work in the life of someone who sinned greatly against the Lord. To deny Christ (three times) is no small, insignificant sin. Russ Ramsey observes, "If a disciple as close to Jesus as Peter can fail as epically as he did and still find himself firmly in the grip of the love of Christ, then you and I—when we doubt or when we struggle or when we fear or even when we fail—will not be separated from His love either."[15] Ultimately, Peter's fragile and

---

14. See Celebrate Recovery, accessed August 6, 2020, www.celebraterecovery.com.

15. Russ Ramsey, "Encounters with Christ: Peter's Reinstatement," He Reads Truth, accessed June 25, 2020, http://hereadstruth.com/2016/04/01/encounters-with-christ-peters-reinstatement.

humbling moment with the resurrected Jesus alters the future trajectory of his life. He goes on to do amazing works of ministry, writes two significant letters in the New Testament (1 and 2 Peter), and even dies a martyr for the sake of the one he loves so much, the Lord Jesus Christ. God would not allow Peter to lose his faith and salvation because of a vulnerable moment of weakness and sin. God uses even Peter's denial of Christ to embolden him to do even more remarkable works of ministry in spite of his failures.

At Morehouse College's 135th commencement, Robert F. Smith, the founder, chairman, and CEO of Vista Equity Partners and the commencement speaker, shared this stunning news with the graduating class of 2019: "My family is going to create a grant to eliminate your student loans!"[16] Now, these graduating students were not expecting such a grand and generous gesture. Since Smith's kindness and generosity came to fruition, what will these graduates do in response? How will they pay forward the unmerited grace they received and find positive ways to channel resources for the good of others? God's grand gesture of erasing debt for sins and sinners is not something that could've been paid off by a billionaire's hard-earned income. Rather, it's been paid with the blood of his Son. We can pray for ourselves and our listeners that God will use those who have been forgiven much to accomplish great works for his kingdom. Pray for your listeners that they will find restoration and healing in Christ for even their worst and vilest offenses. Ask God to use your ministry of presence and proclamation to build up people's souls and repurpose them for the expansion of God's kingdom.

Principles for Preaching on Painful Sins

Preaching on Combating Sins

One of the primary ways we can preach on sin is to combat it head-on. Remind your listeners regularly that they are on the front lines of a field of spiritual land mines full of explosive sins. These sins want to seize

---

16. Allison Klein, "Billionaire Robert F. Smith Pledges to Pay Off Morehouse College Class of 2019's Student Loans," *Washington Post*, May 19, 2019, https://www.washingtonpost.com /lifestyle/2019/05/19/billionaire-robert-f-smith-pledges-pay-off-morehouse-college-class-s -student-loans. See also Taylor Nicole Rogers, "The Billionaire Who Dished Out $34 Million to Pay Off Student Loans for an Entire College Class Says America's Student Loan System Is a 'Catastrophe,'" *Business Insider*, October 24, 2019, https://www.businessinsider.com/robert -f-smith-americas-student-loan-system-catastrophe-2019-10.

their attempts toward Christlikeness. In Genesis 4, God says to Cain upon receiving his offering, "Why are you angry? Why is your face downcast? If you do what is right, will you not be accepted? But if you do not do what is right, sin is crouching at your door; it desires to have you, but you must rule over it" (4:6–7). Might it be the case that our attitudes toward sin have only become increasingly lax as time moves forward?

Those wary of moralistic and legalistic preaching may be hesitant to preach outspokenly about sin, because they're concerned not to offend anyone in the pews. Preachers can be timid and less vocal, to the detriment of God's people. Franklin Andreen's assessment of American Christianity is harsh but perhaps spot-on in some pockets: "With all the latest gadgets and comforts of our modern Laodicean Age, churches today 'don't need' conviction to draw the people in and keep them drooling. The formula is simple: cater to their fleshly comforts and sprinkle in just enough of the Word to give it the appearance of Christianity. The result, unfortunately, is a Church full of baby Christians who never grow beyond the fundamentals of the faith."[17] Andreen maintains that Christianity is spinning in circles because of a lack of conviction about sin. Is it possible that he's correct? Do we cater to the culture and even secretly crave sin rather than be convicted about it? In order to defeat sin through the power of the Holy Spirit, we must wage war with it using a daily, weekly, monthly, yearly regimen. Talk about sin from the pulpit. Speak out against its evils. As Paul exhorts Timothy, help your listeners to "fight the good fight of the faith" (1 Tim. 6:12).

Preaching on Preventing Sin and the Consequences of Sin

Dave Carder's book *Anatomy of an Affair* recounts the common pitfalls of how an affair evolves and erupts in a marriage. He maintains, "Most of the people I've counseled in their recovery had thought they would be immune to betraying their spouse. At least they never married thinking that they would do that. Few realized they were even susceptible to falling into the arms of someone they weren't married to—or even thought it possible that they could come close!"[18] The same principle can apply to

17. Franklin Andreen, *Conviction of Sin: The Lacking Ingredient in Modern Day Church Growth* (Hawley, MN: Flame Church of Hawley, 2017), 1–2.
18. Dave Carder, *Anatomy of an Affair: How Affairs, Attractions, and Addictions Develop, and How to Guard Your Marriage against Them* (Chicago: Moody, 2017), 9.

any type of sin. "I never thought I could do that or be capable of doing that particular sin," we tell ourselves. With this in mind, it's fundamental that preachers preach not only about postfall consequences but also about the prevention of sin. Are we spiritually attentive to what's going on in our lives? Do our listeners watch their own souls?

When I was growing up, my father would often tell me that wisdom is not just learning from my own mistakes but also, and even more importantly, witnessing the mistakes of others and not falling into the same snares. Take, for example, a sermon preached on the familiar story of David's adultery with Bathsheba in 2 Samuel 11. Although we ought to be slow to fabricate knowledge and imagination of all that went on in David's mind prior to his fall, what would a sermon look like that challenged our listeners to consider the areas of vulnerability and susceptibility in their lives and that even scared them away from fanciful, sexual thoughts at the office, gym, church, and elsewhere? We can preach on the consequences of David's sin, his adultery, his murder, his cover-up. We can also preach regularly on prevention of sin so that our listeners will fear the Lord, which we are told is the beginning of wisdom (Prov. 9:10; cf. 1:7).

Striking a Balance between God's Holiness and Forgiveness

Lastly, it's critical that listeners know that, with God, there is compassion, mercy, and forgiveness for sin. Yes, countless verses describe God's righteousness, holiness, justice, wrath, judgment. These attributes must be preached about as well. At the same time, in our preaching, we are painting a multidimensional portrait of who God is and what he looks like. As we preach on the holiness of God, we also communicate about the heavenly Father who runs toward us (Luke 15), about Jesus Christ, the Son who died for us while we were yet sinners (Rom. 5:8), and the Holy Spirit who intercedes for us with wordless groans (8:26).

Like the woman mentioned earlier in this chapter who had an abortion, we need to use those painful memories to receive God's love and forgiveness. Casey Tygrett explains: "*We engage our memories in tandem with God because they are the starting points for who we are now and who we have yet to become.* . . . Allowing the Spirit of Jesus to redeem and renew past pain for the sake of our formation is not perfect or painless in and of itself. Any process of change requires a form of dying, of letting go of structures and conceptions [and memories] that hold us in the place of suffering or stagnancy."[19] This precious woman and others don't simply need this memory to fade; they need to be completely forgiven. They need to be forgiven by God just as they need to forgive themselves.

Does this mean we shouldn't preach sternly against sin? No. Should we avoid mentioning that there are consequences for our sinful actions and behaviors? No, again. Should we shiver to bring up past sins and pains? Not if God is bringing up this event to bring healing and restoration. It's always a delicate balance, isn't it? How could I possibly know every pain and shame in the congregation? I simply can't. The preacher is God's messenger. God uses the Word to convict us. He rouses memories that require his comfort, compassion, forgiveness, and transformation. Our responsibility is to choose words wisely that can make the difference in the listeners' ears. Speak the truth with love and grace. We want listeners to leave the sanctuary brimming with confidence that they truly have been forgiven by their heavenly Father—for any sins committed (1 John 1:9). We want them to take Jesus at his word that Christians can "go now and leave [their] life of sin" (John 8:11) using his strength and power. We want them to live out their courageous call as empowered disciples who have already received the power of the promised Holy Spirit and to be his witnesses (Acts 1:8).

Conclusion

Preaching on painful sins involves the work of the Holy Spirit. Left to our own devices, we will merely wound already wounded souls. Pray that God will use his Word to transform the minds and hearts of his people. By its very nature, sin is painful. It tears. It separates. It wounds. It permeates. It destroys. Our congregants are lugging around sins—past, present, and even future. Use your pulpit ministry, the Word of God, and your pastoral presence to help them overcome these painful sins by trusting in the Lord to accomplish his will in their lives.

19. Tygrett, *As I Recall*, 13 (emphasis original).

Discussion Questions

1. If you were to confess to a trusted friend, what sins are you struggling with privately today that only God knows about?

2. What are the sins that hold your congregants captive?

3. How can you cultivate a congregation of openness, transparency, and vulnerability where sin can be confessed without judgment?

4. What types of sin can you preach against in the pulpit, and are there any sins that you should refrain from preaching on? Why or why not?

"The God of Fourth Chances"

Sermon on John 21:15–25

> **HOMILETICAL IDEA:** God uses broken, forgiven, and restored people, like you and me, to change the world.

There's a website out there called www.weareonlyhuman.com. It's a website where people share their stories of how they have made different mistakes. Stories include taking advantage of the open bar, buying a custom-built computer from a friend, choosing the wrong moving company, painting my room myself, and the list goes on and on.

Although many of these stories are more humorous and lighthearted than sad, the question I want to ask you today is, Have you ever really messed up in life? If we're honest, all of us have. Maybe we've told a lie at work and have lost our job as a result. Maybe we've gossiped about a close friend only to have that person find out, and now we no longer speak to that person. Maybe we've cheated on an exam and gotten caught in the act. Maybe we've failed our spouses and families in different ways. Maybe we've committed a sin that we never want anyone to know about. Well, I'm pretty certain that each of us has at some point done something we're not proud of.

As we come to the final chapter in John's Gospel we meet a character in the Bible who really messed up in the Christian life. His name was Simon Peter. How did he mess up? He was one of Jesus's closest disciples, but when he was confronted about knowing Jesus in a difficult moment, he bailed on Jesus and denied him three times. Friends, what happens when we mess up profoundly in the Christian life? Peter failed Christ three times in this moment. How does Jesus respond to us when we have really blown it? Is there a fourth chance for Peter and for us?

Turn with me in your Bibles to John 21:15.

I. When we receive a fourth chance, we can love Jesus by caring for others.

Prior to these verses we have just read, the disciples were having some difficulty catching fish. For whatever reason, the nets were empty. After Jesus's resurrection, he reappears and comes to the disciples on the shore and miraculously fills their nets with fish. They share a Michelin-rated seafood dinner (okay, maybe not quite that savory), and Jesus begins a conversation with Simon Peter.

What does Jesus say in verse 15? He says, "Simon son of John . . ." Notice, he uses Simon's full name. And each time Jesus asks him the same question, he uses his formal name Simon son of John. It's like when your parents want your full attention and use your full name, as in "Matthew D. Kim, come down here!" In the same way, Jesus wants Peter's full attention. So he says, "Simon son of John."

What does Jesus ask him? Three times he asks in different ways, "Do you truly love me?" The first time in verse 15, Jesus asks, "Do you love me more than these?" What's going on here? What is Jesus referring to when he says "these"?

It can mean one of several things: He's referring either to fishing, to the fish themselves, to being around his fellow disciples, or to something completely different. Remember, Peter has sinned badly. After following Christ for three years, he went back to his former occupation, fishing. In essence, he took a short break from ministry. So Jesus is asking him, "Do you love me and your calling to serve me more than you love your friends and your career as a fisherman?"

Obviously Peter knows what "these" refers to, and he responds clearly and confidently, "Yes, Lord, you know that I love you." And Jesus says, "Feed my lambs." Jesus says, "If you truly love me, then you'll feed my lambs."

What if Jesus asked you this question: Do you truly love me more than *these*? What would *these* represent for you? For some of us, he might ask, "Do you love me more than your children?" For others, he might ask, "Do you love me more than your financial security?" For others, he might ask, "Do you love me more than your hobbies and free time?" How would we answer Jesus?

Thankfully, Jesus's love for us does not depend on what we do for him. But then why does he command Peter to feed and take care of his sheep?

He wants Peter to experience full restoration. He wants Peter to experience the forgiveness of his sins. "Even though you messed up, Peter, it's okay. I forgive you. I want you to go back to a life of ministry." Peter denied Christ three times. So Jesus asks him three times whether Peter truly loves him or not. If Peter does love Jesus, then he'll continue being a fisher of people, a minister of the gospel.

Do you truly love Jesus? Do you fully grasp his forgiveness? Will you forgive yourself for your shameful sins? If we can say yes, the evidence of our love for him will be that we will want to care for others and bring them into the family of God. Stated another way, when you receive a fourth chance, love Jesus by caring for others.

Jimmy Dorrell is the pastor of Church under the Bridge, a ministry that actually meets underneath a bridge. This church ministers to the least of these. They are about one thing: bringing good news to those who need the gospel most, such as widows, orphans, drug addicts, prostitutes, and the homeless, the people many of us wouldn't want to associate with. This is what he says: "A blessed church is one that blesses others, not one that has blessings."[1] Did you catch that? "A blessed church is one that blesses others, not one that has blessings." When we understand the grace of God—the fact that we've received multiple chances from the Lord when we mess up—we will want to care for others.

Jesus tells us today: If we claim to love him, we will feed his sheep and take care of the flock. This is not only for pastors. This is for all sinners saved by grace. We can care for the flock in many ways. Maybe we can pray for someone who's hurting. Maybe we can share God's love with a close friend who's suffering from depression. Maybe we can tell our neighbor about Jesus's love and forgiveness. Maybe we can bring food to someone on the street corner. When we receive a fourth chance, we can love Jesus by caring for others.

II. When we receive a fourth chance, we can follow Jesus to the end, even to death.

At the end of verse 17, Peter is hurt emotionally by Jesus's persistent asking. Peter said, "Lord, you know that I love you." But Jesus asks two more

---

1. See Jimmy Dorrell, *Trolls and Truth: 14 Realities about Today's Church That We Don't Want to See* (Birmingham, AL: New Hope, 2006), 161.

times. By the third time, Peter is sensitive and frustrated. Jesus sounds like a parent who nags like a broken record. After Peter responds for the third time, Jesus gives him the following analogy in verse 18: "When you were younger you dressed yourself and went where you wanted; but when you are old you will stretch out your hands, and someone else will dress you and lead you where you do not want to go." What is Jesus saying here? He's telling Peter a simple truth. Jesus predicts the future. He's telling Peter that by the end of his life his arms are going to be stretched out on a cross, and he's going to be crucified. In fact, according to a church tradition, at the end of Peter's life he was nailed to a cross upside down. He died the most horrific death of all the disciples.

Jesus says to him, "Follow me!" Follow me to your grave. Follow me! When Jesus lived on this earth, he never promised that we would have a cushy life. I'm sorry to disappoint us, but the Christian life is not the prosperity gospel. Jesus never said that if we follow him we will be comfortable. In fact, he promised us just the opposite. He says in Mark 8:34: "Whoever wants to be my disciple must deny themselves and take up their cross and follow me." If we are truly committed to following Jesus, we die to ourselves. We may not die as a martyr, but we will die to our desires and dreams so that God's desires and dreams will become a reality in our lives.

Will we follow Jesus as Jesus intended for our lives? Following Jesus is serious business. People around the world are serving Jesus at the expense of their own comfort and safety. Missionaries are living in houses made of dung and clay. Some people are eating insects and repulsive things for the sake of Christ. Some brothers and sisters in Christ are risking their lives so that the name of Jesus might reach villages in the most rural places. Jesus says to Peter, "Follow me!" He's saying to every person here, "Follow me!" "Follow me without any conditions. Follow me at all costs. Follow me!"

William Kelly was a promising Bible student in the late 1800s. Kelly was noticed by several professors at Trinity College in Dublin. They encouraged him to make a name for himself through scholarship. When Kelly showed disinterest, one professor asked him, "But Mr. Kelly, aren't you interested in making a name for yourself in the world?" To this he responded, "Which world, gentleman?"[2]

2. S. Hutson Camperson, *Go for the Gold: A Life of Excellence* (Murfreesboro, TN: Sword of the Lord, 1996), 28–29.

How do we follow Jesus? Do we follow Jesus only when it's convenient for us? Or do we follow Jesus unconditionally? Do we want to leave a legacy here on earth or in heaven? The second principle Jesus shares through Peter is this: when we receive a fourth chance, we can follow Jesus to the end, even to death. It may not be a physical death, but it will involve dying to ourselves and to our dreams.

The familiar story is told of missionary Jim Elliot, who died as a martyr for Jesus at the young age of twenty-eight at the hands of the Huaorani Indians in Ecuador. His famous words "He is no fool who gives what he cannot keep to gain that which he cannot lose" live on in Christian history. But seldom is he quoted for saying this also: "I know that my hopes and plans for myself could not be any better than He has arranged and fulfilled them. Thus may we all find it, and know the truth of the Word which says, 'He will be our Guide even until death.'"[3]

Friends, how committed are we to Jesus? Do we have this level of commitment to die to ourselves so that Christ may be exalted through our lives? No matter how grave our sins, Jesus can forgive. Jesus can restore. Jesus can heal. Jesus can still use us. Would you take a moment now to confess any sins that are preventing you from living for God? Take a few moments now. Ask the Spirit to search your heart. Give those sins to the Lord.

I pray that I would have this type of faith. We pray that we would be able to die to all of our hopes and dreams so that we may live passionately for the name of Jesus Christ. That we would do whatever it takes to bring glory to Christ! Will you take your fourth chance and use it to follow Jesus wholeheartedly? Friends, when we receive a fourth chance, we can follow Jesus to the end.

III. When we receive a fourth chance, Jesus focuses on how *we* live our lives.

Peter seems a little bothered by Jesus's focus only on him. Jesus seems to be picking on Peter today. Peter senses this and he's not happy about it. He's mad that Jesus asks him three times whether he loves him or not. And now Peter turns and sees that the disciple whom Jesus loves is following

3. Elisabeth Elliot, *Shadow of the Almighty: The Life and Testament of Jim Elliot* (Peabody, MA: Hendrickson, 1958), 270.

them. Peter sees another disciple and says to Jesus, "Hey Jesus, what about him? Why aren't you giving him a hard time? Why is the focus all on me? Yeah, I know I messed up. I denied you three times. Let's put that in the past!" What Peter does here is a natural human response.

Have you ever done this? Let's say you're listening to a sermon on a particular topic. And rather than saying to yourself, "I'm so glad I'm here to listen to this message; I really needed to hear that," you say to yourself, "I wish so and so was here. She really needs this message more than I do." That's how Peter responds to Jesus at this moment.

But how does Jesus respond to Peter's outburst? In verse 22, Jesus hits on a very appropriate subject: comparison. As we go through the Christian life, it is hard not to compare ourselves with others. The mass media tell us to compare. We're told that we never have enough. We shouldn't be satisfied. But when we compare, we fall into judgment and lose our joy. What do I mean?

When we compare ourselves with others, we fall into the trap of judging another person. We become overly spiritual. "Hey, how come I'm cleaning up the fellowship hall and that lazy person over there is sitting there with his arms folded?" "Hey, how come I give 10 percent of my income to God and that person over there—I just saw him put $1 into the offering basket?" "Hey, how come I'm living in this modest home and yet that person is living in a mansion?" "Hey, how come I'm trying to be a good steward by driving a Honda Civic and that person is driving a high-end luxury vehicle?" "Hey, how come I pray for two minutes at the dinner table and that other person just starts eating as soon as he sits down?" And the comparison goes on and on. When we do this, we judge and we lose our joy. We forget to be thankful.

Conclusion

What matters to Jesus is how Peter lives his life! He wants Peter to not be distracted by how so-and-so lives his life. The same goes for us. When we have received a second, third, or fourth chance, we will be concerned not with how others live but only with how we live. What Jesus wants us to take from this message is this: God uses broken, forgiven, and restored people, like you and me, to change the world for the sake of Christ. God doesn't use seemingly perfect people. He uses people just like Peter, who is like you and me with our failures, our mistakes, our sins, our lack of faith. And when we experience the power of restoration and forgiveness, we will love Christ by serving him, following him, and living to please him. God uses broken, forgiven, and restored people to change the world for the sake of Christ. Will you join by committing yourself fully to him today?

Conclusion

Pain and suffering are mired in human frailty across our congregations and are even embodied in the pulpit, if we're willing to be so vulnerable. As we have witnessed throughout these pages, preaching on people's pain is challenging, messy, perplexing, even heart-wrenching. There are no simple answers and solutions. So, why do it? Why bring up hurtful things from our past or their past, our present or their present, our future or their future? Why make people feel uncomfortable with gratuitous lament? Why preach and unintentionally give them any false sense of hope? Do we want to perpetuate the prosperity gospel?

We began this journey with a hypothetical scenario: Would you preach only on success or only on suffering? Obviously, the answer is neither. Preachers don't preach only on one extreme or the other. However, we might follow up with these questions: Do we see the value and significance of intentionally incorporating more sermons on pain and suffering as we set the preaching calendar? And will we do it? Will you preach on the pain of the biblical author or characters in your Scripture passage? Will you be sensitive to the Holy Spirit when he prompts you to acknowledge and empathize with the hurts of your people? If you answered yes to any of these questions, then I have accomplished one of my goals in writing this book.

It's overwhelming to consider all of the people who are suffering quietly or even publicly in the worship service. Yes, their physical bodies are present in the sanctuary, but their minds and hearts are often elsewhere trying to make sense of and cope with the woes, quandaries, and even miseries of life. Naysayers will jest that no sermon can sufficiently address the myriad pains in the room. To this skepticism or dissent I would agree. No sermon can heal every wound and speak to every need. Yet God has spoken and has revealed himself through Scripture. He knows that so much of life is laden with pain, suffering, guilt, shame, and even embarrassment. He wants Christians to know that in the midst of such perplexing conundrums and toils he is there. He is listening. He is not silent. He is present. He is sovereign over every *Sitz im Leben*—to borrow the words of German theologians.

All we can do as preachers is present our listeners with the truth of God's Word and the truth of who God is. Preaching on pain involves more than simple proclamation. It requires active participation and empathy. We can listen to their pain. We can sit beside them and pray for them. We can be a loving, pastoral presence. The choice of whether to follow or deny God during our trials is up for grabs. It's up to the listener to make his or her choice. When challenges come, we can choose to cling to Christ and the hope of our salvation or go the opposite way of distrusting his promises and even abandoning the faith. We as preachers want to teach our listeners to suffer well even when God's provision and answers are not what we were hoping for. Yes, this fact is hard to accept.

Wallie Amos Criswell—better known by his initials W. A.—the influential preacher of First Baptist Church of Dallas, Texas, once testified:

> There is only one joy greater than preaching or teaching the Word, and that joy is this: One day soon we will see the Author of the Word face to face. God Himself will hold us in His arms and take us home. In the meantime, all He asks of us is that we go on loving the Word and sharing it in our own ways, that we remain faithful to the Word, that we win the lost to Christ. And when our trials come, when we feel pain and suffering, when our tears flow again, it is our joy and comfort to lift our faces heavenward and to go on standing on the promises of God.[1]

Whether preacher or parishioner—God promises that he is here with us before, during, and even after our initial pain. He is who he says he is, Immanuel, God with us. How will we respond to pain and suffering? What will we do in spite of it? How will we choose to live the rest of our days even if in God's sovereign plan he does not heal our diseases, chronic pains,

---

1. W. A. Criswell, *Standing on the Promises* (Dallas: Word, 1990), 248–50.

mental health issues, terminal illness, even if he provides no immediate resolution to our broken finances, allows those we love to perish on earth, does not restore every broken relationship, permits all kinds of evils and injustices, and even cares enough to have us suffer from the consequences of our poor decisions and sins committed?

How is a Christian any different from a non-Christian? It's often in how we respond to pain and suffering. This does not mean that trials and tribulations are easy to live with. How do we demonstrate hope in Christ to a world that remains preoccupied and overwhelmed by anxiety, worry, and fear? When trials come and even linger, will we still worship God? Will we still love him? Will we still serve him? Will we still preach God's Word faithfully? Will we still share the gospel of Jesus Christ with the lost? Will we still be disciples and continue to make them? Will we seek first his kingdom and his righteousness? Will we receive God's comfort and try to comfort others in their pain? Jesus recognized how hard it would be for Christians to trust in him during these last days. In fact, he even asks rhetorically in Luke 18:8, "However, when the Son of Man comes, will he find faith on the earth?"

A key difference between a Christian and a nonbeliever manifests itself in how we deal with pain and suffering in this life. Christians respond to life's afflictions with praise and prayer (2 Cor. 1:3–11) to the God who is intimately involved in our lives. His promises are true in times of plenty and in times of want: "Never will I leave you; never will I forsake you" (Heb. 13:5, quoting Deut. 31:6). In times of distress, Christians respond like King David: "But David found strength in the LORD his God" (1 Sam. 30:6). Christians look only to the Lord in turbulent times, because "God is our refuge and strength, an ever-present help in trouble" (Ps. 46:1), and they heed God's Word sans worry when he says, "Be still, and know that I am God" (v. 10). Christians grieve but "do not grieve like the rest of mankind, who have no hope" (1 Thess. 4:13). Christians are called to "rejoice always, pray continually, [and] give thanks in all circumstances; for this is God's will for [us] in Christ Jesus" (1 Thess. 5:16–18). Christians "cast all [their] anxiety on [Jesus] because he cares for [them]" (1 Pet. 5:7). Similar passages to encourage believers in the midst of pain and suffering are numerous. What's your favorite? As we wait for the Lord's return, let's remember to pray for, preach to, and be present with the people in pain in our community, in our congregation, and in our care.

I close with the following vulnerable words from a prayer penned by the Puritan Robert Hawker (1753–1827). We can utter the same prayer:

> So when my poor heart is afflicted, when Satan storms, or the world frowns, when I suffer sickness, or when all your waves and storms seem to go over me, what relief it is to know that you, Jesus, see me. And that you care!
>
> So help me, Lord, to look to you, and remember you. And oh! That blessed Scripture: "In all their affliction he was afflicted, and the angel of his presence saved them; in his love and in his pity he redeemed them; he lifted them up and carried them all the days of old." Amen.[2]

Come quickly, Lord Jesus!

---

2. Robert Hawker, "A Prayer in Time of Suffering," *Lexham Press* (blog), March 20, 2020, https://blog.lexhampress.com/2020/03/20/a-prayer-in-time-of-suffering. The Bible verse Hawker quotes is Isa. 63:9. The language in the prayer has been updated for a modern audience.

Worksheet
for Understanding Pain

Exploring the Preacher's Pain

1. How have you suffered in the past?

2. What pains are you experiencing today?

3. Take some time to pray about and explore your pain and suffering in the following areas. List your struggles below:

Physical pains

Psychological pains

Emotional pains

Relational pains

Economic pains

Spiritual pains

Pain from sins

4. To whom have you spoken about these pains?

5. How has God healed or not healed you from the pains?

6. How might these various pains be entering the pulpit with you when you preach?

Understanding the Listeners' Pains

Individual Inventory of Pain and Suffering

Member	Type of Pain	Length of Pain
1.		
2.		
3.		
4.		
5.		
6.		
7.		
8.		
9.		
10.		

Church Inventory of Pain and Suffering

Type of Pain	Length of Pain
1.	
2.	
3.	
4.	
5.	

Nine Preparatory Questions for Preaching on Pain

1. Which passage will I preach on?

2. What type of pain/suffering is revealed in the text?

3. How does the Bible character or biblical author deal with the pain?

4. How does this pain in the text relate to our listeners' pain?

5. What does this pain say about God and his allowance of pain?

6. How does God / Jesus / the Holy Spirit help us in our suffering?

7. How can our preaching show care and empathy?

8. How can we share this pain in Christian community?

9. *How will God use our suffering to transform us and bring himself glory?*

Clarity for Preaching on Pain

1. Scripture text/topic. This sermon is based on

_____

and addresses the topic of _____.

2. Pain(s) in the text. This passage talks about the following pain(s):

_____

_____.

3. Big idea of the sermon. The main idea of the sermon is:

_____

_____.

4. Purpose of the sermon. After hearing this sermon, I want my listeners to:

_____

_____.

5. Biblical author's tone in the text. The author writes with this/these tone(s)/mood(s):

_____

_____.

6. The preacher's tone. In my word choice and tone of speech, I want to be:

_____

_____.

7. God's hope/promise in the text. God offers the following hope or promise:

_____

_____.

8. Postsermon pastoral care. After this sermon, I will do the following to care for God's people:

_____

_____.

Scripture Index

Subject Index